Hiroshima and Peace Studies

From the First Atomic Bombing to the Treaty
on the Prohibition of Nuclear Weapons

Hiroshima City University
Faculty of International Studies Book Series: Volume 13

Hiroshima and Peace Studies

From the First Atomic Bombing to the Treaty
on the Prohibition of Nuclear Weapons

Edited by
Yoshiaki Furuzawa
Yasuhiro Inoue
Michael Gorman

Hiroshima, 2023
KEISUISHA

Hiroshima City University
Faculty of International Studies Book Series: Volume 13

Published by KEISUISHA Co., Ltd.
1-4 Komachi Naka-ku Hiroshima 730-0041 JAPAN
ISBN978-4-86327-619-2 C3036

Contributors

FUJIWARA, Yubi: Lecturer in the Faculty of International Studies at Hiroshima City University. Her specialties include Linguistics, Chinese language, and Chinese language education. Her recent publications include *Teaching Chinese in East and Southeast Asia* [Dongya yu Dongnanya diqu zhi Huayu Jiaoyu] (Wunan Culture Enterprise, 2020).

FURUZAWA, Yoshiaki: Associate Professor in the Faculty of International Studies at Hiroshima City University. He occasionally carries out fieldwork in Kenya and Sierra Leone. He writes about police reform policy in post-conflict and transitional societies as well as peacebuilding policy in general. He is co-editor of *Hybrid Statebuilding* [Haiburido na Kokkakensetu] (Nakanishiya Publishing Co., 2019).

GORMAN, Michael: Professor of American Literature in the Faculty of International Studies at Hiroshima City University in Japan. His research interests include rural American culture as well as environmental, multicultural, and transnational literatures. His recent publications include "Where Pagodas Rise on Every Hill: Romance as Resistance in 'A Son of the Celestial'" (*Cather Studies,* 2021) and "Climates of Violence, Spirits of Resistance: Chang-rae Lee's *On Such a Full Sea* and Louise Erdrich's *Future Home of the Living God*" (*Transpacific Ecocriticism,* 2019).

HALLETT, Brien: Professor at the Matsunaga Institute for Peace at the University of Hawaii, Manoa, where he teaches courses in peace and conflict resolution, with a special interest in the thought of Gandhi, Martin Luther King, and Vaclav Havel. Hallett is the author of *Declaring War* (Cambridge University Press, 2012) and *The Lost Art of Declaring War* (University of Illinois Press, 1998).

HIGUCHI, Toshihiro: Assistant Professor of History at Georgetown University. He studies the international history of the nuclear age with a focus on its scientific, technological, and environmental aspects. He also writes about the environmental history of modern Japan in the Pacific world. Higuchi is the author of *Political Fallout: Nuclear Weapons Testing and the Making of a Global Environmental Crisis* (Stanford University Press, 2020).

INOUE, Yasuhiro: Professor of Media Studies in the Faculty of International Studies at Hiroshima City University. He was a news reporter at Japanese national newspapers, *Mainichi Shimbun* and *Yomiuri Shimbun*. His most recent publications include *How the World Understands Hiroshima* [Sekai wa Hiroshima wo dou rikaishiteiruka?] (Chuokouron Shinsha, 2021) and *Atomic Bomb Myths and Information Manipulation in the US* [Amerika no Genbaku shinwa to jouhou sousa] (Asahi Shimbun Publications, 2018).

KAWASAKI, Akira: Executive Committee Member of Peace Boat. International Steering Group member of the International Campaign to Abolish Nuclear Weapons (ICAN). His recent publications include *Nuclear Weapons: From Prohibition to Abolition* [Kakuheiki: Kinshi kara Haizetu he] (Iwanami Shoten, 2021). He received the Hiroshima Peace Center Foundation's Kiyoshi Tanimoto Peace Prize in 2021.

KIM, Yeongho: Professor of Comparative Politics in the Faculty of International Studies at Hiroshima City University, and the Dean of the Faculty since 2020. His research interests include comparative politics, international relations, and contemporary Korean studies. He is the author of *South Korean Attitudes toward Japan in ROK - Japan Relations* [Nikkan Kankei to Kankoku no Tainichikodo] (Sairyusha, 2008).

MATSUNAGA, Kyoko: Associate Professor in the Graduate School of Humanities and Social Sciences at Hiroshima University, and a former Fulbright fellow at the University of Nebraska-Lincoln. She specializes in Indigenous American literature, nuclear/atomic literature, and environmental literature. She is the author of *American Indigenous Writers and Nuclear Literature* [Hokubei senjuumin bungaku to kaku bungaku] (Eihosha, 2019).

MORI, Shigeaki: Mori received the Distinguished Service Award from the

United States–Japan Foundation in 2017. At the age of eight, Mori was blown off a bridge 2.5 km from the hypocenter by the atomic bombing. As an independent historian, he tracked down the family members of 12 American POWs who were killed by the atomic bomb in Hiroshima. He published a book titled, *The Unknown History of the American Soldiers Killed by the Atomic Bomb* (Genbaku de shinda Beihei hishi) and won the Kikuchi Kan Prize in 2016 for non-fiction.

NAGAI, Mariko: Professor of Japanese Literature and Creative Writing at Temple University Japan Campus. Nagai has received the Pushcart Prizes both in poetry and fiction (nominated five times in total). Her most recent publications include *Dust of Eden: A Novel* (Albert Whitman & Co., 2014), *Irradiated Cities* (Les Figues, 2017), *Under the Broken Sky* (MacMillan/Henry Holt /Christy Ottaviano Books, 2019), *Body of Empire* (Tarpaulin Sky Press, 2022) and *The Sword of Yesterday* (Little, Brown/Christy Ottaviano, 2023).

OGURA, Keiko: Ogura received the Hiroshima Peace Center Foundation's Kiyoshi Tanimoto Peace Prize in 2013. Ogura was married to Mr. Kaoru Ogura in 1962, who later became the director of the Hiroshima Peace Memorial Museum. After her husband passed away in 1979, she became an interpreting coordinator for international peace-movement visitors. In 1984, she established Hiroshima Interpreters for Peace (HIP) which supports foreign visitors, including journalists and peace activists. Since then, she has been speaking in English about her atomic bombing experience to foreign people from school children to diplomats.

OTA, Ikuko: Professor of International Law and Human Rights in the Faculty of International Studies at Hiroshima City University. She has published widely on the legal questions related to the "implementation of international public interests under the pressure of universal commodification accompanied by market globalization," specifically in the fields of human rights in Japanese society. In addition to her scholarly work, utilizing expertise as a former legal advisor for the Division of the Ocean, the Japanese Ministry of Foreign Affairs, she has actively contributed to the local community in her hometown of Hiroshima.

SATO, Shiro: Professor in the Faculty of Bioindustry at Tokyo University of Agriculture. His major field of interest is Japan's nuclear disarmament and non-proliferation policy within the context of Japan's security policy. His most recent publications include *International Politics of Nuclear Weapons and Hibakusha* [Kaku to Hibakusha no Kokusaiseijigaku] (Akashi Shoten, 2022) and *Reading E. H. Carr* [E.H. Carr wo yomu] (eds. with Seiko Mimaki and Kosuke Shimizu, Nakanishiya Publishing Co., 2022).

SAURAS, Javier: Sauras is a multimedia journalist. As a reporter, he has worked on issues of human rights and development across the globe. He has been a news-wire correspondent in China, and he has covered the consequences of the Fukushima nuclear disaster in Japan, the civil war and famine in South Sudan, and elections and crises in Latin America. His work appears in *Al Jazeera English*, *El País*, *Zeit Online*, and *Internazionale*, among other outlets.

TAGAWA, Gen: Professor of Cultural Anthropology in the Faculty of International Studies at Hiroshima City University. He has carried out field research in southern Ethiopia since 1994. He is co-editor of *Comparative Ethnography of African Elderhood* [Afrika no Rojin] (Kyushu University Press, 2016).

TAKEDA, Yu: Associate Professor in the Faculty of International Studies at Hiroshima City University. He teaches history of modern Japan, and his research interests rest with Japanese diplomacy during the late Cold War. He is the author of *Economic Superpower Japan and Its Cooperation with the US* [Keizaitaikoku Nihon no Taibeikyocho] (Minerva Shobo, 2015) and *Japanese Nuclear Diplomacy* [Nihon no Gensiryoku Gaiko] (Chuo Koron Shinsha, 2018).

TANAMI, Aoe: Associate Professor in the Faculty of International Studies at Hiroshima City University. She specializes in Middle Eastern Regional Studies focusing on Palestinian Society and Culture since the Mandate era. She has worked as an Arabic Instructor at the Foreign Service Training Institute of the Ministry of Foreign Affairs of Japan. Her most recent publication is *The Ethnic Cleansing of Palestine* [Palestine no Minzokujoka] (Hosei University Press, 2017).

YOSHIE, Takafumi: Associate Professor in the Faculty of International Studies at Hiroshima City University. He specializes in Cultural Anthropology and Latin American Area Studies. His main publications are *The Document Networks in the Modern Hispanic World* (editor, National Museum of Ethnology, 2019) and *The Andean World: Dynamics of Negotiation and Creation* (co-author, Sekaishisosha, 2012).

YUASA, Masae: Professor of Sociology in the Faculty of International Studies at Hiroshima City University. She has been working on Japan's pacifism and anti-nuclear social movements in Hiroshima. She is the author of *Challenging Nuclear Pacifism in Japan: Hiroshima's Anti-nuclear Movements after Fukushima* (Routledge, forthcoming). She recently supported Hiroshima "black rain" survivors' trials, writing opinion papers for the Hiroshima Court.

Acknowledgements

The majority of contributors to this book have been involved in the summer program called HIROSHIMA and PEACE (H&P) organized by the Faculty/ Graduate School of International Studies, Hiroshima City University. Since its start in 2003, more than 700 people from over 50 countries have attended the program to learn and discuss about peace. This book pays tribute to its 20 years of history. We are grateful to everyone who has contributed to and participated in this program over the past 20 years.

We are also grateful to the family of the photographer Mr. Wakaji Matsumoto (1889 - 1965) for giving us permission to use a photograph he took of Hiroshima City before the Second World War (circa 1938) for the front cover of this book. Some of us may recall the scene of US President Barack Obama embracing Mr. Shigeaki Mori – an A-bomb survivor (*hibakusha*) – at the Hiroshima Peace Memorial Park during his historic 2016 visit to Hiroshima, the first ever by a sitting US President. A photo of that event can be found in Mr. Mori's account of the episode in Perspective 2 of this book. When we learned that the photographer who took the photo in 2016 was a grandchild of Mr. Matsumoto, we were surprised that a coincidence brought the two photos together in this book.

Last but not least, we also would like to thank the Dean and Associate Deans of the Faculty/Graduate School of International Studies for their support and to Hiroshima City University for providing funding for the book's publication.

from Hiroshima City,

Yoshiaki Furuzawa
Yasuhiro Inoue
Michael Gorman

Contents

PART II
Hiroshima and Its Various Narratives

Contents

Introduction

Yoshiaki Furuzawa

"No more Hiroshimas, no more Nagasakis, no more war, no more *hibakusha*." This famous statement was delivered by Senji Yamaguchi—a Nagasaki A-bomb survivor—at the United Nations second special session on disarmament in New York in June 1982. While more than 40 years has passed since the speech, in October 2022, according to US President Joe Biden, for the "[f]irst time since the Cuban missile crisis, we have a direct threat of the use [of a] nuclear weapon" (Fossum et al. 2022). On the other hand, it was only ten years ago when former US President Barack Obama laid out his vision for a "world without nuclear weapons" in April 2009 and only few years ago when the Treaty on the Prohibition of Nuclear Weapons entered into force in January 2021. The international context surrounding Hiroshima has entered a turbulent era, which was further aggravated by the unexpected invasion of Ukraine since February 2022. While a claim was made that we are supposedly living in the "most peaceful time" in human history (Pinker 2011), it seems in the distant past when people discussed whether humanity has reached the "End of History" (Fukuyama 1992).

In this difficult time, Hiroshima remains a symbol of peace. In 2019 before the global COVID-19 pandemic, the Hiroshima Peace Memorial Museum received a record number of annual visitors, approximately 1,750,000—29 percent of whom were visitors from overseas. Many dignitaries have recently visited Hiroshima. For example, former US President Obama visited Hiroshima in 2016 and became the first sitting US president to visit Hiroshima (former US President Jimmy Carter visited Hiroshima in 1984 after his presidency). A Group of Seven summit is also scheduled to convene in Hiroshima in 2023. It is, however, also important to remember that Hiroshima was not necessarily destined to be a symbol of peace from the beginning of its reconstruction process.

   More than 77 years has passed since the atomic bombs were dropped on Hiroshima and Nagasaki in August 1945. Hiroshima became a peace memorial city officially in 1949 when the Hiroshima Peace Memorial City Construction Law was passed unanimously in both chambers of the Diet, followed by a referendum in Hiroshima City. What seems natural in today's Hiroshima was not necessarily a given during its reconstruction process. On August 6, 1945, the world's first deployed atomic bomb was dropped on the Japanese city of Hiroshima at 8:15 in the morning. The bomb—often referred to as "Little Boy" in contrast to "Fat Man" the one dropped on Nagasaki on August 9, 1945—exploded 600 meters above the city. The bomb burnt down roughly 92 percent of buildings and caused an estimated 140,000 deaths within the first year after the bombing, and resulted in increased long-term side effects of radiation among survivors. In the early stage of reconstruction in 1946, there was also talk about rebuilding the city elsewhere and leaving the ruined areas as a commemorative graveyard for eternal peace (Shinoda 2008). While there were rumors that nothing would grow in Hiroshima for decades to come, the city of Hiroshima remained where it stood, and still stands there today as the home for approximately 1,200,000 people (as of October 2022). While the Atomic Bomb Dome was named as a UNESCO World Heritage site in 1996, the Hiroshima City Council only decided to preserve the dome in 1966 after two decades of divided discussion over its preservation (Fuchinoue 2011). Just as the post-war reconstruction literally started the day after the atomic bombing, people's efforts made Hiroshima City what it is today.

   While the international context surrounding Hiroshima is quite challenging (especially after February 2022), Hiroshima is also facing challenges within. More than 75 years has passed since 1945, the average age of atomic bomb survivors—known as *hibakusha*—reached 84.53 years old in 2022.[1] It was reported that the number of atomic bomb survivor certificate holders fell below 150,000 for the first time in 2019 and has fallen to 118,935 in March 2022 (Tanaka 2019; Higuchi 2022). While the city and people of Hiroshima prepare for the time when *hibakusha* from

Hiroshima are no longer with us, how to pass down their messages of peace to following generations is an important challenge to be tackled today. By incorporating short essays written by two survivors of the bomb dropped on Hiroshima, it is our hope that this book will contribute, however minimally, to pass on their messages of peace in English.

Another aim of this book is to draw various messages of peace from the case of Hiroshima. Some may read this book with the following questions in their minds: What lessons can we draw from the case of Hiroshima? How can the link between Peace Studies and Hiroshima be illustrated? While people rightly associate the term "Hiroshima" to the policy discussion of nuclear disarmament, one can also rightly ask whether the nexus between Peace Studies and Hiroshima can be much broader. A remark made by Filippo Grandi, the United Nations High Commissioner for Refugees, during his visit to Hiroshima in 2016 highlights this point:

> No place in the world symbolizes humanity's devastating relationship with war more than Hiroshima. No city speaks to us about humanity's aspiration to peace like Hiroshima... Never has the suffering of ordinary people as a consequence of war been so acute, so devastating, so lasting. Hiroshima knows what it means for ordinary people to be left at the mercy of absolute destruction (Grandi 2016).

Messages of peace from Hiroshima can be diverse—as illustrated by the following chapters—depending on from which angle Hiroshima is analyzed from. This is illustrating an importance of interdisciplinary approach. Though mostly published in Japanese, Peace Studies works related to Hiroshima grew in its size over the years. This book hopes to provide a glimpse of the research linked to Hiroshima that has been carried out in the past seven decades. This book does not claim to cover everything, but hopefully it will be a good starting point for readers' further study.

This book is divided into two parts, accompanied with short papers titled Perspectives: Part I "Hiroshima and Nuclear Weapons" and Part II

"Hiroshima and Its Various Narratives." Part I "Hiroshima and Nuclear Weapons" starts with Chapter 1 "Contributions of *Hibakusha* Testimonies toward Banning Nuclear Weapons: The 1996 ICJ Advisory Opinion, the 2015 Humanitarian Pledge, and the 2017 TPNW" by Ikuko Ota, which clarifies how *hibakusha* testimonies (narratives with faces and names from "under the mushroom cloud") have contributed as a driving force, and illustrates how the humanitarian, step-by-step approaches have worked in a complementary manner to strengthen nuclear disarmament. Chapter 2 "A Conceptual Approach to Realize the Non-use of Nuclear Weapons" by Shiro Sato examines ways to prevent the use of nuclear weapons from the perspective of International Politics and Security Studies, referring to concepts such as nuclear deterrence, security dilemma, reassurance, and nuclear taboo. Chapter 3 "'To Save Lives and End the War'—Cause or Coincidence" by Brien Hallett examines the political question of whether or not the atomic bombings "ended" the war and "forced" Japan to surrender. Chapter 4 "International Perspectives of the Hiroshima Atomic Bombing: Moral Act or War Crime" is written by Yasuhiro Inoue, Javier Sauras, Yubi Fujiwara, Yeongho Kim, Aoe Tanami, and Takafumi Yoshie. It examines conflicting understandings of Hiroshima by investigating the way in which major world newspapers have portrayed the 1945 atomic bombing of Hiroshima. Chapter 5 "*The New York Times*: Transition from Accomplice to Questioner of the Atomic Bombing" by Yasuhiro Inoue traces how the *New York Times* has changed its stance about the 1945 atomic bombing of Hiroshima over time.

Part II "Hiroshima and Its Various Narratives" starts with Chapter 6 "What We Talk About When We Talk About Hiroshima" by Mariko Nagai, which sheds light on both what we talk about and what we do not necessarily talk about when we talk about Hiroshima. Chapter 7 "Inheriting 'Hiroshima Heart': Imaginary and Institution in Cornelius Castoriadis' Social Theory" by Masae Yuasa explores the meaning of "inheriting atomic-bomb experiences" in Hiroshima by referring to the term "Hiroshima Heart"— which was institutionalized as a core policy of Hiroshima City's peace administration since the late 1970s. Chapter 8 "Hiroshima, Nagasaki, and the Environmental Age" by Toshihiro Higuchi provides another perspective. He views what happened in Hiroshima and Nagasaki as an environmental disaster, and examines how the Hiroshima and Nagasaki bombings changed the ways we think about nature and its relationship to humans in the nuclear age. Chapter 9 "Layered Landscapes, Transplanted Tragedies" by Michael Gorman explores Naomi Hirahara's fictional representation of the trauma affecting Japanese American *hibakusha* and their families. Chapter 10 "(Post)Colonial Atomic Bomb Literatures" by Kyoko Matsunaga examines how Han Su-san's novel *Battleship Island*—which portrays experiences of Korean *hibakusha*—disrupts the "master narrative" of existing Atomic Bomb Literature by viewing it through the lens of East Asian colonial history. Chapter 11 "Space and Time of Atomic Bomb Memorials and Monuments in Urban Hiroshima" by Gen Tagawa provides an overview of memorials and monuments representing the A-Bomb damage within urban Hiroshima.

Three points should be mentioned to readers before ending the Introduction. First, because of the interdisciplinary nature of this book—which is visible from the structure of the book—each author's writing style is respected. Second, it is also important to express our gratitude to publishers and *Hiroshima Peace Research Journal* for their understandings to translate some chapters which were originally written in Japanese. More detailed acknowledgements can be found at the end of each chapter when relevant. Third, the photos and tables in each chapter/perspective were taken/made by each author unless otherwise stated.

While this book focuses on the case of Hiroshima, it also hints at the necessity for a global dialogue about peace to learn about each other's experiences, and to deepen our understandings of the term "peace." While many agree that the term "positive peace"—that is, a situation more than merely a cessation of physical violence, while addressing the structural and cultural violence within a society—is what we should aim for, there is unfortunately no magical formula to realize "positive peace." As each place has its own history and culture, within each local context, there can be various messages of peace with different emphasis. Because peace can be seen as an ongoing process, rather than an end point, global dialogue on peace is crucial. This book is a humble step toward such efforts from the city of Hiroshima.

Notes

[1] Within the context of Hiroshima and Nagasaki, the term *hibakusha* refers to atomic bomb survivors. Recently, the term *hibakusha* also includes victims exposed to nuclear tests or nuclear power plant accidents, who are often referred to as *global hibakusha* (Jacobs 2022).

References

Fossum, Sam, Collins, Kaitlan, and LeBlanc, Paul (2022) "Biden offers stark 'Armageddon' Putin's nuclear threats," CNN, October 7. <https://edition.cnn.com/2022/10/06/politics/armageddon-biden-putin-russia-nuclear-threats/index.html>

Fuchinoue, Hideki (2011) "Peace Monuments and Reconstruction," in Darryl R.J. Macer, (ed.), *Asian-Arab Philosophical Dialogues on Culture of Peace and Human Dignity.* Bangkok: UNESCO, pp.56-71.

Fukuyama, Francis (1992) *The End of the History and the Last Man.* New York: The Free Press.

Grandi, Filippo (2016) "Conflict and Displacement: Talking about Refugees in the City of Peace," a speech given at the Hiroshima Peace Cultural Foundation. November 26. <https://www.unhcr.org/admin/hcspeeches/583c04da7/conflict-displacement-talking-refugees-city-peace.html> (Accessed on November 28, 2021).

Higuchi, Koji (2022) "Hibakusha hajimete 12mannninn sita mawaru [A Number of Hibakusha goes below 120,000 for the first time]," *Chugoku Shimbun*, July 1.

Jacobs, Robert A. (2022) *Nuclear Bodies: The Global Hibakusha.* New Haven: Yale University Press.

Pinker, Steven (2011) *The Better Angels of Our Nature.* New York: Viking Books.

Shinoda, Hideaki (2008) "Post-war Reconstruction of Hiroshima as a Case of Peacebuilding," in Hideaki Shinoda, (ed.), *Post-war Reconstruction of Hiroshima.* Hiroshima: Institute for Peace Science-Hiroshima University, pp.2-24.

Tanaka, Michiko (2019) "Hibakusha 15 mannin wo shitamawaru: Tetyo syojisha heikin 82.65sai [Number of A-bomb Survivor's Certificate holders falls below 150,000, average age now 82.65]," *Chugoku Shimbun*, July 2.

PART I
Hiroshima and Nuclear Weapons

Chapter 1
Contributions of *Hibakusha* Testimonies toward Banning Nuclear Weapons: The 1996 ICJ Advisory Opinion, the 2015 Humanitarian Pledge, and the 2017 TPNW

Ikuko Ota

1. The Unresolved Divide within the International Community over Nuclear Deterrence

On January 22, 2021, the Treaty on the Prohibition of Nuclear Weapons (TPNW)[1] entered into force at midnight local time in each of the ratifying countries. For the first time in history, an international treaty banning nuclear weapons as inhumane became legally effective. The TPNW was adopted by the United Nations (UN) in July 2017 with the support of 122 countries (with one opposed and one abstention), or about 60 percent of the UN member states. The non-nuclear-weapon countries and civil society in support of the TPNW have adopted the humanitarian approach, stigmatizing nuclear weapons as an absolute evil with which humanity cannot coexist. As of January 2023, 92 countries had signed the treaty; 68 had ratified it and are official states parties.

As UN Secretary-General António Guterres has recognized (United Nations 2019, 2021), the TPNW is consistent with existing legal frameworks for nuclear disarmament, including the Treaty on the Non-Proliferation of Nuclear Weapons (NPT) and the Comprehensive Nuclear Test Ban Treaty (CTBT). However, the nine nuclear-weapon countries and their allies, including Japan (hereinafter referred to collectively as "nuclear deterrent states"), refused to participate even in the negotiation process for the TPNW at the UN.[2] They have insisted that, though concerned about the inhumanity of nuclear weapons, they cannot yet abandon, given the increasingly severe international situation, nuclear deterrence for security reasons. Instead, they have chosen a step-by-step approach that would, allegedly in a realistic and practical manner, delegitimize nuclear weapons and more toward the end goal of nuclear abolition.[3]

Amid the unresolved divide within the international community over nuclear deterrence, on February 24, 2022, Russia invaded Ukraine. While the invasion itself is a violation of the UN Charter, Russia is directly challenging the three pillars of the NPT regime involving 191 countries, which has constituted the core of international security since 1970. From the outset of the invasion, Russia has referred to the possibility of using nuclear weapons (denial of "nuclear disarmament"), then attacked nuclear power plants and nuclear-related facilities in Ukraine (denial of "peaceful use of nuclear energy"), and by occupying them, obstructed timely and appropriate inspections by the International Atomic Energy Agency (IAEA) (denial of "nuclear non-proliferation"). With the use of nuclear weapons becoming a reality, the NPT Review Conference, which had been postponed many times due to the COVID-19 pandemic, was held in August 2022 for the first time in seven years. However, due to the opposition of Russia, a unanimous agreement could not be reached, and the Review Conference closed without adopting a final document, as was the case at the previous conference in 2015 (United Nations 2022c; Ministry of Foreign Affairs of Japan 2022). While confidence in the NPT regime was shaken, and even the raison d'etre of the treaty could be questioned, on October 5, Russian President Putin signed a presidential decree ordering the Zaporizhzhia nuclear power plant, located in the unilaterally annexed territory of Ukraine, to be under Russian government ownership and control. The following day, on October 6, US President Biden warned that the danger of nuclear war has reached its highest point since the Cuban Missile Crisis of 1962. And regarding the recent Japanese situation in the Far East, while North Korea is estimated to have about 300 ballistic missiles that can reach Japan and China has more than 600, North Korea's nuclear and missile programs are advancing, and the threat of a Taiwan contingency is also rising as the Xi Jinping administration enters an unprecedented third term at the Communist

Party Congress in October 2022.

Given the views described above, in this chapter, the author demonstrates how the humanitarian and step-by-step approaches, which are often seen as symbolic of the division between nuclear deterrent states and non-nuclear weapon states, in fact, have worked in a complementary manner to strengthen every party's obligation to negotiate and complete nuclear disarmament (Article VI of the NPT). In light of the circumstances leading to the 2017 TPNW, the focus is on the 1996 Advisory Opinion of the International Court of Justice (ICJ) and the 2015 Humanitarian Pledge. In doing so, the author also clarifies how the testimonies of *hibakusha* (narratives with faces and names from "under the mushroom cloud") have contributed, as an irreplaceable driving force, toward adopting these legal documents. Lastly, the author offers some thoughts regarding the shift from "utilitarian use" to "absolutist ban" of nuclear weapons and what Japan can do for a nuclear-free world.

2. The 1996 ICJ Advisory Opinion as Point of Departure: Toward a "Double Obligation" for Nuclear Disarmament Negotiations

Section 2 deals with the starting point of the TPNW, the ICJ's 1996 Advisory Opinion regarding the "Legality of the Threat or Use of Nuclear Weapons" (The 1996 Advisory Opinion) (International Court of Justice 1996).[4] This Section focuses on the process leading to the unanimous ruling by ICJ judges that interprets Article VI of the NPT in a way that strengthens the disarmament obligations of the NPT parties without rejecting the step-by-step approach, that is to say, also encompassing the nuclear deterrent states.

The 1996 Advisory Opinion was issued in response to the question: "Is the threat or use of nuclear weapons in any circumstance permitted under international law?" as stated in a UN General Assembly resolution (UN Doc. A/RES/49/75K) adopted in December 15, 1994. This resolution was adopted in response to campaigning by a loose network of international

NGOs called the "World Court Project," launched in 1992. This Project was inspired by A-bomb exhibitions and testimonies around the world by A-bomb survivors from Hiroshima and Nagasaki, which began to be held actively around the time of the United Nations Special Session on Disarmament in 1978.[5]

In accordance with Article 66 of the ICJ Statute, the ICJ determined that the UN and any state entitled to appear before the Court may provide information on the question. Oral statements were made in the fall of 1995 by the representatives of 22 countries. Of these, 15, including Egypt, Mexico, Costa Rica, Malaysia, the Philippines, Zimbabwe, and several countries of the South Pacific, asserted that nuclear weapons are illegal, while Germany and Italy stated that the Court should avoid making a judgement. The US, UK, France, and Russia agreed that no judicial decision should be made, but advocated "conditional legality," that is, any decision can be made only on the specific circumstances of a given use.

From Japan, on November 7, 1995, the mayors of Hiroshima and Nagasaki appeared before the court asserting the illegality of the weapons, describing in detail the effects of the atomic bombings and the inhumanity of nuclear weapons. The 1963 Tokyo District Court decision in the *Shimoda Case*, claiming compensation against Japan brought by the residents of Hiroshima and Nagasaki, clearly declared the atomic bombings to be a violation of existing international law (Fujita 2011:1-75), but the Japanese government officially stated only that "the use of nuclear weapons is clearly contrary to the spirit of humanity that gives international law its philosophical foundation." Japan did not offer an opinion as to whether all use would be illegal (NHK Hiroshima 1997: 70-129).

On July 8, 1996, the 14 judges of the ICJ proclaimed unanimously in their Advisory Opinion (paragraph 105), at Point (2) F, that, "…there exists an obligation to pursue in good faith and bring to a conclusion negotiations leading to nuclear disarmament in all its aspects under strict and effective international control." This proclamation clearly interpreted Article VI of the NPT as a "double obligation," that is, 1) to negotiate for disarmament in good faith (obligation of ways), and 2) to bring the negotiations to a precise conclusion—total and permanent nuclear disarmament (obligation of results). This interpretation led first to the ICJ trials by the Marshall Islands. In 2014, they submitted to the ICJ the cases on "the Obligations Concerning Negotiations Relating to Cessation of the Nuclear Arms Race and to Nuclear Disarmament," asserting non-compliance with Article VI by the nine nuclear weapon states. The second result of the ICJ's interpretation in the 1996 Advisory Opinion was the drive for negotiations toward a treaty that totally bans nuclear weapons (Souza Schmitz 2016; Eto 2019: 392, 405-411).

The critical aspect of the Opinion that played a major role in the ban treaty movement is articulated in Paragraph 105, at Point (2) E. The first sentence of Point (2) E says, "The threat or use of nuclear weapons would generally be contrary to the rules of international law applicable in armed conflict, and, in particular, the principles and rules of international humanitarian law." The second sentence states that "…in view of the current state of international law, and of the elements of facts at its disposal, the court cannot conclude definitively whether the threat or use of nuclear weapons would be lawful or unlawful in an extreme circumstance of self-defense, in which the very survival of a state would be at stake." In the interview of 2014 by Fumihiko Yoshida (editorial writer for the *Asahi Shimbun*), then-President of the ICJ Mohammed Bedjaoui described the drafting process of Point (2) E as follows:

> The court has noted that there is this kind of tension between humanitarian law, which would prohibit the use of nuclear weapons because of their indiscriminate effect, and the right of self-defense which would be allowed, in some extreme cases, in order to let a state survive. These two points would be in contradiction, in some frontal conflict. Consequently, as a sort of compromise, we had concluded as [Point (2) E] in the advisory opinion (Yoshida/*The Asahi Shimbun* 2014).

As a consequence of compromise, the second sentence of this Point has been perceived as a "loophole" by nuclear deterrent states, leaving them room to interpret that the Court was allowing for the legal use of nuclear weapons in extreme situations. However, the real intent of then-President Bedjaoui was to proclaim (i.e., make known officially to the public) an advisory opinion incorporating the above-mentioned Point (2) F, which states that NPT parties have a "double obligation" to negotiate and, then, to actually bring about the abolition of nuclear weapons, under the condition that five of the 14 judges are from a nuclear weapon state (Bedjaoui, Kurosawa, and Ida 2015).

With this objective in mind, he did not vote against Point (2) E, which says that "the use of nuclear weapons would generally be illegal [in light of international humanitarian law], but in extreme situations, the Court cannot decide [because all states have the right to self-defense]." Considering that it would be difficult to reach a majority decision and adopt the Opinion itself, he dared to vote in favor, thinking it would be better to put his true intent in a "Declaration" to be published with the Opinion. For voting to adopt Point (2) E, the court was split seven in favor to seven against, including three judges voting against who were concerned with the word "generally" and require the Court to remove any ambiguity regarding the illegality of threat or use of nuclear weapons. Thereafter, then-President Bedjaoui cast the deciding vote in accordance with the ICJ rules and Point (2) E was adopted (*Asahi Shimbun* 2014).

Then-President Bedjaoui stated the following in the interview by Yoshida in 2014:

> [The oral statements by the mayors of Hiroshima and Nagasaki have] just reinforced considerably my feeling about the fact we needed to do everything we could do. As president of the ICJ, I listened to the mayors of Nagasaki and Hiroshima, that's an imperishable memory. The two of them have been extremely moving, and they showed us very well that nuclear weapons are the weapons of evil. They told us about the inexpressible suffering of their populations. … [A] judge of the ICJ, is, after all, a human

being like everyone else. He has perfect mastery of international law, he must be, as a judge, working in a perfect spirit of independence. That is perfectly right but he is also a human being, a man who has political convictions, and these convictions are something very personal which cannot be excluded in his judgments. He makes his judgment from the law, not from his personal feelings. But in this case, in this eminently political matter, we have to express ourselves, our opinion, based not only on the laws, but also on our consciousness, too (Yoshida/*The Asahi Shimbun* 2014).

3. The 2015 "Humanitarian Pledge," a Turning Point: Embodying "Effective Measures" for Nuclear Disarmament

Section 3 examines how non-nuclear weapon states and international NGOs have positioned the TPNW as an "effective measure" under Article VI of the NPT that "closes the legal loophole" created when the Advisory Opinion left open a possible justification for nuclear deterrence.

In September 1996, two months after the Advisory Opinion was issued, Malaysia attempted to "fill the loophole" in the second sentence of Point (2) E. As a major non-aligned power with the presidency of the UN General Assembly, Malaysia drafted a resolution that was presented as a "Follow-up to the Advisory Opinion of the International Court of Justice on the Legality of the Threat or Use of Nuclear Weapons." That resolution stated that the UN General Assembly "urges all States to fulfil that obligation immediately by commencing multilateral negotiations in 1997 leading to an early conclusion of a nuclear-weapons convention prohibiting the development, production, testing, deployment, stockpiling, transfer, threat or use of nuclear weapons and providing for their elimination." Malaysia called for informal consultations with New Zealand, Australia, Indonesia, and others. On December 10, the resolution was adopted by a vote of 115 in favor (including China), 22 against (the US, Russia, the UK, France, and other nuclear weapon states and their allies), and 32 abstentions (including three

NATO member states—Denmark, Iceland, and Norway—and Japan). It has since been adopted every year by majority vote.[6]

Furthermore, in 1997, Costa Rica submitted to the UN General Assembly a Model Nuclear Weapons Convention (MNWC) drafted by the International Association of Lawyers Against Nuclear Arms (IALANA) and other international NGOs. In 2007, a revised version of MNWC modeled on the Chemical Weapons Convention was prepared and submitted by Costa Rica and Malaysia to the NPT Preparatory Committee, where it was put on the agenda for discussion (Kawasaki 2018: 27-28).

In April 2009, US President Barack Obama made a speech in Prague calling for a "world without nuclear weapons." This speech led to his Nobel Peace Prize in October that year. With this wind at their back, one year after, the International Committee of the Red Cross (ICRC), headquartered in Switzerland, which usually abides strictly by its principle of political neutrality, made a major policy change from a humanitarian perspective. Although it has expressed concern about nuclear weapons since 1945, this time it declared officially that the ICRC could not offer rescue or relief after a nuclear explosion. That is, in April 2010, a month before the NPT Review Conference began in May that year, again with the intention of "closing the loophole" in the Advisory Opinion, the ICRC presented a statement by President Jakob Kellenberger entitled, "Bringing the era of nuclear weapons to an end." Quoting Marcel Junod, who entered Hiroshima immediately after the atomic bombing and later conveyed the reality of the bombing to the world, the statement asserts that, "The ICRC finds it difficult to envisage how any use of nuclear weapons could be compatible with the rules of international humanitarian law," and the debate regarding nuclear weapons "…must be conducted not only on the basis of military doctrines and power politics…. The currency of this debate must ultimately be about human beings, about the fundamental rules of international humanitarian law, and about the collective future of humanity" (Kellenberger 2015: 883).

At the NPT Review Conference held in New York shortly thereafter, the Swiss Foreign Minister argued that humanitarian concerns should be placed at the center of the discussion on nuclear disarmament, and the final document (Plan of Action), which was unanimously accepted, including by the nuclear deterrent states, included this text: "The Conference expresses its deep concern at the catastrophic humanitarian consequences of any use of nuclear weapons and reaffirms the need for all States at all times to comply with applicable international law, including international humanitarian law" (United Nations 2010: 19; Ministry of Foreign Affairs of Japan 2010).

The adoption of the final document at the 2010 NPT Review Conference, which was inspired by the ICRC president's statement, generated considerable momentum for the "humanitarian initiative," reframing the negotiations from a military/political perspective to a humanitarian perspective. This reframing led to two parallel diplomatic actions at the NPT Preparatory Committee meeting in May 2012 (Bernard 2015: 504-506; Kmentt 2015: 685-704).

The first action was continued adoption, by the NPT Preparatory Committee and the UN General Assembly, of joint statements by non-nuclear weapon states across the globe expressing concern about the inhumanity of nuclear weapons and calling for them to be made explicitly illegal under international law (Ministry of Foreign Affairs of Japan 2020).[7]

The second action was in response to these joint statements. Three international conferences on the humanitarian impact of nuclear weapons were held (in Norway with 127 countries in March 2013; in Mexico with 146 countries in February 2014; and in Austria with 158 countries in December 2014). India and Pakistan, both nuclear weapon states, participated in all three of these conferences. The United States and the United Kingdom participated in the third conference. In addition to scientifically examining the harms nuclear weapons have inflicted through bombings and testing, the risks of accidental use and accidents involving nuclear weapons were discussed. A number of *hibakusha* (atomic bomb survivors of Hiroshima and Nagasaki and victims contaminated by nuclear tests) also participated in these conferences. Describing their experiences, they impressed upon the participating states the "unspeakable suffering inflicted on ordinary citizens by nuclear weapons." Based on both testimony and scientific fact, a common understanding emerged: humanitarian relief would be extremely difficult in the event of a nuclear explosion in a densely populated area, and the use of nuclear weapons would not in any way be consistent with international humanitarian law (Ministry of Foreign Affairs of Japan 2014).

These two diplomatic actions led to a turning point at the close of the third conference, attended by 158 states. In addition to the Chair's summary, Austria released a document later renamed the "Humanitarian Pledge for the Prohibition and Abolition of Nuclear Weapons." Citing the need to urgently and fully implement their obligations under Article VI of the NPT, the Pledge called on all NPT states parties to "identify and pursue effective measures to fill the legal gap for the prohibition and elimination of nuclear weapons." The Pledge also stated its intention "to cooperate with all stakeholders to achieve this goal." The following month, in January 2015, Austria sent its Pledge to all UN member states for signature. Due in part to intensive lobbying by ICAN and other NGO networks, by the time the NPT Review Conference began in April that year, about 70 countries had endorsed the Pledge (107 countries by the end of the conference; Japan was not among them) (United Nations 2015; Kawasaki 2017: 53).

Thus, the movement for a legal prohibition of nuclear weapons from a humanitarian perspective converged on the phrase "effective measures for nuclear disarmament," as stipulated in Article VI. At the 2015 NPT Review Conference, the New Agenda Coalition[8] and other countries that endorsed the Humanitarian Pledge discussed "effective measures" almost synonymously with "a legal ban." Nuclear deterrent states opposed a legal ban, arguing that "effective measures" meant steadily advancing the step-by-step approach. The draft final document prepared by the chair included a recommendation to establish an Open-Ended Working Group (OEWG) under the UN General Assembly to discuss "effective measures," including legal provisions for a nuclear-weapon-free world. (The Review Conference ended without adopting a final document due to conflict regarding a Middle East Nuclear-Weapon-Free Zone Initiative). At the UN General Assembly in October that year, Mexico submitted a draft resolution to establish the

OEWG, which was adopted by a majority vote (Japan abstained). After discussions in the OEWG, by resolution 71/258, a United Nations conference to negotiate a legally binding instrument to prohibit nuclear weapons, leading towards their total elimination, was convened at the UN in March 2017, leading to adoption of the TPNW in July the same year (Kawasaki 2017, 53-56; Imanishi 2019: 83-88).[9]

4. The TPNW: A Prohibition-First Treaty Envisaging Later Participation by the Nuclear Weapon States

Section 4 summarizes the TPNW[10] based on the considerations mentioned above.

In general, treaty preambles describe the philosophy, purpose, and background of the treaty in question. The 24 paragraphs of the TPNW preamble refer to the inhumanity of nuclear weapons, which result in "catastrophic humanitarian consequences," hence the need for abolition, the necessity of a prohibition treaty due to concerns about stalled nuclear disarmament and the modernization of nuclear weapons, and the need to respect and strengthen existing nuclear disarmament regimes, including the NPT and CTBT. Furthermore, the wording of Point (2) F in the ICJ Advisory Opinion, which is the origin of the TPNW, is mentioned in paragraph 17, and the *hibakusha*, the moral force behind the TPNW, are mentioned in paragraphs 6 and 24.

The main text of the TPNW consists of 20 articles. The text draws on existing disarmament treaties, including the Chemical Weapons Convention, the Anti-Personnel Landmines Convention, and the Cluster Munitions Convention. In the processes leading to these conventions, countries and NGOs collaborated on an international campaign to resist pressure from major powers, basing the inhumanity of the regulated weapons on the suffering of their victims. In content and structure, the TPNW again follows these precedents; it is a comprehensive ban on the production, use, stockpiling, and transfer of weapons. In other words, it is a prohibition-first treaty, with details of the elimination (disposal) process and verification system to be worked out after its ratification. This allowed the treaty to enter into force without the participation of nuclear weapon states and without their disposal and verification technology and know-how.

Article 1 of the TPNW, in the same language as the NPT, refers to "nuclear weapons and other nuclear explosive devices" as "inhumane weapons." On that basis, it prohibits all activities related to nuclear weapons—making (developing, testing, producing, manufacturing), possessing (acquiring, possessing, storing, placing in a territory, establishing, deploying), allowing entry into a territory (transferring, receiving), use (including the threat of use), and cooperating with (assisting, encouraging, soliciting)—all without exception (i.e., without "loopholes").[11]

In addition, Articles 2 to 4 present the basic process for dismantling nuclear weapons, assuming that nuclear weapon states will join the TPNW. They also set forth the fundamentals regarding declaration obligations, safeguards, and verification of elimination. With regard to verification, the articles stipulate the procedures to be followed in cases where a state party voluntarily eliminates its nuclear weapons and then joins the TPNW, and in cases where a state party first joins the TPNW and then eliminates its nuclear weapons. In both cases, a "competent international authority" (to be established) will be responsible for verification, and a safeguards agreement will be concluded with the IAEA to ensure that no declared nuclear material has been diverted from "peaceful nuclear activities" and that no undeclared nuclear material or nuclear activities exist. Moreover, the state parties will be obliged to report on the progress of elimination periodically.

Article 6 provides for victim assistance and environmental restoration. Based on humanitarian and human rights principles, state parties are obligated to provide medical, social, and economic assistance to people affected by the use of nuclear weapons or by nuclear testing. They are also obligated to restore environments contaminated by previous activities related to the use of nuclear weapons and nuclear testing.[12]

Article 8 provides for meetings of state parties to "consider and, if necessary, decide issues relating to the application or implementation of the Treaty and on further measures for nuclear disarmament." The UN

Secretary-General is required to convene the first meeting within one year of entry into force to begin considering specific measures, such as the verification of any destruction of nuclear weapons that takes place. Thereafter, meetings will take place every two years. The first Conference of the Parties was held on June 21-23, 2022, in Vienna, and adopted the action plan and political declaration for the TPNW's goal of a world free of nuclear weapons, while reaffirming the complementarity of the TPNW with the international disarmament and nonproliferation regime, including the NPT (United Nations 2022a, 2022b).

A review conference stipulated Article 8 will be held five years after entry into force and every six years thereafter to "consider the operation of the Treaty and progress toward its objectives." Both the meetings of state parties and the review conferences may "invite" non-parties to the TPNW; international organizations including the United Nations, the ICRC, and relevant NGOs may attend as observers. Other provisions include the entry into force conditions (Article 15) and the relationship between the TPNW and existing international agreements (Article 18).

5. Narratives from "Under the Mushroom Cloud" Paving the Way toward a New Future after Russia's Aggression against Ukraine

As examined in the above Sections, the testimonies of *hibakusha* (narratives with faces and names from "under the mushroom cloud") became a driving force leading to, first, the ICJ's Advisory Opinion, and then to a new movement in nuclear disarmament negotiations, which had been stalled "above the mushroom cloud." The new movement was based on a humanitarian approach derived from the inhumanity of nuclear weapons. A third outcome of *hibakusha* narratives was the process that led to the TPNW. Despite opposition from the nuclear deterrent states, the negotiations at the UN started by, in a complementary manner, utilizing the step-by-step approach for "effective measures for nuclear disarmament," as stipulated in Article VI of the NPT. A fourth outcome was the treaty itself, adopted with the approval of 122 countries, with entry into force in little more than three years. It was as if people of different nationalities and ages, moved by *"sonzai no araware* [the manifestation of existence]"[13] of the *hibakusha*, who had found and carried the humanitarian mission in the midst of the extremes of human suffering and hardships, linked the two approaches and passed the baton within the constraints of their respective positions and roles.

As the Chair's Summary of the fourth conference on the humanitarian impact of nuclear weapons (June 20, 2022, Vienna) clearly points out, Russia's invasion of Ukraine underscores, among others, three facts: first, "nuclear weapons do not prevent major wars, but rather embolden nuclear-armed states to start wars"; second, "a security paradigm based on the theory of nuclear deterrence" is fragile; third, "the immediate humanitarian emergency and long-term consequences of nuclear weapon detonations" are "[w]hat we cannot prepare for, what we cannot respond to, we must therefore prevent" (Republic of Austria 2022).

Then, this last part offers some thoughts regarding what Japan can do for a nuclear-free world while taking into consideration the shift from "utilitarian use" to "absolutist ban" of nuclear weapons.

5.1. To Avoid "Fighting Dirty"

According to philosopher Thomas Nagel of New York University, the logic underlying the "utilitarian use of nuclear weapons" and the theory of nuclear deterrence is this: "[I]f faced with the possibility of preventing a great evil by producing a lesser, one should choose the lesser evil[,]" giving top priority to "what will *happen*" (Nagel 1972:125, 124). However, "the justification for what one did to another person had to be such that it could be offered to him [interpersonally], rather than just to the world at large…" (Nagel 1972:137). Therefore, "directing [one's] attack not at the true target of [one's] hostility, but at peripheral targets that happen to be vulnerable" is "to fight dirty," which means not treating them "with the minimum respect which is owed human beings" (Nagel 1972:135, 134, 139). Given the concept of "fighting dirty," "certain acts cannot be justified no matter what the consequences" (Nagel 1972:128). Based on this logic, "[i]f it is not allowable to do certain things, such as killing unarmed prisoners or civilians, then no argument about what will happen if one doesn't do them can show that doing them would be all right" (Nagel 1972:128). In other words, the absolutist ban on nuclear weapons for nuclear abolition is legitimate because "[one cannot] say to the victims of Hiroshima, 'You understand, we have to incinerate you to provide the Japanese government with an incentive to surrender' " (Nagel 1972:137).

5.2. To Overcome the Dominant Narrative-Framing

If this is the case, then, to encourage nuclear deterrent states to "ban nuclear weapons based on absolutism," Japan must address its own inhumanity as perpetrator during World War II, for example, by acknowledging the Korean *hibakusha* issue hidden behind the A-bomb tragedy. On the other hand, Japan must also continue its efforts to weaken the "framing of nuclear weapons as essential means to end war" or the "trivialization of nuclear damages," recognizing the fact that such narrative framing persists in the newspaper articles regarding the atomic bombings in the US, Britain, and Australia. An example of this effort can be seen in the oral statement before the ICJ by then-Mayor of Hiroshima, Takashi Hiraoka.

During his two terms (eight years) as mayor, Hiraoka frequently faced accusations from Asian countries regarding Japan's war crimes and the framing of the atomic bombings as retaliation for the surprise attack on Pearl Harbor. Critics insisted that Japan was not a victim but a perpetrator, emphasizing that displaying the damage done to Hiroshima was an effort by Japan to present itself as a victim, exonerating itself for the atrocities committed during the war.

Based on this bitter experience, then-Mayor Hiraoka began his statement on November 7, 1995, before the ICJ judges as follows:

> Inscribed on the Cenotaph for the A-bomb Victims, located in Hiroshima's Peace Memorial Park, are the following words: "Let All the Souls Here Rest in Peace: For We Shall Not Repeat the

Evil." Evil indicates *the act of human beings* waging war and developing and using atomic weapons to achieve victory.

I am not here in this Court, however, to debate the responsibility for the dropping of the atomic bombs. Japan also committed shameful acts during World War II. Reflecting upon these acts, I would like to convey to the people of the world what kind of damage befell Hiroshima and appeal for the abolition of nuclear weapons *so that this tragedy is never repeated on the face of this earth.*

Beneath the atomic bomb's monstrous mushroom cloud, human skin was burned raw. Crying for water, human beings died in desperate agony. *Beginning with thoughts of these victims, and imagining our own wives and children as the victims of nuclear war,* it is incumbent upon us to think about the nuclear age and the relationship between human beings and nuclear weapons (emphasis added by author).[14]

5.3. To Pass the Baton by Linking the Humanitarian and Step-by-Step Approaches

Inheriting this wisdom of then-Mayor Hiraoka, what can Japan act for a nuclear-free world?

ICAN, the international NGO that contributed most to the movement toward the adoption of the TPNW, was awarded the Nobel Peace Prize in 2017. Mayors for Peace, an ICAN partner, is also an international NGO that aims to abolish nuclear weapons through the solidarity of 8,237 local governments in 166 countries and regions around the world (as of January 2023). Mayors for Peace was established in 1982 as an organization of local governments responding to a call issued by then-Mayor of Hiroshima Takeshi Araki at the second UN Special Session on Disarmament (Komizo 2019).

Upon the entry into force of the Convention, Kazumi Matsui, the current mayor of Hiroshima and president of Mayors for Peace, said, "The time has come to urge politicians to change their policies. I want the civil society assertion that nuclear weapons are unacceptable to develop into a global movement" (*Chugoku Shimbun* 2021). He also attended, as an observer, the first TPNW state parties meeting of June 2022 in Vienna, and introduced in his speech the implementation of Mayors for Peace initiatives under the "PX Vision (Vision for Peaceful Transformation to a Sustainable World)" (Matsui 2022).[15] Further, Mayor Matsui has demanded that the Japanese government participate in the second meeting of state parties to the TPNW (to be held in New York, November 2023) and also promptly become a state party itself (City of Hiroshima 2022; Mayors for Peace 2022b).

Mayor Matsui's call based on a humanitarian approach will be able to have a better chance of becoming a reality, again by using a step-by-step approach in a complementary manner, for the following reasons.

Japanese premier Fumio Kishida, whose constituency is the city of Hiroshima, has always said that nuclear disarmament is at the center of his life's work. Being true to his words, PM Kishida became the first Japanese prime minister to attend the NPT Review Conference of August 2022. He presented the "Hiroshima Action Plan" in his speech on August 1, 2022, while expressing his strong sense of urgency due to the repeated threats to use nuclear weapons by Russia in its aggression against Ukraine. His Action Plan aims to be a realistic roadmap to the ideal of a world without nuclear weapons by strengthening the NPT regime step by step. After the explanation of the fifth action of his Plan to "promote the accurate understanding on the realities of nuclear weapons use through encouraging visits to Hiroshima and Nagasaki by international leaders and others," he also revealed that it was his own intention for the G7 Summit of May 2023 to be held in Hiroshima. By inviting world leaders to the A-bombed city to learn about the reality of the atomic bombing, PM Kishida believes the G7 Summit will demonstrate from Hiroshima to the world the G7 leaders' firm commitment to never repeat the catastrophe of nuclear weapons (Kishida 2022; Kuriyama and Teraguchi 2022).

Besides, it was a remarkable fact that TPNW was mentioned for the first time in the Japan-proposed draft UN resolution aimed at a nuclear-free world. On October 31, 2022, the draft resolution entitled "Steps to building a common roadmap towards a world without nuclear weapons," submitted by the Government of Japan to the First Committee of the UN General Assembly, was adopted for the 29th year in a row, with the support of 139 countries (with six opposed and 31 abstentions). The draft resolution is expected to be adopted in a plenary meeting of the General Assembly in December 2022 (NHK World-Japan 2022).

Although the Japanese government still refuses to sign the TPNW, it has participated in expert meetings on nuclear disarmament verification, in which the nuclear weapon states are also involved.[16] Encouragingly as well as interestingly enough, among 80 states, the *hibakusha* and NGOs, the Government of Japan attended the fourth conference on the humanitarian impact of nuclear weapons, which was held by the Government of Austria on June 20, 2022, ahead of the first meeting of state parties to the TPNW. The future TPNW meetings of state parties need to establish a concrete verification process for dismantling nuclear weapons, and Japan can contribute to nuclear abolition by attending as an observer, providing its expertise as far as possible.

5.4. To Imagine Optimistically the Future of the Anthropocene

In April 2020, "75 Years after the Atomic Bombings: A Message from Nagasaki" was displayed at the entrance to the Nagasaki Atomic Bomb Museum, which was temporarily closed due to the COVID pandemic. In light of this Anthropocene era, when human activities decisively and negatively affect the Earth's systems, the message read as follows:

> Nuclear weapons, environmental issues, and COVID-19... the way to tackle all these global issues is fundamentally the same: Have a sense of commitment; Extend compassion to others; Imagine the consequences; Take action.
> Let's take a step forward this year as we mark the 75th anniversary of the atomic bombings (City of Nagasaki 2020).

Reading that Nagasaki message in the context of what has been examined in this chapter, it can be said that the solution begins by imagining what it would like to be in a disaster and to actually have one of those "narratives with a face and a name." Therefore, the author will end this chapter with a personal reflection on imagination.

Near the end of July 1995, the author was asked to assist the secretariat of an international conference, and spent several days in a room in the conference center in Hiroshima Peace Memorial Park surrounded by a loud chorus of cicadas. There the author met several times an elderly gentleman with a straight back looking elegant in a three-piece linen suit. He seemed a remarkably light-hearted intellectual.

Toward the end of the conference, the author ventured to ask him, "How can you be so optimistic when dealing with such heavy nuclear issues?" At 86 years of age, he looked at the author with a smile and said, "Ah, it's simple. My ultimate goal is to abolish war. How can we do that if we can't even abolish nuclear weapons?"

Joseph Rotblat lost his wife in a Polish concentration camp when he was still young. He joined the Manhattan Project but resigned before its completion. He served as head of the Pugwash Conference, which was awarded the Nobel Peace Prize of 1995. Eleven years after his passing (in 2005), the first US president of African descent visited the same Peace Park, stood in front of the Cenotaph, and told the world to "imagine being under the mushroom cloud." On that May evening, the author vividly recalled the vision received from that smile of Joseph Rotblat.

Acknowledgements

This chapter is an English version of the following Japanese manuscript: OTA Ikuko (2021), "Kakuheiki-kinshi-joyaku to jindo-teki/dannkai-teki apurouchi [The TPNW and the Humanitarian and Step-by-Step Approaches]" (pp. 321-342) in Inoue (2021). It has been updated in some regards to reflect the change of the global situation due to the Russian invasion of Ukraine after February 2022. The author would like to thank Mr. Steve Leeper at Peace Culture Translations for his work in translating the original Japanese version into English.

Notes

[1] For the original text and other information on the TPNW, see United Nations (2017).

[2] A total of 71 states did not go into the negotiations. Although the Netherlands is a NATO member, its government participated in the treaty negotiations at the request of its parliament, then it voted against adoption.

[3] See, for example, United States Mission to the United Nations (2017) and Ministry of Foreign Affairs of Japan (2017).

[4] Unlike ICJ judgments, advisory opinions are not legally binding, but legal authority is also recognized for treaty interpretations of advisory opinions. Kita (2019), pp. 60-61.

[5] For details, see International Association of Lawyers Against Nuclear Arms (2017).

[6] UN Doc. A/RES/51/45 M, 10 December 1996. *Asahi Shimbun* (1997).

[7] At the first meeting of the NPT Preparatory Committee in May 2012, 16 states (including Switzerland, Austria, Ireland, and NZ, which have adopted their own non-nuclear or neutral policies; Norway and Denmark, which are NATO members; and South Africa, Malaysia, Costa Rica, Mexico, and Indonesia, which have called for nuclear abolition as developing states) jointly issued a statement. The final statement, an Austrian-led joint statement at the time of the NPT Review Conference in April 2015, was signed by 159 states, including Japan.

[8] The six non-nuclear states of Brazil, Egypt, Ireland, Mexico, New Zealand, and South Africa, are actively promoting nuclear disarmament. In response to the declaration of nuclear weapons possession by India and Pakistan in 1998, the above-mentioned six plus Sweden and Slovenia making eight nations initially issued a statement.

[9] The IALANA, an international NGO, has asserted that the legal gap should be interpreted, not as a deficiency in the law, but as a compliance gap in the sense that the parties have not succeeded in abolishing nuclear weapons in accordance with the NPT Article VI. See, Burroughs and Weiss (2015).

[10] The descriptions in this section are based on Abe (2017), pp. 2-3, and Kawasaki (2018), pp. 40-41, 58-61.

[11] It is understood that "military preparation activities" related to nuclear weapons, permission for nuclear weapons "transit," and "financing" of nuclear weapons manufacturing companies are also included in "assistance" under prohibited acts. Kawasaki (2018), p. 59.

[12] For details, see Yamada (2019), pp. 465-477.

[13] See Kurihara (2005), who discusses "*Minamata-byo no shisou* [the philosophy of Minamata disease]" based on the "manifestation of existence" of patients, who had gone through the extreme of human suffering and hardships with Minamata disease, an environmental pollution disease caused by mercury effluent from a local plant in Kumamoto of a large corporation in Japan.

[14] This translation from Mayor Hiraoka's original Japanese statement once appeared on

the website of Hiroshima City. URL: http://www.pcf.city.hiroshima.jp/peacesite/ Japanese/Stage3/3-9/3-9-5-3J.html (accessed on August 6, 2006). The following phrase was on that website and a literal translation from Hiraoka's original Japanese statement (Hiraoka 1996: 116): "Beginning with thoughts of these victims, and imagining our own wives and children as the victims of nuclear war." However, it has been recorded in his official English statement at the ICJ as "With thoughts of these victims as the starting point" (Hiraoka 1995: 23).

[15] In July 2021, in addition to "Realize a world without nuclear weapons" and "Realize safe and resilient cities" that have been set forth as the objectives to lasting world peace, with "Promote a culture of peace" as its third goal, the PX Vision was formulated. Mayors for Peace (2022a).

[16] On IPNDV and the UN GGE on nuclear disarmament verification, see Imanishi (2019), pp. 94-97.

References

Abe, Tatsuya (2017) "Kakuheiki kinshi joyaku [TPNW]," *International Law Association Expert Comment*, No. 2017-1 (October 10), <http://jsil.jp/expert/20171010.html> (accessed on October 15, 2022).

Asahi Shimbun (1997) "Hamon yonda ICJ kankoku, 'ho no shihai' oyobuka [ICJ Recommendation Causes a Stir: Does 'Rule of Law' Apply?]," *Asahi Shimbun* Cross-search Database, April 30.

Asahi Shimbun (2014) "'Ippanteki ni iho,' wareta sanpi: kokusai shiho sai, 96 nen no kankokuteki iken ['Generally illegal,' divided opinion: ICJ, the 1996 Advisory Opinion]," *Asahi Shimbun,* July 31, p.29.

Bedjaoui, Mohammed, Kurosawa, Mitsuru, and Ida, Ryu'ichi (2015) "Kaku to inochi wo kangaeru: Hibaku 70 nen no Hiroshima kara [Thinking about Nuclear Weapons and Life: From Hiroshima on the 70th Anniversary of the Atomic Bombing]," *Asahi Shimbun,* August 22, p.13.

Bernard, Vincent (2015) "A price too high: Rethinking nuclear weapons in light of their human cost (Editorial)," *International Review of the Red Cross*, 97(899), pp.499-506.

Burroughs, John, and Weiss, Peter (2015) "Legal Gap or Compliance Gap?" *Arms Control Today*, Vol. 45 (October). <http://hankaku-j.org/data/02/160325.html> (accessed on October 15, 2022).

Chugoku Shimbun (2021) "Kakuheiki kinshi joyaku ga hakkou, hibakuchi, haizetsu he zenshin negau [The TPNW takes effect, A-bombed city hopes for progress toward abolition]," *Chugoku Shimbun,* January 22.

City of Hiroshima (2022) "Peace Declaration (August 6)," <https://www.city.hiroshima. lg.jp/site/english/158103.html> (accessed on October 15, 2022).

City of Nagasaki (2020) "Hibaku kara 75 nen, Nagasaki karano messeiji [75 Years after the Atomic Bombings: A Message from Nagasaki]," *Facebook* posting (April 10), <https://www.facebook.com/permalink.php?id=462106243843654&story_fbid=2986011698119750> (accessed on October 15, 2022).

Eto, Jun'ichi (2019) "Kaku gunshuku koshou gimu [Obligations to Negotiate Nuclear Disarmament]," in Satoru Taira et al., (eds.), *Kokusai ho no furonthia* [Frontiers of International Law], Tokyo: Nihon Hyoron sha, pp. 391-412.

Finn, Beatrice (2019) "Kakuheiki kinshi joyaku wa koushite jitsugen shita [This is how the TPNW came about]," in Hibiki Yamaguchi, (ed.), *Kakuheiki kinshi joyaku no Jidai* [The Age of TPNW] (RECNA Sosho 4), Kyoto: Horitsu Bunka Sha, pp. 83-101.

Fujita, Hisakazu (2011) *Kaku ni tachimukau kokusaihou* [International Law Confronting Nuclear Weapons]. Kyoto: Horitsu Bunka Sha.

Hiraoka, Takashi (1995) "Oral Statement at the International Court of Justice [public sitting held on November 7]," (Verbatim Record, CR 1995/27, pp.22-32) <https://www.icj-cij.org/public/files/case-related/95/095-19951107-ORA-01-00-BI.pdf> (accessed on October 15, 2022).

Hiraoka, Takashi (1996) *Kibou no Hiroshima* [Hiroshima as a Hope]. Tokyo: Iwanami Shoten.

Imanishi, Yasuharu (2019) "Kakuheiki no haizetsu ni muketa samazama na apurouchi [Various Approaches to the Abolition of Nuclear Weapons]," *Kokusaiho Gaiko Zasshi*, 118(1), pp. 78-99.

Inoue, Yasuhiro, ed. (2021) *Sekai-wa Hiroshima-wo Dou Rikai Shiteiruka* [How the World Understands Hiroshima]. Tokyo: Chuo Koron Shinsha,

International Association of Lawyers Against Nuclear Arms (2017) "World Court Project (October 18)," <https://www.ialana.info/topics/world-court-project/> (accessed on October 15, 2022).

International Court of Justice (1996) "Legality of the Threat or Use of Nuclear Weapons (1994-1996), Advisory Opinion of 8 July 1996 (July 8)," <https://www.icj-cij.org/en/case/95> (accessed on October 15, 2022).

Kawasaki, Akira (2017) "Kakuheiki no hi-jindosei kara kakuheiki kinshi joyaku he [From the Inhumanity of Nuclear Weapons to the TPNW]," in Hiroshima Peace Institute, (ed.), *Sengo 70 nen wo koete* [Beyond the Seventy Years After World War II]. Hiroshima: HPI Booklet No.3, pp. 49-69.

Kawasaki, Akira (2018) *Shinpan: Kakuheiki wo kinshi suru* [New Version: Banning Nuclear Weapons], Tokyo: Iwanami Booklet No.978.

Kellenberger, Jakob (2015) "Bringing the era of nuclear weapons to an end [Speech given to the Geneva Diplomatic Corps on April 20, 2010]," *International Review of the Red Cross,* 97(899), pp. 883-886.

Kishida, Fumio (2022) "General Debate Speech by Prime Minister KISHIDA Fumio at the Tenth Review Conference of the Parties to the NPT (August 1)," <https://japan.kantei.go.jp/101_kishida/statement/202208/_00001.html> (accessed on October 15, 2022).

Kita, Yasuo (2019) "Kakuheiki kinshi joyaku dai VI jou niokeru kakugunnshuku gimu [Nuclear Disarmament Negotiating Obligations in Article VI of the Treaty on the Non-Proliferation of Nuclear Weapons]," *Kokusaiho Gaiko Zasshi*, 118(1), pp. 51-77.

Kmentt, Alexander (2015) "The development of the international initiative on the humanitarian impact of nuclear weapons and its effect on the nuclear weapons debate," *International Review of the Red Cross*, 97(899), pp. 681-709.

Komizo, Yasuyoshi (2019) "Kakuheiki kinshi joyaku no tenbou to heiwa shuchokaigi no teian[Prospects for the TPNW and a Proposal of Mayors for Peace]," in Hiroshima Peace Institute, (ed.), *Heiwa no tobira wo hiraku* [Opening the Door to Peace]. Hiroshima: HPI Booklet No. 6, pp. 51-80.

Kurihara, Akira (2005) *"Sonzai no araware" no seiji* [The Politics of "Manifestation of Existence"]. Tokyo: Ibunsha.

Kuriyama, Hirotaka, and Teraguchi, Ryoichi (2022) "Japan PM Kishida Pushes 'Hiroshima Action Plan' for Nuke-free World," *Yomiuri Shimbun,* August 2, <https://japannews.yomiuri.co.jp/politics/politics-government/20220802-49050/> (accessed on October 15, 2022).

Kurosawa, Mitsuru (2019) "Kakuheiki no nai sekai he mukete [Towards a World Without Nuclear Weapons]," in Yamaguchi, Hibiki (ed.), *Kakuheiki kinshi joyaku no Jidai* [The Age of TPNW] (RECNA Sosho 4). Kyoto: Horitsu Bunka Sha, pp. 60-82.

Matsui, Kazumi (2022) "Statement by MATSUI Kazumi, President of Mayors for Peace and Mayor of Hiroshima First Meeting of States Parties to the Treaty on the Prohibition of Nuclear Weapons Vienna, Austria (June 21)," <https://www.mayorsforpeace.org/wp-content/uploads/2022/file-2206-1MSP_TPNW_speech_Hiroshima_E.pdf> (accessed on October 15, 2022).

Mayors for Peace (2022a) "The Hiroshima Appeal: Commemorating the 40th Anniversary of the Establishment of Mayors for Peace [adopted at the 10th General Conference of Mayors for Peace] (October 20)," <https://www.mayorsforpeace.org/wp-content/uploads/2022/file-2210-10th-GC_Adopted_Hiroshima-Appeal_E.pdf> (accessed on October 31, 2022).

Mayors for Peace (2022b) "Letter of Request to the Japanese Government Calling for the Promotion of Actions to Abolish Nuclear Weapons [adopted by total 1,737 Japanese local governments at the 10th Japanese Member Cities Meeting of Mayors for Peace] (October 20)," <https://www.mayorsforpeace.org/wp-content/uploads/2022/file-2210-10th-GC_Adopted_Letter-of-Request-to-the-Japanese-Government_J.

pdf> (accessed on October 31, 2022).

Ministry of Foreign Affairs of Japan (2010) "2010 nen kakuheiki fukakusan joyaku (NPT) unyo kento kaigi gaiyo to hyoka [2010 NPT Review Conference: Summary and Evaluation] (May 28)," <https://www.mofa.go.jp/mofaj/gaiko/kaku/npt/kaigi10_gh.html> (accessed on October 15, 2022).

Ministry of Foreign Affairs of Japan (2014) "Dai 3 kai kakuheiki no jindouteki eikyo ni kansuru kyodo kaigi [The Third Conference on the Humanitarian Impact of Nuclear Weapons] (December 25)," <https://www.mofa.go.jp/mofaj/dns/ac_d/page24_000380.html> (accessed on October 15, 2022).

Ministry of Foreign Affairs of Japan (2017) "Statement by H.E. Mr. Nobushige TAKAMIZAWA, Ambassador Extraordinary and Plenipotentiary, Permanent Representative of Japan to the Conference on Disarmament at the High-level Segment of the United Nations Conference to Negotiate a Legally Binding Instrument to Prohibit Nuclear Weapons, Leading Towards Their Total Elimination (March 27)," <https://www.mofa.go.jp/mofaj/files/000243024.pdf> (accessed on October 15, 2022).

Ministry of Foreign Affairs of Japan (2020) "Kakuheiki no jindouteki ketsumatsu ni kansuru kyodo suteitomento [Joint Statement on the Humanitarian Consequences of Nuclear Weapons] (March 19)," <https://www.mofa.go.jp/mofaj/dns/ac_d/page23_002806.html> (accessed on October 15, 2022).

Ministry of Foreign Affairs of Japan (2022) "The Tenth NPT Review Conference, Statement by Foreign Minister HAYASHI Yoshimasa (August 27)," <https://www.mofa.go.jp/dns/ac_d/press1e_000317.html> (accessed on October 15, 2022).

Nagel, Thomas (1972) "War and Massacre," *Philosophy & Public Affairs*, (1) 2, pp. 123-144.

NHK Hiroshima Kaku Heiwa Purojekuto [Nuclear Peace Project] (1997) *Kakuheiki Saiban* [Nuclear Weapons Trial]. Tokyo: NHK Shuppan.

NHK WORLD-JAPAN(2022) "UN panel approves Japan-proposed draft resolution aimed at nuclear-free world (November 1)," <https://www3.nhk.or.jp/nhkworld/en/news/20221101_12/> (accessed on November 3, 2022).

Ota, Ikuko (2005) "Hiroshima dorimingu: taishosei no ronri, shinso-minshushugi, Kokusaiho" [Hiroshima Dreaming: Logic of Symmetry, Deep Democracy and International Law]," in Chiwaki Shinoda, et al., *Shinwa, Shocho, Bunka* [Myths, Symbols and Cultures]. Nagoya: Rakurou Shoin, pp. 609-644.

Republic of Austria (2022) "Chair's Summary (which is presented in a purely national capacity) [The 2022 Vienna Conference on the Humanitarian Impact of Nuclear Weapons] (June 20)," <https://www.bmeia.gv.at/fileadmin/user_upload/Zentrale/Aussenpolitik/Abruestung/HINW22/Chair_s_Summary.pdf> (accessed on October 15, 2022).

Sekai kaku higaisha fouram jikkou iinnkai [Executive Committee of the World Nuclear Victims Forum](2020) *Kaku no nai mirai wo!* [A Future Without Nuclear Weapons!] (Held in Hiroshima in November 2015, Record of the Report of the Forum & Postscript).

Souza Schmitz, Maitê de (2016) "Decision of the International Court of Justice in the Nuclear Arms Race Case," *Harvard International Law Journal Online* <https:// harvardilj.org/2016/11/decision-of-the-international-court-of-justice-in-the-nuclear-arms-race-case/> (accessed on October 15, 2022).

Suzuki, Tatsujiro (2017) *Kakuheiki to genpatsu* [Nuclear Weapons and Nuclear Power Plant]. Tokyo: Kodansha Gendai Shinsho.

Takemine, Seiichiro (2020) "Sekai no kakujikken higai hoshou seido no horiokoshi to kokusai hikaku kenkyu [Digging up the world's nuclear test damage compensation system and international comparative study]," *Kankyo to kougai*, 50(2), pp. 8-13.

United States Mission to the United Nations (2017) "Joint Press Statement from the Permanent Representatives to the United Nations of the United States, United Kingdom, and France Following the Adoption (July 7)," <https://usun.usmission. gov/joint-press-statement-from-the-permanent-representatives-to-the-united-nations-of-the-united-states-united-kingdom-and-france-following-the-adoption/?_ ga=2.240804995.1427172340.1619607002-386081561.1619607002> (accessed on October 15, 2022).

United Nations (2010) "Final Document (Vol.I) [2010 Review Conference of the Parties to the Treaty on the Non-Proliferation of Nuclear Weapons, May 3-28,]" NPT/ CONF.2010/50 (Vol.I), <https://documents-dds-ny.un.org/doc/UNDOC/GEN/N10/ 390/21/PDF/N1039021.pdf?OpenElement> (accessed on October 15, 2022).

United Nations (2015) "United Action with Renewed Determination Towards the Total Elimination of Nuclear Weapons," UN Doc. A/RES/70/48 (December 11).

United Nations (2017) "Treaty on the Prohibition of Nuclear Weapons," <https://www. un.org/disarmament/wmd/nuclear/tpnw/> (accessed on October 15, 2022).

United Nations (2019) "Elimination of Nuclear Weapons 'Only Real Way' to Allay Fear of a Constant Threat, Guterres Insists," *UN News* (September 26), <https://news. un.org/en/story/2019/09/1047712> (accessed on October 15, 2022).

United Nations (2021) "Secretary-General's Video Message on the Occasion of the Entry Into Force of the Treaty on the Prohibition of Nuclear Weapons (January 22)," <https://www.un.org/sg/en/content/sg/statement/2021-01-22/secretary-generals-video-message-the-occasion-of-the-entry-force-of-the-treaty-the-prohibition-of-nuclear-weapons> (accessed on October 15, 2022).

United Nations (2022a) "Draft Vienna Action Plan [of the 1st Meeting of States Parties of the Treaty on the Prohibition of Nuclear Weapons]," TPNW/MSP/2022/CRP.7 (June 23), <https://documents.unoda.org/wp-content/uploads/2022/06/TPNW.MSP_.

2022.CRP_.7-Draft-Action-Plan-new.pdf> (accessed on October 15, 2022).

United Nations (2022b) "Our Commitment to a World Free of Nuclear Weapons [Draft Vienna Declaration of the 1st Meeting of States Parties of the Treaty on the Prohibition of Nuclear Weapons]," TPNW/MSP/2022/CRP.8 (June 23). <https:// documents.unoda.org/wp-content/uploads/2022/06/TPNW.MSP_.2022.CRP_.8-Draft-Declaration.pdf> (accessed on October 15, 2022).

United Nations (2022c) "Tenth Review Conference of the Parties to the Treaty on the Non-Proliferation of Nuclear Weapons," <https://www.un.org/en/conferences/npt2020> (accessed on October 15, 2022).

Yamada, Hisanori (2019) "Kakuheiki kinshi joyaku (TPNW) dai 6 jou oyobi dai 7 jou no kentou [Examination of Articles 6 and 7 of the Treaty on the Prohibition of Nuclear Weapons (TPNW)]," in Satoru Taira et al., (eds.), *Kokusaihou no furonthia* [Frontiers of International Law]. Tokyo: Nihon Hyoron sha, pp. 455-477.

Yoshida, Fumihiko (2014) "NUKE JUDGMENT, Part 2/ Bedjaoui: 18 Years Later, ICJ Opinion on Eliminating Nuclear Weapons More Important Than Ever," *The Asahi Shimbun* (August 1). <http://ajw.asahi.com/article/behind_news/politics/AJ201408010080> (accessed on August 4, 2017).

Remembering Hiroshima

"Which country dropped such a cruel bomb?" Immediately after my talk about my experience of the atomic bombing, a seven- or eight-year-old American girl asked me this question. For a second, I was at a loss for words.

"I'm sorry. It's your country. It is the USA."

"Oh!" She covered her mouth with her hands. I saw that both her eyes were filled with tears.

Every year, many people visit the Hiroshima Peace Memorial Museum from overseas, including students, teachers, peace activists, politicians, and the media. Recently the number of families with children is increasing among tourists.

I am one of the survivors belonging to the Hiroshima Peace Memorial Museum. As a witness to as well as a survivor of the Hiroshima atomic bombing, I am working for foreign visitors by talking about the Hiroshima atomic bombing.

It is not easy for me to recall that fearful day. I cannot erase the hideous scene I saw in 1945 from my mind. And yet, the unforgettable memory of that day is getting stronger and clearer after the invasion of Ukraine.

The most difficult and embarrassing moment for me is to talk about the Hiroshima bombing with American children.

My experience on August 6, 1945, was as follows:

> I was eight years old and in the second grade of elementary school living with my brothers and sisters in the north area of Hiroshima City, 2.4 kilometers from the hypocenter.
> On August 6, 1945, I was on the road alone near my house. All of a sudden, a blinding, bluish-white flash enveloped me. And then a tremendous roar came, followed by a furious blast. I was

blown back and thrown down on the road by the blast. In the darkness, dust, dirt, rubble, and debris attacked me and I blacked out. When I woke up, everywhere was just pitch dark in the strange silence. I walked toward my house in the thick, gray dust. Everything in my house was smashed and scattered everywhere. The ceiling and roof tiles were blown away. Hundreds of shattered pieces of window glass penetrated into the walls and pillars.

Within an hour or so, my brother, 13 years old, came home and reported that the whole city was completely destroyed. He had been in the field north of Hiroshima JR (Japan Railway) station. When he was exposed to the bomb, he was looking up at the B-29 bomber. He even saw the tiny dot – the atomic bomb – and he could recognize that the bomb was released from the aircraft.

Hearing my brother's story, I walked out of the gate of the house. Then suddenly I encountered rows of burned and injured people fleeing on the road. Their clothes, legs, and arms were torn into tatters. A long wordless line of victims, like goats, passed by me, bleeding all over their bodies. Some of their faces and lips were swollen. Some were squatting. Some were lying down. Some were on the road; some were on the stone steps. I saw an enormous number of injured and dying victims in front of me.

All night on the 6th, the entire city just kept on burning. My partially destroyed house was full of injured people. My house was filled with a bad smell – blood, puss, dirt, burnt hair, and filth.

In those days, almost all the girls in the city tried not to talk about the bombing. The reason for not focusing on the bombing was that we girls and our mothers were afraid of discrimination and prejudice against our getting married. There were rumors that atomic bomb survivors would not live long or that they might have a deformed child because of the radiation.

I used to interpret hibakusha testimonies into English, but I didn't tell about my own experience until one time when I was asked to talk with American students. They pushed me to tell about my story, maybe because

Photo: Yasuhiro Inoue

they didn't like interpretation (it takes double the time). I had kept silent for more than 50 years and did not talk about my experiences. But I thought that talking with American students is the most important, because America is a big country with nuclear weapons.

In September 2022, I was invited to talk about my experiences for the event "Remembering Hiroshima" held by the University of Idaho, as a keynote speaker. I asked the host if I could visit an elementary school and talk about Hiroshima with children. I wanted to find out how to teach them about nuclear weapons.

It is very painful to recall that day in 1945 for both audience and A-bomb survivors. I have been stumped for many years, trying to find a way to convey the fearfulness and savagery of nuclear weapons. It is very difficult for even adults to comprehend the reality of atomic bombing and radiation. I think it is even more difficult for children. Especially for American children who live with nuclear weapons.

I was prepared for the difficult challenge—to talk about the true story of the Hiroshima atomic bombing to children.

Therefore, when I gave my presentation to the children, I used watercolor pictures by a Motomachi high school student, instead of using more frightening pictures from the Peace Memorial Museum.

After my speech, I added information about some of the warm help given by American citizens: the Schmoe house, built by American people, where Hiroshima Maidens, girls with keloids, were taken care of by American citizens. They lived together there for a year or so—a beautiful story to learn about reconciliation and better understanding.

My keynote speech ended with a standing ovation.

The next day, another session for children ended with many children and parents who were standing in a line to hug me and give me their brief comments.

After hugging me, one girl handed me a strip of yellow paper. It read:

Thank you!
You are amazing.
Love, Sandra.
P.S.
You have a heart of gold.
You are so brave.

Tracking Down American Servicemen Killed by the Atomic Bomb and President Obama's Visit to Hiroshima

Barack Obama, as the first sitting president of the United States, visited Hiroshima on May 27, 2016. The long-awaited visit finally became a reality. Offering floral tribute at the Atomic Bomb Memorial, giving a 17-minute speech, making a stop at the Hiroshima Peace Memorial Museum, and speaking with a couple of hibakushas—all of these were done within a very short visit. This could lead some people to regard President Obama's trip to Hiroshima as "unsubstantial." Drawing such a conclusion is totally wrong.

Each part of President Obama's visit carried historical significance. As one of the guests who was there, I would like to express my opinions about his speech.

I was in the front row when the president gave his speech. He opened

Photo: City of Hiroshima

the remark with dignity. "Seventy-one years ago, on a bright, cloudless morning. . ."

"Why do we come to this place, to Hiroshima? . . . We come to mourn the dead, including. . . a dozen Americans held prisoner."

I was surprised. That was about what I have done! Hearing the president's words, I was almost in tears. I was sure that the president spoke in his own voice. In the middle of the speech, there was a phrase, "(D)o not want more war." I was surprised again.

These words were spoken to me by an American bomber pilot, Captain Thomas Cartwright. His bomber was shot down, and he was caught and held as a captive in Hiroshima. He was transferred to Tokyo before the atomic bombing so he survived. However, his crew members died in Hiroshima.

The captain, while he was a prisoner of war (POW), thought, "I will work to help others if I survive and go back to the US alive." "Do not want more war." After the war, the captain entered a prestigious university in the US, earned his Ph.D. in agriculture, and then became a professor.

The president again mentioned what I have done. "(T)he man who sought out families of Americans killed here, because he believed their loss was equal to his own."

I was hugged by President Obama. I have long been searching for the families of American servicemen who were killed by the atomic bomb. I cried tears because I thought that my efforts were rewarded in this way.

The family members of the American POWs were delighted with the coverage about the president and me. They had thought that their loved ones had died for nothing. The families, however, were moved when they saw the victims acknowledged by the president and the nation.

A famous Japanese journalist, Akira Ikegami, interviewed me at the Peace Park where I met the president, and asked me what I would do in the future. I answered, "I think that I would be a bit famous thanks to President Obama. I will work to help human beings from now. This is my mission." I was using the same words as Captain Thomas Cartwright.

I received a phone call on October 14, 2020, from a Catholic nun who was working at a nursing home in Hiroshima. She said that she had met five crew members from the atomic bombing missions including the B-29s Enola Gay and Bockscar when they came to her nursing home. She said that she had spoken with them in English.

According to the sister, the five crew members were Richard Nelson (Enola Gay), Charles W. Sweeney, Frederick C. Bock (Great Artiste), George W. Marquardt (Necessary Evil), and Charles Donald Albury (Bockscar). During their visit, they donated a lot to the nursing home and prayed together in the church.

They came in secrecy because they believed that they were not supposed to come to Hiroshima. However, the sister made up her mind that the fact about a trip made to Hiroshima by several crew members who dropped the atomic bombs in Hiroshima and Nagasaki must be passed down to the following generations.

The day was November 30, 1989. Their visit was a display of remorse.

(Originally written in Japanese. Translated into English by Yasuhiro Inoue)

Chapter 2
A Conceptual Approach to Realize the Non-use of Nuclear Weapons

Shiro Sato

Nearly 77 years have passed since the first atomic bomb was dropped on a Japanese city. "Little Boy," a uranium atomic bomb dropped on Hiroshima, instantly reduced the city to ashes on August 6, 1945, at 8:15 a.m. The death toll was estimated at 140,000 as of the end of December 1945. Setsuko Thurlow[1] described the devastation in her Nobel Peace Prize speech on December 10, 2017:

> Processions of ghostly figures shuffled by. Grotesquely wounded people, they were bleeding, burnt, blackened and swollen. Parts of their bodies were missing. Flesh and skin hung from their bones. Some with their eyeballs hanging in their hands. Some with their bellies burst open, their intestines hanging out. The foul stench of burnt human flesh filled the air (Thurlow 2017).

Nuclear weapons cause enormous destruction due to the synergistic effects of blasts, heat rays, and radiation. They indiscriminately kill innocent people. Even if *hibakusha*, the nuclear weapon victims, survive the horrors of atomic bombings, they continue to suffer physically and mentally from radiation damage. In addition, *hibakusha* suffer social discrimination and prejudice. The use of nuclear weapons, undoubtedly, is inhumane.

Nevertheless, there are 12,705 nuclear weapons in the international community as of January 2022. The United States is estimated to possess 5,428 nuclear warheads, Russia has 5,977, the United Kingdom 225, France 290, China 350, India 160, Pakistan 165, Israel 90, and North Korea 20 (SIPRI 2022). These nuclear states (and their allies) have not signed the

Treaty on the Prohibition of Nuclear Weapons (TPNW). Therefore, it follows that the risk of nuclear weapons being used remains. The question arises: how can the international community prevent the use of nuclear weapons under the present situation? One obvious answer would be to abolish nuclear weapons worldwide. But, how can we prevent the use of nuclear weapons until they are abolished?

This chapter examines the ways to prevent the use of nuclear weapons in the international community from the perspective of International Politics and Security Studies. This chapter particularly focuses on the concepts of "nuclear deterrence," "security dilemma," "reassurance," and "nuclear taboo." The first section of this chapter deals with the concept of "nuclear deterrence," which is the classical way of preventing states from using nuclear weapons in international politics through the promise of nuclear retaliation and destruction. Nuclear deterrence, however, has the risk of causing a "security dilemma" by multiplying anxiety and fear among states. Therefore, "reassurance" should be focused on. The second section focuses on the "nuclear taboo," which is a normative approach to refrain states from using nuclear weapons. This section discusses the significance and challenge of nuclear taboo and considers the case of Hiroshima to realize the non-use of nuclear weapons.

Before discussing the non-use of nuclear weapons in detail, we must clarify the central concept of the "use" of nuclear weapons, which entails the "consequence" of using nuclear weapons. In addition, the "threat" of using nuclear weapons is only a "means"; however, it may not always be associated with the "consequence."

1. Nuclear Deterrence, Security Dilemma, and Reassurance

1.1. Nuclear Deterrence

On February 24, 2022, Russian President Vladimir Putin addressed the nation and threatened to use nuclear weapons against Ukraine and the member states of the North Atlantic Treaty Organization (NATO):

As for military affairs, even after the dissolution of the USSR and losing a considerable part of its capabilities, today's Russia remains one of the most powerful nuclear states. Moreover, it has a certain advantage in several cutting-edge weapons. In this context, there should be no doubt for anyone that any potential aggressor will face defeat and ominous consequences should it directly attack our country (Putin 2022).

This is a common example of foreign policy based on "nuclear deterrence." Nuclear deterrence can be defined as the threat of using nuclear weapons to stop the other side from unwanted behavior. This is the most classical way of preventing states from using nuclear weapons. The logic is that the "threat" will discourage the other side from using nuclear weapons.

For nuclear deterrence to work:

(1) one side must have the intention and capability to threaten nuclear retaliation
(2) the other side must recognize that the threat is believable (credibility)
(3) there must be a means of communication for the situations described in (1) and (2)
(4) both sides need to act rationally to satisfy the conditions in (1), (2), and (3)

The question now arises—will nuclear deterrence work? It is important to quote the report of Secretary-General, Kurt Waldheim, at the 35th Session of the United Nations General Assembly in 1980. The report, titled *Comprehensive Study on Nuclear Weapons*, pointed out the workability of nuclear deterrence as follows:

Perhaps the most severe criticism which could be addressed towards a system of security based on the concept of nuclear deterrence relates to the problem of what happens if deterrence fails. It is argued that deterrence has thus far prevented a world conflict, and consequently that deterrence has worked. Apart from the fact that many other factors of a historical, political and other nature have to be considered in that context, it is a truism to say that deterrence works, because that statement will hold true only until history disproves it (United Nations General Assembly 1980: 102-103, para. 297).

It is apparent in this extract that the success of nuclear deterrence depends on the "consequence." Nuclear deterrence works as long as nuclear weapons are not used. However, if nuclear weapons are used, it may be because one of the deterrence reasons did not work. Thus, the success or failure of nuclear deterrence cannot be asserted definitively. This is the uncertainty of nuclear deterrence.

1.2. Security Dilemma and Reassurance

It is important to remember that nuclear deterrence has the risk of causing a "security dilemma" by amplifying anxiety and fear among states. The term was first coined by John H. Herz (Herz 1950). Robert Jervis further developed this concept and described it as "an increase in one state's security can make others less secure not because of misperception or imagined hostility, but because of the anarchic context of international relations" (Jervis 1976: 76).

The main causality of the security dilemma, whether "misperception or imagined hostility" or "the anarchic context of international relations," is beyond the scope of this chapter. However, it needs to be mentioned that nuclear deterrence could cause a security dilemma and a nuclear arms race as long as nuclear deterrence is a "threat" commitment. The threat of using nuclear weapons could cause anxiety and fear in the other nuclear states. As a result of this, they would attempt to build up their nuclear forces, placing all the nuclear states into a vicious cycle of further anxiety and fear.

Hence, the focus should be on the concept of "reassurance," which is the logic of mutual restraint and promises of not using nuclear weapons. This "promise" commitment is expected to remove or ease anxiety and fear among the states. In other words, reassurance is "the process of building trust" (Kydd 2005: 184).[2] From this viewpoint, reassurance is an important security measure to remove or ease security dilemmas (Kydd 2005: Ch 7). An example of reassurance is the no first use (NFU) of nuclear weapons.[3] This is the second measure to realize the non-use of nuclear weapons. The NFU is a promise that nuclear weapons will not be used first when exercising the right of self-defense.[4] However, it leaves open the option of using nuclear weapons for a counterattack if another state makes the first use of nuclear weapons. Therefore, this commitment does not mean complete refrainment from the use of nuclear weapons. In any case, the declaration of the NFU limits the circumstances of nuclear weapon use. It may help reduce the role of nuclear weapons in security policies and encourage nuclear disarmament and non-proliferation measures.

1.3. Nuclear Deterrence and the NFU

It is important to examine the relationship between nuclear deterrence and the NFU (See, Table 1). Nuclear deterrence and the NFU differ in character in terms of the threat or restraint of nuclear weapon use. There is, therefore, a possibility of conflict at the foreign policy level, such as whether nuclear deterrence or the NFU should be implemented. Yet, both nuclear deterrence and the NFU ensure security from nuclear threats. In addition, both share the problem of enhancing the "credibility" of their commitments; if the credibility is low, the other side may take unwanted actions, such as launching a nuclear attack.

Table 1: Nuclear Deterrence and the NFU

	Type of Commitment	Means	Objective	Problem
Nuclear Deterrence	threat	threaten to use nuclear weapons	non-use of nuclear weapons	credibility
NFU	promise	restraint to use nuclear weapons		

Hence, while nuclear deterrence and NFU have the potential to compete in foreign policies, they share the same objective and challenge. Therefore, it is not necessarily a question of choosing between the two concepts.[5]

2. Nuclear Taboo

So far, this chapter has examined the concepts of nuclear deterrence and NFU of nuclear weapons as security measures to achieve the non-use of nuclear weapons in international politics. Given these concepts, and from an ethical perspective, we can consider the third approach for the non-use of nuclear weapons—nuclear taboo. As per the norm, we should not use nuclear weapons because it is morally unacceptable. It has long been pointed out by scholars of International Politics that one of the reasons for the non-use of nuclear weapons since 1945 is related to normative reasons. For instance, Joseph S. Nye, Jr. acutely pointed out:

> Ever since the first bomb was dropped by the United States on Hiroshima, there was a lingering sense that nuclear weapons were immoral, that they went beyond the realm of what was acceptable in war. Though that normative restraint is hard to measure, it clearly suffused the debates over nuclear weapons and was one reason for the unwillingness of states to use them (Nye 2009: 148).

In addition, Hedley Bull mentioned the following about the normative restraint on using nuclear weapons:

> What is novel about deterrence in the age of nuclear weapons is that states have been driven to elevate it to the status quo of a prime object of policy by their reluctance to use nuclear weapons in actual war (Bull 2002: 114).

These passages clarify that the ethical debate surrounding the use of nuclear weapons has been an important deterrent in its use since 1945. Nina Tannenwald explored this ethical aspect from the perspective of International Politics[6] and propounded the concept of "nuclear taboo" by conducting case studies of the Korean War, the Vietnam War, and the Gulf War (Tannenwald 2007).

2.1. Nuclear Taboo

Tannenwald defines "nuclear taboo" as the "powerful *de facto* prohibition against the first use of nuclear weapons" (Tannenwald 2007: 10). Hence, she limits the "use" of nuclear weapons to the "dropping or launching of nuclear weapons" other than during nuclear tests (Tannenwald 2007: 2 [n. 4]). Nuclear taboo is "not the behavior (of non-use) itself but rather *the normative belief about the behavior*" (Tannenwald 2007: 10) and restrains the behavior of nuclear powers. This norm originated in Hiroshima (Tannenwald 2007: Ch 3). Nuclear taboo is widespread, yet not universal and has not become a sufficiently strong norm (Tannenwald 2007: 59). Furthermore, it is not accepted by the military, although the norm is gradually being shared among American citizens and leaders (Tannenwald 2007: 59). It is noticeable that Tannenwald did not deny the existence of nuclear deterrence as a factor of the non-use of nuclear weapons. She claims that nuclear deterrence is not enough for the non-use of nuclear weapons and that nuclear taboo must be considered as well (Tannenwald 2007: 4-5). In effect, she tried to show that nuclear taboo was more important than nuclear deterrence as a factor for the non-use of nuclear weapons.

Opinions vary about nuclear taboo; it faces two objections. One is the discourses that deny it; the other is the weakness of its degree. The first criticism, i.e., discourses that deny nuclear taboo, recognizes its existence. However, it asserts that nuclear taboo explains only half of the fact. The *Review of International Studies* featured nuclear taboo (Vol. 36, No. 4, October 2010). For example, Farrell (2010) examined the 2002 Nuclear Posture Review, which specified the use of nuclear weapons against rogue states and pointed out that the nuclear taboo explained only half of the facts. In addition, Eden (2010) claimed that the Single Integrated Operational

Plan (SIOP) represented a plan to use nuclear weapons that was incompatible with nuclear taboo.

The second criticism is the weakness of the degree of nuclear taboo. For instance, T. V. Paul, in his book *The Tradition of Non-use of Nuclear Weapons*, criticized that the norm of non-use of nuclear weapons was not a taboo, rather just a "tradition," even though he positively recognized the existence of the norm (Paul 2009). According to him, while taboos are prohibitive, traditions do not include strict prohibitions (Paul 2009: 5). In other words, taboos cannot be broken; however, traditions can be broken or bent. Since nuclear states still have the option of using nuclear weapons, Paul indicated that nuclear weapons had not been used since 1945 due to tradition, i.e., an informal social norm. He called the tradition of the non-use of nuclear weapons "self-deterrence" (Paul 2009: 31). Furthermore, Paul discussed the tradition of the non-use of nuclear weapons in the aforementioned issue of *Review of International Studies* in 2010. He asserted that if nuclear nations used nuclear weapons on non-nuclear states, they and their leaders would have to pay the price in the form of reputation damage in the international community; this price had solidified the tradition of non-use of nuclear weapons (Paul 2010).

These criticisms of nuclear taboo are valid. Tannenwald would need to examine the implications of nuclear taboo and the discourses that deny its existence. However, it is important to note that in the context of this chapter, the existence of a social norm against the use of nuclear weapons, whether as a taboo or a tradition, has not been criticized much. Hence, nuclear deterrence is not the sole reason for the non-use of nuclear weapons since 1945. The norm of non-use of nuclear weapons, too, restrains their use.

2.2. Nuclear Deterrence and Nuclear Taboo

Let us consider the relationship between nuclear deterrence and nuclear taboo (See, Table 2). Nuclear deterrence is an attempt to material restrain the use of nuclear weapons through the threat of using them. The logic is to suppress violence through violence. In contrast, a nuclear taboo is an attempt at normative restraint by fostering the norm of their use being morally unacceptable. The logic is to suppress violence through non-violence. In effect, nuclear deterrence and nuclear taboo are different in terms of their use of violence. However, they both share the goal of creating conditions that make the use of nuclear weapons difficult.

Table 2: Nuclear Deterrence and Nuclear Taboo

	Means	Objective	Problem
Nuclear Deterrence	violence (material approach)	non-use of nuclear weapons	uncertainty
Nuclear Taboo	non-violence (ethical approach)		

It is important to note that nuclear deterrence and nuclear taboo share the same problem. The success of nuclear deterrence cannot always be assured (the uncertainty of nuclear deterrence) because the functionality of nuclear deterrence can only be judged based on the consequences. Similarly, it cannot be guaranteed that the norm of nuclear taboo will always be abided by (the uncertainty of nuclear taboo). Hence, nuclear deterrence and nuclear taboo may not be able to prevent the use of nuclear weapons. Therefore, the second paragraph of the Preamble to the TPNW is extremely important. Because it mentions that the abolishment of nuclear weapons "remains the only way to guarantee that nuclear weapons are never used again under any circumstances." In other words, the abolishment of nuclear weapons remains an important approach to be considered to realize the non-use of nuclear weapons.

2.3. Positive and Negative Impact of Nuclear Taboo

Nuclear taboo has a specific positive and negative impact on international politics. By propagating the story of the inhumanity of nuclear weapons, *hibakusha* raise awareness in the international community about the immorality of nuclear weapon use. This fosters and reinforces a nuclear taboo against nuclear weapon use, which, in turn, creates a situation in which nuclear weapons are unlikely to be used. This is the positive impact of nuclear taboo. The testimony of *hibakusha* is an important political act to achieve the non-use of nuclear weapons.

At the same time, nuclear taboo faces the paradox that the narratives of inhumanity would strengthen the grounds for nuclear deterrence. *Hibakusha* testimonies tell us that nuclear weapons should never be used because of their inhumane consequences. However, because of this, a state may attempt to develop and/or possess nuclear weapons to avoid the inhumane consequences of their use. The nuclear test conducted by Pakistan in 1998 is an example of this situation. Pakistan's then Prime Minister, Nawaz Sharif, stated that one of the reasons for conducting the nuclear test was to avoid the tragedies of Hiroshima and Nagasaki.[7] The report, entitled *Comprehensive Study on Nuclear Weapons*, pointed out this ironical paradox:

> But it is one of the more ominous paradoxes of history that the horror and tragedy of Hiroshima and Nagasaki should have imposed upon military planners the desire, as well as the compulsion, to obtain, in ever increasing numbers and sophistication, the weapons that had demonstrated this horrendous capability for destruction (United Nations General Assembly 1980: 150, para. 490).

The details cannot be discussed here due to limitations of space; however, *hibakusha* testimonies of the horror and tragedy of Hiroshima demand strengthened norms for nuclear taboo to weaken the justification of nuclear deterrence.

Conclusion

We close this chapter with the role of *hibakusha* in the non-use of nuclear weapons in the international community. In the previous section, we highlighted that the testimony of *hibakusha* strengthened the perception that nuclear weapon use is morally impermissible. This perception fostered and reinforced the nuclear taboo against their use and consequently created conditions that made the use of nuclear weapons difficult. In other words, *hibakusha*, who speak of the inhumanity of nuclear weapons, are attempting to create a normative deterrent for the use of nuclear weapons in international politics.

In addition, eyewitness testimony of atomic bomb survivors not only strengthens nuclear taboo but also "stigmatizes" and "delegitimizes" nuclear weapons. A prime example is the TPNW, which was adopted in July 2017 and enforced in January 2021. As of September 2022, the TPNW has been signed by 91 countries and regions, and ratified by 68 countries and regions. This treaty prohibits the development, testing, manufacture, acquisition, transfer, use, or threat to use of nuclear weapons under Article 1. It is based on the recognition that the use of nuclear weapons would have "catastrophic humanitarian consequences" (Preamble, paragraph 2) and is "mindful of the unacceptable suffering of and harm caused to the victims of the use of nuclear weapons (hibakusha), as well as of those affected by the testing of nuclear weapons" (Preamble, paragraph 6). Hence, it is no exaggeration that the *hibakusha* narratives have made a significant contribution to the TPNW enactment in the international community.

Despite these positive impacts, it is noteworthy that the horror and tragedy of Hiroshima continue to strengthen the justification for nuclear deterrence, as mentioned in the previous section. In addition, the *hibakusha* testimony is a "relativization" of the "universality" of Hiroshima, which becomes a roadblock. If the *hibakusha* narrative of inhumanity emphasized only the victim aspect of Japan, it would appear to people outside Japan that the country's aggressor aspect was being denied. As a result, the universality of Hiroshima would be relativized, which would make it difficult for the nuclear taboo to penetrate deeply into the international community. To resolve this problem, we must first recall the following questions. That is, to borrow Tadashi Ishida's phrase, "What did the atomic bombs do to human beings? And what should human beings do about it?" (Ishida 1986: 104). Ishida's question has the potential to go beyond the relativization of Hiroshima because it provides an opportunity to rethink the definition of human dignity.

Notes

[1] Setsuko Thurlow was exposed to the atomic bomb in Hiroshima at the age of 13. She met a Canadian man in Hokkaido when she was a student at Hiroshima Jogakuin University and they married after graduation. She now lives in Toronto, Canada. She has spoken about the inhumanity of nuclear weapons in Canada, the US, and other countries, even before she worked with the International Campaign to Abolish Nuclear Weapons (ICAN).

[2] "Defensive realism" holds that states can build cooperative relationships through reassurance. "Offensive realism" considers that states cannot build cooperative relations through reassurance because they are always in confrontational relationships. From the perspective of offensive realism, reassurance is a part of "appeasement" policy (Montgomery 2006). In response, Tang (2007) contends that reassurance as an appeasement policy confuses the means and ends of reassurance. On defensive realism and offensive realism, see Snyder (1991).

[3] China is the only nuclear state that has declared NFU. Since its first nuclear test in October 1964, China has consistently and unconditionally declared NFU. However, its modernization and deployment of nuclear weapons, incompatible with this declaration, have cast doubt on its credibility.

[4] The concept of NFU is similar to that of the "sole purpose" of nuclear weapons. NFU declares a situation in which nuclear weapons are "used" while the sole purpose declares the purpose of "possessing" nuclear weapons (Panda and Narang 2021). The US administrations of Barack Obama and Joe Biden considered the sole purpose of nuclear weapons, yet decided against adopting it because their allies were concerned that the declaration would reduce nuclear deterrence.

[5] A declaration of NFU, while consistent with the concept of nuclear deterrence, could legitimize the retaliatory use of nuclear weapons in the event of nuclear deterrence failure. Consequently, NFU may jeopardize nuclear disarmament and sustain the dangerous illusion that the use of nuclear weapons is acceptable (Johnson 2009).

[6] "Social constructivism" focuses on non-material factors such as norm and identity in the field of International Politics.

[7] The *Chugoku Shimbun*, May 29, 1998. <https://www.hiroshimapeacemedia.jp/abom/98abom/Pakistan/index.html> (Accessed on November 22, 2022).

References

Bull, Hedley (2002) *The Anarchical Society: A Study of Order in World Politics*. 3rd ed. New York: Columbia University Press.

Eden, Lynn (2010) "The Contingent Taboo," *Review of International Studies*, 36(4), pp.

831-837.

Farrell, Theo (2010) "Nuclear Non-use: Constructing a Cold War History," *Review of International Studies*, 36(4), pp. 819-829.

Herz, John H. (1950) "Idealist Internationalism and the Security Dilemma," *World Politics*, 2(2), pp.157-180.

Ishida, Tadashi (1986) *Genbakutaiken no shisouka: han-genbaku ronsyuu I* [On Thought-Building of Atomic Bomb Experiences: Anti-Atomic Bomb Essay Series I]. Tokyo: Miraisha.

Jervis, Robert (1976) *Perception and Misperception in International Politics*. Princeton: Princeton University Press.

Johnson, Rebecca (2009) "Security Assurances for Everyone: A New Approach to Deterring the Use of Nuclear Weapons," *Disarmament Diplomacy*, 90 (Spring). <http://www.acronym.org.uk/dd/dd90/90sa.htm> (Accessed on November 7, 2022).

Kydd, Andrew H. (2005) *Trust and Mistrust in International Relations*. New Jersey: Princeton University Press.

Montgomery, Evan Braden (2006) "Breaking Out of the Security Dilemma: Realism, Reassurance, and the Problem of Uncertainty," *International Security*, 31(2), pp. 151-185.

Nye, Joseph S., Jr. (2009) *Understanding International Conflicts: An Introduction to Theory and History*. 7th ed. New York: Longman.

Panda, Ankit, and Narang, Vipin (2021) "Sole Purpose Is Not First Use: Nuclear Weapons and Declaratory Policy," *War on the Rocks* (February 22, 2021). <https://warontherocks.com/2021/02/sole-purpose-is-not-no-first-use-nuclear-weapons-and-declaratory-policy/> (Accessed on November 7, 2022).

Paul, T. V. (2009) *The Tradition of Non-use of Nuclear Weapons*. Stanford: Stanford University Press.

Paul, T. V. (2010) "Taboo or Tradition? The Non-use of Nuclear Weapons in World Politics," *Review of International Studies*, 36(4), pp. 853-863.

Putin, Vladimir (2022) Address by the President of the Russian Federation, February 24, 2022. <http://en.kremlin.ru/events/president/news/67843> (Accessed on October 26, 2022).

SIPRI (2022) *SIPRI Yearbook 2022: Armaments, Disarmament and International Security Summary*. <https://www.sipri.org/sites/default/files/2022-06/yb22_summary_en_v2_0.pdf> (Accessed on October 26, 2022).

Snyder, Jack (1991) *Myths of Empire: Domestic Politics and International Ambition*. Ithaca: Cornell University Press.

Tannenwald, Nina (2007) *The Nuclear Taboo: The United States and the Non-use of Nuclear Weapons Since 1945*. Cambridge: Cambridge University Press.

Tang, Shiping (2007) "Correspondence: Uncertainty and Reassurance in International

Politics," *International Security*, 32(1), pp. 193-200.

Thurlow, Setsuko (2017) Nobel Lecture by the Nobel Peace Prize Laureate 2017, ICAN, delivered by Beatrice Fihn and Setsuko Thurlow, Oslo, 10 December 2017. < https:// www.nobelprize.org/prizes/peace/2017/ican/lecture/> (Accessed on October 26, 2022).

United Nations General Assembly (1980) *Comprehensive Study on Nuclear Weapons: Report of the Secretary-General* (A/35/392, 12 September 1980).

Perspective 3   *Akira Kawasaki*

Treaty on the Prohibition of Nuclear Weapons and Japan's Choice

The Treaty on the Prohibition of Nuclear Weapons (TPNW) is a humanitarian disarmament treaty that comprehensively and completely prohibits nuclear weapons and provides pathways for their total elimination. The treaty also provides assistance for the victims of the use and testing of nuclear weapons. It was adopted at the United Nations in July 2017 with the support of 122 states and entered into force in January 2021. The first meeting of states parties (MSP) was held in Vienna in June 2022, with over 80 states in attendance, including observer states, international organizations, the International Committee of the Red Cross (ICRC), and NGOs from around the world.

Despite the slogan of a world without nuclear weapons that Japan continues to repeat, it has shown no intention to join the treaty. Rather, the government boycotted the UN conference to negotiate the treaty and has voted against the UN resolutions to promote it. Japan has said, "We share the goal of a world without nuclear weapons but take a different approach from the treaty," "We need to engage nuclear-weapon states but none of them has joined the treaty," and "Humanitarian aspects of nuclear weapons are important but at the same time we need to consider the severe international security environment." Even Fumio Kishida, a representative of Hiroshima who became Prime Minister in 2021, has not changed this position despite having admitted that the TPNW is "an important treaty that could be regarded as a final passage to a world without nuclear weapons."

The fundamental reason for Japan's reluctance to joining the treaty is the country's reliance on the nuclear deterrence extended by the United States. The TPNW clearly rejects the concept of nuclear deterrence. In its preamble, the treaty considers that any use of nuclear weapons would be contrary to the principles and rules of international humanitarian law. Article 1 prohibits development, testing, production, possession, use, threat of use and deployment of nuclear weapons "under any circumstances." It also prohibits "assisting, encouraging or inducing" anyone engaged in any of the prohibited activities listed above.

Under the Japan-US bilateral security arrangement, Japan asks the US to protect Japan with its armed forces that include nuclear weapons. This means that Japan is encouraging US possession of nuclear weapons, and would eventually assist the US in using nuclear weapons on Japan's behalf. Indeed, the US has repeatedly committed to defend Japan "using its full range of capabilities, including nuclear" (Kishida-Biden Joint Statement, 13 January 2023), while Japan strengthens the alliance, " including extended deterrence by the U.S. that is backed by its full range of capabilities, including nuclear" (National Security Strategy, 16 December 2022).

Article 9 of the Japanese Constitution "forever renounce[s] war as a sovereign right of the nation and the threat or use of force as means of settling international disputes," and prohibits the maintenance of armed forces. The Japanese government's interpretation is, however, that the right to self-defense cannot be denied and that possession of "the minimum level" of self-defense force is allowed. Indeed Japan maintains strong Self-Defense Forces (SDF) and has been among the world's top-10 military spenders. The government has held its interpretation that nuclear weapons are theoretically not excluded from "the minimum level" of self-defense although it would never choose that option, given the Three Non-Nuclear Principles declared in 1967.

Nowadays Japan's SDF is expanding its overseas roles and strengthening its ties with the US military, including through the Japan-US defense cooperation guidelines and the security laws enacted in 2015 permitting the conditional exercise of the right of collective self-defense. Japan is thus becoming an active, integral part of the US forces to deter adversaries, including with the threat to use nuclear weapons. So the moral question should be raised for the country which experienced the devastation of the atomic bombings and is now relying on the threat to use these very weapons of mass destruction, which are now prohibited under international law. The question of constitutionality of Japan's being an integral part of the US military should also be examined.

It would take time though, for Japan to reconcile its two conflicting faces —being both the nation of Hiroshima and Nagasaki and an active part of the US nuclear posture—especially in the wake of North Korea's provocations, the rise of China and the war in Ukraine. Nonetheless, the Japanese public consistently support nuclear disarmament with many public opinion polls showing that over 60-70 percent of people support Japan joining the TPNW. There are several immediate actions Japan can take in the long-term pursuit of that goal.

One is to participate in international efforts to assist the victims of the use and testing of nuclear weapons and remediation of the environment contaminated by nuclear testing. Articles 6 and 7 of the TPNW provide the positive obligation of states parties and international cooperation in that regard. The Vienna Action Plan, adopted at the first MSP in June 2022, includes concrete actions in this area and joint efforts of states parties, the Red Cross and NGOs are underway. Creating an international trust fund for this purpose is being discussed. Drawing on the lessons of Hiroshima, Nagasaki, and Fukushima, Japanese NGOs jointly presented recommendations to the first MSP, emphasizing that the affected people must be at the center of the process of victim assistance. The Japanese government is also encouraged to participate in and contribute to this process.

The other area to which Japan can and should contribute is nuclear disarmament verification. The TPNW provides that states parties discuss ways to credibly verify irreversible nuclear disarmament and get ready for the time that a nuclear-armed state joins the treaty. International organizations to be in charge of such verification need also to be designated. This is an issue relevant to efforts to denuclearize the Korean Peninsula. Japan's active participation would thus be a benefit for the world, including Japan itself.

The MSP is open even for non-signatory states to attend. Indeed, five countries that have a policy of relying on the US extended nuclear deterrence

—Australia, Belgium, Germany, the Netherlands, and Norway—did participate in the first MSP. Finland, Sweden, and Switzerland also participated, while Japan's Kishida chose not to.

But now is a good time for Japan to reconsider its position, and choose to participate in the second MSP to be held in New York in November 2023, at least as an observer. The vicious cycle of nuclear threats is being promoted both in Europe and East Asia. Joining the emerging international legal norm against nuclear weapons would help stop that cycle. Japan's joining the TPNW would not only restore its moral authority but also have a cascading impact for a safer world without nuclear weapons.

Chapter 3
"To Save Lives and End the War"
– Cause or Coincidence

Brien Hallett

So they left us to live with the legacies of the war.
The question is, Do we have the courage to overcome them?
Tsuyoshi Hasegawa (303)

With the disintegration of the Soviet Union in 1990, the Soviet archives from World War II finally became available to historians. Combining the new materials found there with that of the well-known Japanese and American resources, historian Tsuyoshi Hasegawa's 2005 *Racing the Enemy* presents the most complete picture yet of the diplomatic and military maneuvers that led inexorably to Japan's surrender in August 1945. Since history is as much about the present and future as it is about the past, Hasegawa concludes his book by identifying three "legacies" that political courage has yet to surmount.

For the Russians, there is the legacy of Stalin's imperialist occupation of the southern Kurils in the days after the Japanese surrender. This land grab has created the intractable "Northern Territories question," frustrating all attempts to negotiate a treaty of peace between Japan and Russia in the years since 1945. As a result, fully normalized Russo-Japanese relations have not been possible (300-1).

For the Japanese, there is, first, the myth of victimization, a less than full-hearted acknowledgment of their role as perpetrators in the Second World War in the Asia-Pacific region. Closely connected to the first is the role of the Emperor, Hirohito, in supporting the military's aggression and his failure to take personal responsibility for that role and abdicate in 1945 (301-2).

For the Americans, there is the myth that the atomic bombings of Hiroshima and Nagasaki "ended the war and saved lives" (298-300).

Of the three "legacies," the one that most affects the world as a whole is the third: the American belief that the atomic bombings "ended the war and saved lives." This is the case because the American "legacy" is the cornerstone of our Nuclear Age, an uncomfortable, self-contradictory age "where safety will be the sturdy child of terror and survival the twin brother of annihilation," as Winston Churchill once defined it (1955). For, if uncontrolled nuclear chain reactions are powerful enough to end a world war, then they are surely powerful enough to prevent future wars. Or, at least, they are if one ignores the Korean, Vietnam, Afghanistan, Iraqi, and many other wars. And, as long as all the wars fought after 1945 are ignored, a large nuclear stockpile is undoubtedly a rock solid foundation upon which to base national security.

While superficially logical, Churchill's elegant oxymora are plausible only so long as the foundational myth of our Nuclear Age can be sustained, only so long as evidence exists that atomic bombs actually "ended the war and saved lives." Unfortunately, the evidence no longer exists, if it ever did. The Soviet archives are now open, the missing documents are now available, and as Hasegawa concludes, "Therefore, even without the atomic bombs, the war most likely would have ended shortly after the Soviet entry into the war [on August 8, 1945]—before November 1 [the date for Operation Olympic, the invasion of Kyushu]. . . this book demonstrates, this myth [that the bombs "ended the war and saved lives"] cannot be supported by the historical facts" (Hasegawa 2005: 296, 299).

1. Monster or Savior?

But, if archival research now demonstrates that the myth is truly a confection without historical substance or support, one must remember the emotional sources of the myth. At the time, in August 1945, the world ached with exhaustion and fatigue over a war that had lasted far too long. It was a sullen world, morose at the prospect that the bloodshed would continue on indefinitely, the locus of the slaughter having shifted from Germany to Japan. But, then, completely unexpected, as the American veteran Paul Fussell recalled:

> When the atomic bombs were dropped and news began to circulate...that we would not be obliged to run up the beaches near Tokyo assault-firing while being mortared and shelled, for all the fake manliness of our facades we cried with relief and joy. We were going to live. We were going to grow up to adulthood after all (1981: 29).

True, this elation and euphoria was counterbalanced by the distress and trauma of the hibakusha in Hiroshima and Nagasaki, those like Shinoe Shoda who remembered, "The large skull/is the teacher's./Gathered around it,/smaller skulls" (Nakano 1995: 74). Crucially though, at the time, the balance was uneven. The tragedy of the hibakusha was all but lost among strikingly similar tragedies of countless other victims of the war: the victims of the fire bombings of Tokyo, Dresden, Hamburg, and many other cities; or the victims of the Nazi Holocaust, the Rape of Nanking, the Bataan Death March; or any of a thousand and one other atrocities that had occurred during the war. In contrast to those horrors, the unimaginable euphoria of the Japanese surrender was unlike anything else that occurred during the war. It ended the butchery. In this elated state of mind, the atomic bombings were seen as saviors, not monsters. For, what else can one call the unimaginable power of a bomb that "ended the war and saved lives?"

2. Cause or Coincidence

But, to say that the atomic bombs were saviors of the war weary, and not the monsters described by the hibakusha, tells us little about the Japanese surrender and the ending of the war. For a soldier still stationed in Europe, like Paul Fussell, to say that the atomic bombings ended the war is merely to point out an interesting coincidence: during the early weeks of August

1945, Japan surrendered, and, coincidently, several atomic bombs were also dropped. The coincidence is, of course, undeniable. In order to move beyond undeniable coincidences to verifiable causation, one must dig out coherent evidence. One must produce evidence that the atomic bombings not only "ended" the war but in point of fact actually "caused" or "forced" the Japanese to surrender.

As Hasegawa's research has once again demonstrated, the atomic bombs were clearly coincidental with, and not causal of the Japanese surrender, "On the basis of the available evidence, however, it is clear that the two atomic bombs on Hiroshima and Nagasaki alone were not decisive in inducing the Japanese to surrender" (Hasegawa 2005: 298). But long before this archival evidence was available, the simple logic of the situation should have driven people to deny the seductive allure of Churchill's oxymora: How is it possible for safety to be the sturdy child of terror or survival the twin brother of annihilation? A terrified child does not feel safe. Annihilation does not result in survival. How, then, is it possible for uncontrolled nuclear chain reactions to either "end wars or save lives?"

Before Hasegawa's archival research, the traditional starting point for serious discussions of the effects of the atomic bombings was the United States Strategic Bombing Survey (USSBS). In the words of its executive director, Paul Nitze, the evidence led inexorably to Hasegawa's conclusion:

> Based upon a detailed investigation of all the facts and supported by the testimony of the surviving Japanese leaders involved, it is the Survey's opinion that certainly prior to 31 December 1945, and in all probability prior to 1 November 1945 [the planned date for Operation Olympic, the invasion of Kyushu], Japan would have surrendered even if the atomic bombs had not been dropped, even if Russia had not entered the war, and even if no invasion had been planned or contemplated (USSBS 1946, 13).

Paul Nitze's conclusion is undoubtedly true; Japan was indeed utterly defeated by the summer of 1945, and its leaders knew it. This hard and unavoidable truth, however, is unhelpful. Yes, the entire course of the American war in the Pacific—the cumulative effect of each battle, of each Japanese defeat, from Pearl Harbor to Okinawa—is surely the ultimate reason Japan surrendered, but to say that everything caused the surrender is to argue that nothing in particular caused it, which is an unproductive position to take. Something more is needed.

That something more is to observe that the claim that the atomic bombings "ended" the war and "forced" Japan to surrender raises an essentially political question. Prime Minister Suzuki and his colleagues in the Supreme Council for the Direction of the War were politicians struggling with fundamentally political issues. To understand why they surrendered when they did, one must, therefore, investigate the politics and policy choices that surrounded them in the early weeks of August 1945.

To begin such an investigation, one must divide the claim that the atomic bombings "ended" the war and "forced" Japan to surrender into its two constituent parts: first, that atomic bombings "caused" or "forced" Japan to surrender and, second, that this "saved" lives. Taking the second claim first, one is immediately struck by its hypothetical character. The fact of the matter is that the Home Islands were not invaded. Moreover, as the USSBS and others have documented, there is considerable evidence that they never would have been invaded. Therefore, how is it possible to draw a solid conclusion from something that did not happen? Had I been killed while driving home last evening, one could conclude definitively that I had died in an auto accident last evening. However, since I was not killed yesterday evening, it is not possible to conclude much of anything. Why my life was spared last evening will forever remain an unresolvable mystery.

Moreover, because the claim that the atomic bombings "saved" lives is hypothetical, estimating the number of lives "saved" is extraordinarily difficult. Just how difficult is best illustrated by observing the exponential growth between 1945 and 1955 in the number of American lives "saved."

3. How Many Lives Were Saved?

On August 9, 1945, the day Nagasaki was bombed, President Harry S. Truman told the nation in a radio address that he had ordered the atomic bombs dropped "to save the lives of thousands and thousands of young Americans" (*NY Times* August 10, 1945, 12). Two years later, in a February 1947 article in *Harper's*, former Secretary of War Henry L. Stimson estimated that over a million American casualties would have been sustained in the invasion of Japan (1985 [1947]). In 1953, Winston Churchill estimated American casualties at a million American lives lost, which implies five times as many wounded (638), while, in his 1955 *Memoirs* (417), Truman revised his 1945 estimate from "thousands" to 500,000 American lives lost.

What makes these escalating estimates suspect is not so much their deviation from Truman's original 1945 estimates but rather their unacceptable statistical consequences: During the Pacific War, the ratio of Americans killed to total American casualties was 1 to 5, while the ratio of American to Japanese dead was 1 to 22. As a result, on the high side, Churchill's figure of a million American dead implies five million American casualties or 31.25 percent of the entire American armed forces of 16 million and 22 million Japanese killed or 226.8 percent of the entire Japanese armed forces of 9.7 million (of which only 2.5 million were deployed in Japan itself). On the low side, Truman's figure of a half million American dead, 70 percent more than the 292,000 Americans actually killed in all of World War II, implies 2.5 million American casualties and 11 million Japanese deaths or 113.4 percent of the entire strength of the Japanese armed forces. Clearly, the post-1945 casualty estimates bear no relation to reality. In point of fact, we now know from declassified documents, that Truman's initial estimate of "thousands and thousands" of lives "saved" reflects the casualty estimates made by General MacArthur and the Joint Chiefs of Staff. In 1945, General MacArthur's staff had estimated that the American losses for Operation Olympic, the invasion of Kyushu planned for November 1, 1945, might be more or less the same as those suffered on Luzon—31,000 casualties, 7,000-8,000 deaths. If the war continued after that, making an invasion of the Kanto plain necessary, the worst case estimate for the two operations was 20,000 American deaths, but most probably less than 15,000. Consequently, if any American lives were to be "saved" by the atomic bombings, the most probable number was 7,000 to 8,000, although the number might rise to 15,000 to 20,000 if an invasion of the Tokyo area were to take place (Miles 1985; Bernstein 1986).

But consider the matter further: In point of fact, the not-quite-believable-statistical evidence does not speak to the heart of the matter. Namely, the Japanese surrendered. The war ended. Even if no lives were saved, "causing" or "forcing" the end of the war alone would clearly and fully justify the dropping of the atomic bombs. More, if a causal connection could be established between the atomic bombings in Hiroshima and Nagasaki and the Japanese decision to surrender in Tokyo, that would demonstrate the transcendent power of the bomb, a "deterrent" power which could perhaps prevent future wars. It would confirm Churchill's oxymoronic assertion that "safety will be the sturdy child of terror and survival the twin brother of annihilation." This being the case, what political circumstances or inferences exist that might lead one to believe that the atomic bombs possessed the transcendent power to "cause" the Japanese to surrender?

4. Who Surrendered?

In order to answer this question, one must first answer another question: Who surrendered? President Truman and his advisors in Washington? Or, Premier Suzuki and his advisors in Tokyo? Once asked, the answer to this preliminary question seems obvious enough. However, almost without exception, it has been systematically ignored. Instead of focusing on the situation in Tokyo, most discussions focus on the situation in Washington. Instead of asking "Who surrendered?" the discussion always begins by asking why Truman allowed the bombs to be dropped. As is well known, Truman allowed the atomic bombs to be dropped because he and his advisors could think of no reason not to drop them. As he put it on more than one occasion: "The question was whether we wanted to save our people and Japanese as well and win the war, or whether we wanted to take a chance on winning the war without killing all our young men [by dropping the atomic bombs]" (Giovannitti and Freed 1965: 321). When faced with a Hobson's choice like this, the decision is a foregone conclusion. Yet, to say that the bombs were dropped because Truman and his advisors in Washington believed that they would "end the war and save lives" is not to say that Premier Suzuki and his advisors in Tokyo actually surrendered for those reasons. The irrelevance of what was thought or believed in Washington could not be more complete.

Turning, therefore, to the situation in Tokyo, a simple common sense political considerations offers, *if not proof*, at least some understanding of what did and did not motivate Premier Suzuki and his government to surrender when they did. Namely, the fact that, if the atomic bombs did "cause" or "force" the Japanese to surrender, then one should be able to identify a chain of causation that would link the dropping of the first atomic bomb on Hiroshima at 8:15 am August 6, 1945 to the initial Japanese surrender offer on August 11, 1945.

5. A Chain of Causation?

The first news of the Hiroshima bombing reached Tokyo about noon on the sixth but would not have caused any great interest since it was not unusual for whole Japanese cities to be devastated by American bombings. Sixty-four had already gone up in smoke. Therefore, it was not until the next day, August 7, after more complete reports had been received from Hiroshima and after President Truman's announcement of the atomic bombing had been received and translated, that officials in Tokyo became aware that something unusual had happened. Enemy propaganda, however, is not to be relied upon. The Americans said it was an atomic bomb, but was it really? The Cabinet did not think so, as Chief Cabinet Secretary Sakomizu has said, "President Truman [in his statement] mentioned that it was an atomic bomb but we didn't believe what he said" (Giovannitti and Freed 1965: 266). And, indeed, it was not until 5:00 pm on August 8 that Dr. Taro

Takemi finally confirmed officially that the bomb was an atomic bomb (Takemi 1983: 618).

While some Japanese officials learned of these results that night, most would not have heard of Dr. Takemi's results until the next morning, August 9. August 9th, however, was an unusually portentous day. Not only did it include the bombing of Nagasaki at 10:58 am, but it was also the day the Suzuki government began the process that led to surrender. From 10:00 in the morning until 8:00 that evening, the Supreme Council for the Direction of the War spent all of August 9 discussing—not the atomic bombings—but the Potsdam Ultimatum for unconditional surrender in light of the Soviet entry into the Pacific War the day before (Butow 1961: 150-176; Hasegawa 2005: 203-9).

It was during these protracted and fruitless discussions that the news of the Nagasaki bombing reached the Supreme Council for the Direction of the War at shortly after noon. But ten hours of discussion resolved nothing. The same ministers repeated yet again the very same arguments that they had been using for over six months. At 8:00 pm, the meeting adjourned in deadlock. At this time, the Supreme Council for the Direction of the War went to the Imperial Palace where, at 11:30 pm, the fateful Imperial Conference took place at which the Emperor stated his personal preference for surrender (Butow 1961: 175-6; Hasegawa 2005: 209-14).

While the final surrender was not accepted by Secretary of State James Byrnes for another four days, midnight August 9-10 was the moment when the logjam was broken and Japan's surrender became only a formality. Consequently, if one were to argue that the atomic bombings "caused" or "forced" Japan to surrender, then one would be obliged to demonstrate that the bombs exerted their influence during the four-day period from August 6, 1945 to the early morning hours of August 10, 1945. But more realistically, one would have to demonstrate that they exerted their influence during the twenty-hour period which began when the decision makers received confirmation from their own scientists that the Hiroshima bomb was indeed an atomic bomb on the morning of the 9th and 3 or 4 o'clock on the morning of the 10th after the Imperial Conference, when the Cabinet took its decision to surrender.

Such an argument would have to demonstrate that during this twenty-hour period the two-dozen or so old men who ruled Japan could have put aside all their preoccupations with running the war and deciding the fate of their country and come to grips with the horrible reality that is an atomic bomb. The argument would have to demonstrate that during this crucial twenty-hour period these old men could comprehend the physical properties of an uncontrolled nuclear chain reaction, that they could comprehend the *then unknown* biological and environmental effects of the massive exposure to radiation, that they could understand how the atomic fires vaporize steel and bone and brick, and that they could come to this understanding without having seen an atomic explosion, without having seen movies of an atomic explosion, without having seen pictures of the victims of an atomic explosion, in short, without any of the information that is available to us now. Consequently, when one examines the events of August 6 to 10, 1945 in detail, it becomes extremely difficult to identify any causal chain that would link the suffering of the victims in Hiroshima and Nagasaki to the decision-makers in Tokyo. Indeed, the fact that these devices are almost unimaginable in their power and devastation forces one to conclude that the two-dozen old men who made the decision to surrender could not have imagined their catastrophic consequences.

However, reflect upon a second common sense consideration: This second consideration is built upon the fact that the primary concern of every politician is either how to get into power or how to stay in power once he has gotten in. Premier Suzuki and his colleagues were politicians. Not only were they politicians but they were politicians who had just gotten into power, having formed a new government on April 7, 1945, following the collapse of Premier Koiso's government in the weeks after the American landings on Okinawa on March 18, 1945. Therefore, it is not unreasonable to conclude that what worried this group of politicians most in August 1945 was not the atomic bombings, but the fear of losing power, the fear of their government collapsing.

6. The Effect of Soviet Entry into the Pacific War?

In light of this most common political fear, one is better able to evaluate the first two possible "causes" of the Japanese surrender listed by Paul Nitze and the USSBS: the atomic bombings and the Soviet entry into the Pacific War. The atomic bombings in no way undermined or threatened the Suzuki government's hold on power; the Soviet entry did. This is the case because the Suzuki government had a policy to deal with the atomic bombings, but no policy to deal with the Soviet entry into the war. The Suzuki government of course had no policy concerning atomic bombings, in particular, the existence of which it was totally ignorant until Hiroshima. But it did have a policy concerning the destruction of whole cities, which was the practical effect of the atomic bombings. It was not a particularly good policy, but it worked. Indeed, it was the same policy that Churchill had developed during the Battle of Britain and that Hitler had followed in Germany when the Allies bombed 61 of the 62 cities in Germany with a population of 100,000 or more. This "policy" was to bury the dead, care for the injured, clear the rubble out of the streets, and ignore the devastation as much as possible. Just as this policy had worked well in Britain and Germany, so it had sufficed in Japan. Having survived the devastation of 64 Japanese cities since March, the Suzuki government was in no danger of falling. After the first 64, who can imagine that the devastation of only two more cities truly threatened Suzuki's hold on power?

In stark contrast though, the Suzuki government had no policy to deal with the Soviet entry into the Pacific War, which occurred on August 8, 1945. To understand why, one must return to April 1945 when, after long and bitter negotiations in the wake of the fall of the Koiso government, Prime Minister Suzuki's colleagues finally agreed upon a two track policy for forming a new government and prosecuting the war. The military track was to complete preparations to repulse the inevitable American invasion of Kyushu. The diplomatic track was to pursue negotiations with Moscow aimed at a renewal of the Soviet-Japanese Neutrality Pact, which was due to expire in April 1946. Then, if those negotiations were successful, the

Suzuki government would ask the Soviets to use their good offices with the Americans to negotiate, first, a conditional surrender and, then, a peace treaty.

That this policy was doomed to failure given Stalin's promise at Yalta to enter the Pacific War three months after the defeat of Nazi Germany is of course not the point. The point is that as long as the Suzuki government had a policy, any policy, it could and would remain in power to sustain the Imperial Institution. However, on August 8, 1945, the worst possible catastrophe happened. The Soviet Union declared war against Japan, three months after the May 8, 1945 surrender of Germany. As a result, the Suzuki government's *only* policy was in shambles. The Suzuki government was going to fall, as it did, for lack of a policy, any policy.

Not only was the government's *only* policy a dead letter, but defeating the American invasion was no longer possible. Supported by the Red Army in Manchuria, Korea, and Hokkaido, the Americans could land in Kyushu with complete confidence of success. Even the most punishing blow that the Imperial Army could deliver to the American landing forces would be of no avail since there was now no way to follow up such a military success diplomatically, the road to Moscow having been closed. More ominous still, total chaos, complete anarchy, was about to break out. Japan had suffered through three changes of government in the last year. Could she survive another? It was very unlikely. Who would lead the new government? What would its policies be? A fight to the death? Can a government be formed based upon a policy of national suicide? Consequently, after the Suzuki government fell, as it had to and did, there would be a prolonged period of internal political crisis in the middle of which would come the American invasion: an invasion and no government to meet it. What could possibly be worse? How could the Imperial Institution survive in such anarchy, without a government to sustain it?

In sum, the Suzuki government had a policy to deal with the rapid destruction of two cities from atomic bombs, a policy tested and proved in 64 other Japanese cities, 61 German cities, and several British cities. However, crucially, the Suzuki government had no policy to meet the Soviet declaration of war; it did not have even the hope of a policy. It was going to fall; Japan was going to descend into anarchy; the Americans and the Soviets would invade, and the Imperial Institution would be destroyed forever. Thus, from the point of view of Premier Suzuki and his advisers in Tokyo, the final straw was the Soviet declaration of war on August 8, 1945. It created a situation in which there were no policy alternatives.

7. Excuses?

To say this however is not to say that the Suzuki government did not find the atomic bombings very useful. As Cabinet Secretary Sakomizu has said, the atomic bombs "provided an excuse" that was very useful as a face-saving device for the military (Giovannitti and Freed 1965: 315). Of course the Imperial Army could have defeated the American landings, but it could not defeat this new, inhuman device, and so on and so forth in like vein. While useful to soften the blow after the decision to surrender had been made, the atomic bombings never threatened the Suzuki government's hold on power. Consequently, it is extremely difficult not to concur with Lieutenant General Seizo Arisue, G-2 of the Army General Staff, "The two things happened at almost the same time. It was a bigger blow for me that Russia joined the war than the atomic bomb. However, when it comes to shock the atomic bomb created such a disastrous scene" (Giovannitti and Freed 1965: 333). General Arisue's opinion is particularly revealing because he headed the official party that was sent to Hiroshima on August 7, 1945 to investigate the "new weapon." While not among the decision-makers, he was nonetheless the highest-ranking Japanese official to actually have seen the effects of the atomic bombings. But if he, who had actually seen Hiroshima, felt that the Soviet entry into the war was the "bigger blow," then what must his superiors who had not seen Hiroshima have thought?

8. Why Were the Bombs Dropped?

This conclusion, however, forces one to ask again why did President

Truman allow the atomic bombs to be dropped. There are, I believe, two reasons. The first reason is made up of one part hope and one part bureaucratic imperative. The hopeful part arose out of a sincere belief that no alternative existed. I have already cited President Truman's words above; here, let me cite the words of his Secretary of State, James Byrnes:

> Any weapon that would bring an end to the war and save a million casualties among American boys was justified and we are talking about dealing with the people who hadn't hesitated at Pearl Harbor to make a sneak attack destroying not only American ships [7 destroyed] but the lives of many American sailors [2,300 military and 60 civilians]. It was our duty to bring the war to an end at the earliest possible moment" (Giovannitti and Freed 1965: 321).

That Byrnes, Truman, and many others in Washington hoped and sincerely believed that the atomic bombings would or did "end the war and save lives" is not to be denied. Yet, crucially, what was hoped for and believed in Washington could not and did not affect what was decided in Tokyo. To move this sincere belief from the realm of coincidence to cause, one must discover a causal link that connects the horrors in Hiroshima and Nagasaki with the decision-makers in Tokyo, a task that cannot be done. The hope, the belief, and the coincidence most certainly existed; the causal connection did not.

The bureaucratic part of the first reason provides the operational mechanism for sustaining the hope by minimizing any reflection on whether to use or not use the atomic bombs. This mechanical, bureaucratic imperative was articulated best by General Leslie R. Groves, Commanding Officer of the Manhattan Engineer District, the code name for the atomic-bomb project, who observed:

> There was never any question in my mind but that we would use the bomb when it was ready... the best way I can think of to have delayed the project would have been to start discussing throughout

the project: "Shall we use the bomb or not when we get it?" (Giovannitti and Freed 1965: 320. See also Rhodes 1986: 688; Hasegawa 2005: 151-2).

Based upon this premise, Groves constructed a self-actuating system. The bombs would be dropped unless someone spoke up and stopped it, as he said: "As far as I [Groves] was concerned, his [Truman's] decision was one of noninterference—basically a decision not to upset the existing plans" (Giovannitti and Freed 1965: 246).

In the end, Truman never actually ordered the atomic bombs to be dropped; he simple remained silent; he did not interfere in the bureaucratic machine set in motion by President Franklin Roosevelt five years beforehand (Hasegawa 2005: 176). Indeed, the only positive, active decision he made with regard to the atomic bombs was to halt their further use after Nagasaki on August 10, 1945. According to the Secretary of Commerce Henry Wallace, "He said the thought of wiping out another 100,000 people was too horrible. He didn't like killing. . . 'all these kids'" (Hasegawa 2005: 202). The Manhattan Engineer District has been authorized to make atomic bombs; it had made the bombs as authorized; therefore, it used the bombs as planned. Who would be so foolhardy to stand in the way and try to stop this well-oiled bureaucratic machine?

This brings us to the second reason. If the bureaucratic imperative itself was not enough reason to drop the atomic bombs, then the clear political consequences of failing to do so were. As General Groves stated with casual brutality:

I said they could not fail to use this bomb because if they didn't use it they would immediately cast a lot of reflection on Mr. Roosevelt and on the basis of that why did you spend all this money [over $2 billion] and all this effort and then when you got it, why didn't you use it? Also it would have come out sooner or later in a Congressional hearing if nowhere else just when we could have dropped the bomb if we didn't use it.   And then knowing American politics, you know as well as I do that there would have been elections fought on the basis that every mother whose son was killed after such and such a date—the blood was on the head of the President (Giovannitti and Freed 1965: 322).

Thus, for both the Japanese and the American governments, the myth that the atomic bombs "ended the war and saved lives" was useful. For the Japanese, it was useful to save face for the Imperial Army and Navy in their moment of utter defeat; for the Americans, it was useful to explain and excuse the horrors of the atomic bombings and, later, after the Cold War grew hot, to justify the continued building of nuclear bombs because they had "ended" one war and would surely "deter" or prevent another, a hope that the Korean, Vietnam, Afghanistan, Iraqi, and many other wars soon dispelled. Moreover, both governments were able to sustain this convenient myth because both the Japanese and the American people were too war-weary to care. Both peoples were too overjoyed with the end of the war to care how it had really ended. With peace at hand, with the slaughter ended, who cared what the actual causes were?

9. Deterrence?

But, still, the uncounted generations born after August 1945 will care. They, who will ultimately control our memory of the atomic bombings, the grandchildren and great-grandchildren of both the American veterans and hibakusha, will inevitably find the testimony of the hibakusha more relevant and compelling than that of the American veterans. For, the lived reality of future generations will not be one of euphoria at the ending of a world war long forgotten, but rather a continuing fear and anxiety over life lived in the ominously abiding shadow of the mushroom cloud. This reality resonates with the terror of the hibakusha, not the euphoria of the American veterans. The bomb is ultimately a monster, and not a savior.

More sobering though, precisely because this monster lacked the power to end the Pacific War, no reason exists to suspect that it ever has or ever will possess the power to "deter" or prevent any future war. Safety, therefore, is not the sturdy child of terror nor is survival the twin brother of annihilation. Why, then, the generations to come will ask, did our grandfathers build these things that only generate fear and anxiety?

References

Bernstein, Barton J. (1986) "A Postwar Myth: 500,000 U.S. Lives Saved," *Bulletin of the Atomic Scientist,* 42(6), pp. 38-40.

Butow, Robert J.C. (1961) *Japan's Decision to Surrender.* Stanford, CA: Stanford University Press.

Churchill, Winston S. (1953) *The Second World War: Triumph and Tragedy*, vol 6. Boston: Houghton Mifflin.

Churchill, Winston S. (1955) Speech in the House of Commons, March 1, 1955. (March 14, 2022), <https://winstonchurchill.org/resources/speeches/1946-1963-elder-statesman/never-despair/>

Fussell, Paul (1981) "Hiroshima: A Soldier's View," *The New Republic,* 185 (August 22 & 29), pp. 26-30.

Giovannitti, Len and Freed, Fred (1965) *The Decision to Drop the Bomb.* New York: Coward-McCann.

Hasegawa, Tsuyoshi (2005) *Racing the Enemy: Stalin, Truman, and the Surrender of Japan.* Cambridge, MA: Harvard University Press.

Miles, Jr., Rufus E. (1985) "Hiroshima: The Strange Myth of Half a Million American Lives Saved," *International Security,* 10(2), pp. 121-140.

Nakano, Jiro, ed. and trans. (1995) *Outcry from the Inferno: Atomic Bomb Tanka Anthology.* Honolulu, HI: Bamboo Ridge Press.

Rhodes, Richard (1986) *The Making of the Bomb.* New York: Simon and Schuster.

Stimson, Henry L. (1985 [1947]) "The Decision to Use the Atomic Bomb," *Harper's Magazine,* February. Reprinted in *SAIS Review,* 5(2), pp. 1-15.

Truman, Harry S. (1945) "President Truman's Report to the People on War Developments, Past and Future," *New York Times*, (August 10, 1945), p. 12.

Truman, Harry S. (1955) *Volume One: Memoirs: Years of Decisions.* New York: Doubleday.

Takemi, Taro (1983) "Remembrances of the War and the Bomb," *The Journal of the American Medical Association,* 250(5), pp. 618-619.

The United States Strategic Bombing Survey (1946) *Japan's Struggle to End the War.* Washington, D.C.: GPO.

Chapter 4
International Perspectives on the Atomic Bombing of Hiroshima: Moral Act or War Crime?

Yasuhiro Inoue, Javier Sauras, Yubi Fujiwara,
Yeongho Kim, Takafumi Yoshie, and Aoe Tanami[*]

1. Conflicting Understandings of Hiroshima

1. 1. Genocide or Peace-Maker?

"Absolute evil," "Never repeat this hell on earth," "The atomic bomb killed hundreds of thousands of innocent people, and many more are still suffering."

These words are quite often printed in newspapers and broadcast on television news programs in Japan, especially around the anniversaries of the Hiroshima and Nagasaki atomic bombings, on the 6 and 9 August respectively. There is no room to debate over the definitions of the atomic bombings, at least in the media narratives and the public discourse in the country. The atomic bombing is absolute evil, period.

When looking at the narratives of the atomic bombings outside Japan, we find different views.

"The atomic bombings destroyed military facilities and forced Japan to surrender," "Ended the war, saved millions of lives, even Japanese lives," "Deserved punishment for Japan's invasion of Asian countries, God's vengeance," "Salvation."

These are actual wordings and portrayals of the atomic bombings that have appeared in the media and even academic articles/books in some countries other than Japan. In other words, they are some of the world's

---

[*] Section 1, 2, and 3 were written by Yasuhiro Inoue. Section 4 was written by Javier Sauras, Section 5 by Yubi Fujiwara, Section 6 by Yeongho Kim, Section 7 by Takafumi Yoshie, and Section 8 was by Aoe Tanami.

understandings of Hiroshima. Of course, these utter justifications are not the only narratives found outside Japan. Harsher and more condemning words and phrases have also been used outside Japan, such as "Genocide," and "A war crime that massacred civilians indiscriminately." Occasionally, the atomic attack is identified with the Holocaust; Hiroshima with Auschwitz (almost never found in the US, though). The understandings of Hiroshima are diverse and, frequently, contradictory.

This chapter investigates the way in which major newspapers around the world portrayed the event of the world's first nuclear attack on Hiroshima, 75 years previously. The goal is to understand and obtain empirical evidence of the diversity and commonness of newspaper coverage of Hiroshima, i.e., framings of Hiroshima (Inoue and Rinnert 2010). Framing is the selection of meanings of an issue to suggest what is involved and promote a particular causal interpretation.[1] The way media frame (or present) an issue influences the way people think about it (public opinions) and eventually the way policies are made.

In this chapter, we examine how the act of using the bomb was framed (e.g., as a justifiable means of ending the war, as a war crime) and/or compared to other historical events (e.g., the Holocaust). Also, the following questions are addressed: to what extent the coverage mentioned the horrible aftermath and delayed effects of radiation on the victims of the bombing; whether the morality and/or legality of the use of the bomb was questioned.

1.2. No Simple Dichotomy in the Understandings

A previous study, which examined international news coverage of the 60th anniversary in 2005, identified four different framings of the Hiroshima bombing (Inoue and Rinnert 2010): (1) salvation/war-ender; (2) atrocity/holocaust; (3) mixed frames (both justified and questionable action); and (4) deserved punishment for Japan. The researchers of this study examined the international coverage of the 75th anniversary (2020) of the atomic bombing and came to a conclusion: A few more framings should be added. The additional framings are: (5) Japan was totally defeated and about to surrender. The Soviet war declaration against Japan (August 8, 1945) was decisive to Japan's surrender; (6) the lessons of Hiroshima are important and universal, i.e., lessons of humanity; (7) the damage of the atomic bombings was not as horrible as other war tragedies, i.e., trivialization of the atomic bombings.

As stated above, newspaper coverage is one of the major factors that influences public opinion. In addition, it more or less reflects public attitudes towards social and political issues. This is the main reason that we chose newspaper coverage for our research: international understandings of Hiroshima. The primary focus of this research was text analysis with reference to those seven framings. Graphical content such as photos and illustrations were also analyzed from the same viewpoints. In addition, we looked at article size and placement (the location of a story in the newspaper such as the front page and the editorial page) as a partial measure of prominence given to the story.

The data for this study are articles (including straight news, features, editorials, and so on) published between August 1 and 16, 2020. The original research collected and examined 194 major newspapers from 55 countries/regions.[2] This chapter primarily presents the results of the United States, the United Kingdom, Spain, China, South Korea, the Middle East, and Latin America with new interpretations by incorporating current international contexts.

For the results of France, Germany, and other countries, please refer to the original research (Inoue, 2021). All the quoted words and sentences from the newspapers are English translations of the originals or the original texts in English. Articles' dates and page numbers are enclosed in parentheses.

2. The United States: The Country that Deployed the First Nuclear Weapon

2.1. The Atomic Bomb Myths: Established Views

The New York Times (*NYT*) played the most crucial role in forming the understandings of the atomic bombing in the US and many other countries because the paper monopolized atomic bomb-related information.[3] The government propaganda, which managed to make *NYT* cooperate and collude in the cover-up of atomic bomb damages (especially radiation), was another decisive player. Other news media and many opinion leaders undoubtedly followed suit in line with *NYT* and the government information management (the next chapter focuses on *NYT* coverage).

In addition, a sense of guilt among Americans for using the most destructive and indiscriminate weapon for the first time would also be a factor. People want to believe what they want: the weapon was used against military targets and ended the war, saved lives. On the other hand, people don't want to believe what they don't: the atomic bomb killed an unimaginable number of Japanese people, civilians. People's unconscious willingness to believe what they want to believe is a major factor in the formation of the understandings.

These players and the factor have established the particular understandings of Hiroshima in the United States: The Atomic Bomb Myths (Inoue 2018). The definition of "myths" in this context is that widely believed but false, baseless, and/or unscientific beliefs/ideas. Many researchers (e.g., Bernstein 1999; Lifton and Mitchell 1995; Wilson 2014) including the author found the Myths in the media and public discourse. The Atomic Bomb Myths can be summarized in the following five beliefs (Inoue 2018):

1. The atomic bomb was used with prior warnings in order to avoid civilian victims. An important military base was targeted and destroyed.
2. The atomic bomb (and its psychological shock) forced Japan to surrender and ended the war sooner.
3. Thanks to the bombs, the US was able to avoid the planned mainland battles (the planned invasion of Japan's mainland). Therefore, the atomic bombings saved 500,000 to 1,000,000 American lives and even more Japanese lives.
4. Americans are a chosen people and "God let us do the merciful act", i.e., atomic bombing. The atomic bombing is salvation

for the US as well as for Japan.

5. Most of the radioactive material of the bomb turned into enormous heat and blast. Therefore, there was little residual radiation. Heat and blast, not radiation, killed (military) people.

Since 1945, most American newspaper coverage on Hiroshima has repeated one or several of the Myths. No deviation from these established views was found in conservative, right-wing, and local newspapers in 2020. However, some major newspapers such as *NYT* and *Los Angeles Times* have broadened their editorial stance to present readers with understandings contrary to the Myths. The transition of *NYT*'s editorial stance from 1945 to 2020 is addressed and discussed in the next chapter. This section deals with the other newspapers and starts with typical justifications for the bombing.

2.2. Consistent Support: *The Wall Street Journal*

"The Atomic Bomb Saved Millions—Including Japanese."

This is the headline of an opinion piece published by *The Wall Street Journal* (*WSJ*) on the 2020 anniversary of the Hiroshima bombing (A17). Its assertion perfectly reflects one of the Atomic Bomb Myths listed above. The writer sprinkles the article with pseudo-evidence and baseless argument, except for one historical fact (estimated numbers of Japanese atomic bomb victims). This chapter is not meant to point out hearsay evidence and baseless argument. However, for readers' reference, the author of this section has drawn lines between historical facts and baseless opinions by adding italicized comments in brackets when necessary. The article starts with "Ended war, saved lives" framing:

A July 1945 U.S. government report estimated that invading the Japanese Home Islands would cost five million to 10 million Japanese lives." *[No government/military documents which support these estimated numbers have been found yet]*

The U.S. government estimated, based on the fierce Japanese

resistance encountered on outlying islands, that the war would last another year and a half-through the spring of 1947. It expected between 1.7 million and four million Allied casualties, including 400,000 to 800,000 fatalities. . . All this (invasion and occupation by the Soviet) was averted. *[The official government document, The United States Strategic Bombing Survey, clearly stated, "Based on a detailed investigation of all the facts, and supported by the testimony of the surviving Japanese leaders involved, it is the Survey's opinion that certainly prior to 31 December 1945, and in all probability prior to 1 November 1945, Japan would have surrendered even if the atomic bombs had not been dropped, even if Russia had not entered the war, and even if no invasion had been planned or contemplated"]*[4].

WSJ's editorial position on the atomic bombing has long been consistent. In 2005, the 60th anniversary, *WSJ* expressed its support of the atomic bombing for the reason that it "hastened World War II to its conclusion" (8/5: A8). This was not just the only article that the newspaper published on the 60th anniversary, but it was *the* editorial of the paper on the day. The editorial justifies the bombing by framing it as the "salvation" myth:

Nuclear weapons are often said to pose a unique threat to humanity, and in the wrong hands they do. But when President Truman gave the go-ahead to deploy Fat Man and Little Boy, what those big bombs chiefly represented was salvation: salvation for. . . all the GIs; salvation for the tens of thousands of Allied POWs the Japanese intended to execute in the event of an invasion; salvation for the grotesquely used Korean "comfort women"; salvation for millions of Asians enslaved by the Japanese. . . Not least, and despite the terrible irony, the bombings were salvation for Japan.

Salvation framing could have a strong effect on readers' image and opinion forming, particularly for Christians. It contends that nuclear weapons are good as long as they are in hands of the right people.

2.3. Total Support: *The Washington Times* and *Chicago Tribune*

One of the most conservative right-wing newspapers in the US, *The Washington Times* (which endorsed Trump in the 2020 US presidential election) strongly supported the atomic bombing not only in text but also with a large illustration. The paper published two "total justification" articles on the Hiroshima anniversary day. One of them, "Our annual August debate over the bombs" (B1) utterly justifies the bombing:

> To Americans and most of the world 75 years ago, each day in early August 1945 that the Japanese war machine continued its work meant that thousands of Asian civilians and Allied soldiers would die.
>
> In the terrible arithmetic of World War II, the idea that such a nightmare might end in a day or two was seen as saving millions of lives rather than gratuitously incinerating tens of thousands.

One of the technological breakthroughs to develop the atomic bomb was the success of the world's first self-sustaining nuclear chain reaction. It was The University of Chicago where the experiment took place in 1942. *Chicago Tribune*'s editorial on August 6, which took up most of a whole page, praised the university and its success with a big photograph of a mushroom cloud (attaching photographs to editorials is quite unusual). The editorial, titled "The Bomb that ended World War II: A haunting anniversary" (13), justifies the bombing by putting it in a local context:

> The debate over whether the decision to drop the bomb was right, was moral, is easily misdirected. Japanese military leaders could not win the war, nor could they bring themselves to concede defeat. Until the A-bombing, fighting was certain to continue at tremendous cost to the people of both America and Japan. The

Aug. 7 Tribune brought reminders. There were 21 U.S. dead after a destroyer hit a mine in the Philippines. There were 33 Chicago-area men reported wounded in various incidents. . . we thought of the untold thousands of other young Americans who avoided the lieutenant's cruel fate because the war ended when it did. That is the sober justification for Hiroshima and Nagasaki.

2.4. Interesting Mix: *The Washington Post*

The Washington Post, acquired by Amazon.com founder Jeff Bezos in 2013, seems to have changed, at least partly, its editorial stance on the bombing from praising to criticizing the bombing. This is surprising because *The Post* was one of the fiercest spearheads denouncing the Smithsonian National Air and Space Museum's atomic bomb exhibition in 1995 and played a major role in the cancellation of the exhibit.[5] Another impressive fact is that in 2020 *The Post* gave more space to the issue than any other newspaper in the US. The paper published a total of eleven articles, amounting to nearly ten pages.

The Post cast light on "inconvenient facts" or taboos, i.e., the atomic bomb killed Americans and many American survivors, hibakusha, still suffer from radiation exposure. One article, "An American who survived the atomic bomb in Hiroshima reflects on the past 75 years" (8/7: A12), features a Japanese American survivor and reveals facts such as the following:

Howard. . . (and his brother) born in California, they were Americans, like their mother and father before them, like unknown numbers of U.S. citizens who were caught in that city on that day and forever after associated with the atomic bomb and the horrors it unleashed.
A dozen servicemen, crew members of aircraft downed in the final days of the war and held as prisoners, died after the bomb detonated. But hundreds, some say thousands, of other Americans also perished or suffered and bore witness.

The Post went far beyond fact-revealing by publishing a scathing opinion article titled "No, it wasn't 'necessary' to bomb Nagasaki" (8/9: B1-2). Written by an American historian (Susan Southard), it flatly denies one of the most essential parts of the Atomic Bomb Myths, the claim that the bombing "ended the war, saved lives":

> (T)here is no historical evidence that the Nagasaki bombing helped bring about Japan's surrender. Before the nuclear attack that morning, Japanese leaders were already panicked over the Soviet Union's massive invasion of Japanese-held Manchuria, 11 hours earlier. As the mushroom cloud rose high above Nagasaki, Japan's leaders were already in a heated debate over whether to surrender and under what conditions; the news of the second atomic bombing had no apparent impact on their deliberations.

This article also raised moral issues about the atomic attack and described what happened to babies, children, and pregnant women in a graphic way. It is worth presenting long quotations from the article here:

> The real problem, however, is that debating the necessity of the bomb keeps us from confronting far more pressing questions. . . (W)ere these mass killings and irradiation of civilians "right"? And what are the implications of continuing to accept our country's official narrative?. . .
> Is it, for example, acceptable to purposely sear the face and body of a 13-year-old boy? Or for a teenage girl to find the charred body of her 9-year-old brother, recognizable only by the name tag on his shredded school uniform? Or for a 12-year-old, who was not injured in the atomic blast, to fall sick a month later with fever, bleeding gums, hair loss and telltale purple spots all over her body. . .
> Is it right that pregnant women whose fetuses were exposed in utero suffered spontaneous abortions, stillbirths and infant deaths,

and many babies who survived birth developed physical and mental disabilities?

While the overall editorial tone about the atomic bombing was critical and fact-revealing, *The Post* also printed an opinion article regarding the event as "moral." This piece, "History not yet repeated" (8/6: A25) was written by George Will, a famous political commentator. Nuclear deterrence (bomb as peace-maker) is the theme of the article. Will's article presents a typical justification of the atomic bombing:

> Seventy-five years ago Sunday, three days after the first use of a nuclear weapon, the second occurred. There has not been a third in the subsequent 27,394 days. One of humanity's remarkable achievements is this absence of something.
> President Harry S. Truman. . . used the bombs to avoid invading Japan. His decision, following the bitter-end Japanese fanaticism on Iwo Jima and Okinawa, was a moral and successful wager on economizing violence.

2.5. Historians' Views: *Los Angeles Times*

The Post was not the only major newspaper in the US that published critical articles denouncing the Myths. The largest newspaper on the West Coast, *Los Angeles Times*, invited American historians to contribute a commentary article that states what are facts and what are baseless. The long headlines of the article summarize its theme and contention: "We didn't need to start the nuclear age—U.S. leaders knew we didn't have to drop atomic bombs on Japan to win the war. We did it anyway. We've been taught that the U.S. had to drop atomic bombs on Japan to end World War II. History proves otherwise" (8/5: A11). The commentary explains the historical evidence:

> The accepted wisdom in the United States for the last 75 years. . .
> Not only did the bombs end the war, the logic goes, they did so in

the most humane way possible.

However, the overwhelming historical evidence from American and Japanese archives indicates that Japan would have surrendered that August, even if atomic bombs had not been used—and documents prove that President Truman and his closest advisors knew it.

The allied demand for unconditional surrender led the Japanese to fear that the emperor, who many considered a deity, would be tried as a war criminal and executed. . .

But the Soviet Union's entry into the war on Aug. 8 changed everything for Japan's leaders, who privately acknowledged the need to surrender promptly. . .

Truman knew that the Japanese were searching for a way to end the war; he had referred to Togo's intercepted July 12 cable as the "telegram from the Jap emperor asking for peace.". . .

3. The United Kingdom: Participant in Making the Atomic Bomb

3.1. British Public Opinion Shift

The United Kingdom was one of the Allied countries and joined the US-led Manhattan Project to develop the atomic bombs. British citizens had long supported the decision to use the atomic bombs for the reason that the bombing ended the war, saved the lives of the British, American, and Japanese people. However, British public opinions about it have changed, becoming more negative over time as the number of war-experienced generations is decreasing. An opinion poll conducted in 2016 demonstrates this turnaround and the generation gap. Overall, 41 percent of British respondents thought the bombing was wrong; 25 percent, right. But for those older than 65 years old, 49 percent regarded it as the right decision and 31 percent as the wrong decision.[6]

This shift in British attitudes towards the atomic bombing is reflected in the coverage of British newspapers. A passage in a major newspaper, *Daily*

Telegraph, demonstrates this: "This past week saw the 75th anniversary of the dropping of the Hiroshima bomb. Across the media it was widely referred to as an 'atrocity'" (8/8: 17).

3.2.   Unrelenting Accusation: *The Guardian/The Observer*

While not all major British newspapers gave significant coverage to the issue, *The Guardian* and its Sunday edition, *The Observer*, not only published the largest number of articles (six) but also denounced the bombing in the severest way among the British newspapers. The newspapers shed light on another taboo, the racial motivation of the atomic attack.

On the 75th anniversary of the Hiroshima bombing, *The Guardian* published a whole page feature, "Nuclear rift: Anniversary of Hiroshima reopens anguished debate over attack" (27), questioning the common wisdom of the atomic bombing: that it ended the war, saved lives. The feature raises doubt by stating, "(W)as this the aircraft [B-29 Enola Gay] that finally ended the second world war, saving hundreds of thousands of lives, or was it the instrument of the mass killing of civilians, which heralded a new age of nuclear terror?" While the feature offers both pros and cons to the question, the page is occupied by far more accusing accounts than supportive ones:

"The use of this barbarous weapon at Hiroshima and Nagasaki was of no material assistance in our war against Japan. The Japanese were already defeated and ready to surrender," wrote the admiral William Leahy, who presided over the combined US-UK chiefs of staff.

Dwight Eisenhower, the general who "won the war" in Europe, recalled his reaction to being told by the secretary of war, Henry Stimson, that the atomic bomb would be used. "I voiced my grave misgivings, first on the basis of my belief that Japan was already defeated and that dropping the bomb was completely unnecessary, and secondly because I thought that our country should avoid shocking world opinion by the use of a weapon."

The Observer touched on an extremely sensitive issue, the racial motivation of the atomic attack, by publishing a whole page feature titled "Don't let the victors define morality—Hiroshima was always indefensible. The decision 75 years ago to use atomic bombs was fueled not by strategy but by sheer inhumanity" (8/9: 35). The feature's revelation of racially driven motives in the atomic attack is intense, relentless, and extensive as follows:

> There is evidence that the Americans had been preparing to use the A-bomb against the Japanese as early as 1943 and that, in the words of General Leslie R Groves, director of the Manhattan Project, the US nuclear weapon programme, "the target. . . was always expected to be Japan."
>
> It's an attitude that may have been driven by the different ways in which the Allies saw their enemy in Europe and in Asia. Germans were depicted as brutal and savage, but the bigotry was restrained to some extent by the fact that they were European and white. The Japanese, however, were particularly despised because they were non-white. . .
>
> It was common for western diplomats to refer to the Japanese as "monkeys" and "yellow dwarf slaves." A former marine, Andrew Rooney, observed that US forces "did not consider that they were killing men. They were wiping out dirty animals." Truman himself wrote: "When you have to deal with a beast you have to treat him as a beast". . .
>
> The Japanese too were vicious, cruel and racist. But Japanese attitudes and atrocities are well known; those of the Allies are often forgotten, because they were the "good guys."

3.3. Lesser and Softer Coverage: *The Times* and *Financial Times*

Two other major newspapers reported on the bombing in a limited manner. Both *The Times* and *Financial Times* decreased the amount of coverage and became less critical in editorial tones from 2005 to 2020.

In 2005, *The Times* published a five-page feature about "Hiroshima

Nagasaki double-bombed survivors"; the newspaper in 2020 carried a "filler" article about the Hiroshima ceremony, several "insignificant" articles, and letters from readers which are supportive of the bombing. Likewise, *Financial Times* did not delve into the historical or moral issues but picked up a film "I Saw the World End" produced by British and Japanese artists shown at London's Imperial War Museum, and a BBC podcast produced by an American journalist whose grandfather was a scientist in the Manhattan Project. Considering that *FT* in 2005 published a total of five articles including the front page cover story and editorial, it is surprising.

As the last example of this section, a book review is singled out in *FT*'s 2005 coverage. That article, titled "How morality went bang," goes beyond an ordinary book review to criticize the atrocity inflicted by the US. For example, the sentence, "Little Boy performed to perfection, scorching, ripping, atomising and carbonising the flesh of 100,000 children, women, and men" suggests that the target was not a military base but civilians. The following remarks in the last paragraph represent the author's assertion:

Today, people are used to living with the bomb. Yet the chances of nuclear attack are probably greater now than in the cold, bipolar world where deterrence held a grim logic. Dropping the atomic bomb on Japanese civilians is arguably the vilest single act one set of human beings has ever perpetrated on another.

4. Spain: Atomic Memories by the Mediterranean Coast

Only one village in the entire world has had over four megatons of nuclear weapons dropped on it with nobody being hurt. On January 17, 1966, a B-52 Stratofortress bomber of the United States Strategic Air Command crashed into a KC-135 refueling plane over Palomares, a coastal town with 400 inhabitants in Southern Spain. The planes were performing a Cold War patrol, part of Operation Chrome Dome that kept the most capable bombers in the US inventory flying towards the Soviet Union on continuous airborne alert. Seven people died in the crash—the entire crew of the KC-

135 and three of the B-52's squad—while four hydrogen bombs, each of them with a payload equivalent to 75 times the force that destroyed Hiroshima and Nagasaki, fell in Palomares. Emergency parachutes should have borne them gently down to the ground, preventing any contamination, but the contingency measures failed. Two of the bombs blew apart on impact, scattering highly toxic plutonium dust. Another one sank to the bottom of the sea.

Within days of the crash, the beach in Palomares became the base for a hectic military deployment involving some 850 American soldiers and scientists, dozens of land and air vehicles, and 14 ships of the Navy Task Force. They were trying to find the nukes and secure them. In 2016, *The New York Times* identified 40 American veterans who helped with the cleanup—21 had cancer, nine had died from it (Philipps 2016). Nine out of the ten Spanish civil guards who watched over the site of the accident in the following years suffered the same fate (Iglesias 2016). Secretary of State Hillary Clinton promised in 2012 that the US government would finish decontaminating the area, but it never happened. Today, there are still nearly 50,000 cubic meters of contaminated soil in Southern Spain. No serious epidemiological study has ever been done in the region (Laynez-Bretones and Lozano-Padilla 2017). In the Spanish public imagination, these atomic memories are very much alive.

The Spanish print press demonstrated a decisive commitment to commemorate the 75th anniversary of the atomic bombings of Hiroshima and Nagasaki, publishing numerous items, from op-eds to news reports, feature articles, interviews with survivors and experts, biographical essays, analytical texts, and special pieces with photos and graphics. Five publications we chose (*El País, ABC, La Vanguardia, La Razón,* and *El Mundo*) represent the marquee print outlets of the country and a wide range of the political spectrum, from social democrats to Catholic conservatives. On average, they have published over 7,000 words and 9 articles each on this issue. Of course, not all coverage is the same. *El Mundo*, a liberal-conservative paper, historically critical of the Spanish socialist party and regional nationalist movements, took the lead with 17 articles and over

12,000 words in the first two weeks of August. *La Vanguardia*, however, a centrist-moderate publication from Barcelona catering to the Catalonian bourgeoisie, published just two brief items of barely 300 words. Nevertheless, something united them all: a harsh, critical editorial stance against the bombings was widely shared across the board. Out of 48 items, only one presented the bombing as a justified action that saved more lives than it took (an interview with British military historian Antony Beevor). None of the coverage framed the bombings as deserved punishment for Japan. Three pieces presented ambivalent stances, developing the US motives to drop the bombs, and exploring consequences and alternatives. The rest were openly reproachful. Terms like holocaust, apocalypse, genocide, hell, extermination, massacre, megadeath, extinction, horror, and annihilation dominated the written texts, while comparisons to the Nazi's Final Solution and concentration camps were also abundant. Many items fitted multiple analytical frames, but we clearly found that presenting the event as an atrocity and casting it as a lesson for humanity to pass on, prevailed over the rest.

While *El Mundo* took the lead in publishing its special during the weekend before the anniversary, the other Spanish papers waited until August 6. The first pro-democracy national newspaper born in Spain after Franco's death in 1975, *El País*, an influential center-left daily widely read in the entire Spanish-speaking world, chose to let survivors tell the story. *ABC*, the oldest still-operating Spanish newspaper, and *La Razón*, the youngest of them all, did the same. Keiko Ogura, hibakusha leader of the Hiroshima Interpreters for Peace (HIP) group, was profiled in three of these papers (*El País, El Mundo,* and *ABC*), after she participated in a video conference organized by the Foreign Press Center of Japan. The journalists focused, consequently, on remarkably similar elements of Ogura's story, who was an 8-year-old elementary school student in 1945.

By letting witnesses like Ogura speak openly on their pages, the Spanish press adopted their memories of the event and the survivors framing of the bombing. Through this penetrating, analytical lens, the papers positioned themselves, and their readers, on the side of the victims. The plethora of survivor stories brought into the light of public discourse not only adopted Spanish citizens' understanding of the bombing and its consequences, but also their conclusions and political agenda: the atomic bombing of Hiroshima was a lesson that humankind should learn from and pass on to future generations, and this lesson implies a message of peace and the elimination of nuclear weapons.

The Spanish press gives Hiroshima a prominent place in the metaphoric atlas of World Peace. The atomic memories of Spanish people, heavily influenced by the 1966 accident in Palomares, attest to the importance of the bombings today. The nuclear tragedy of 1945 is very much alive in Spanish society, as we saw during the two weeks' coverage of the 75th anniversary. The homogeneous treatment of the bombing as an atrocity in Spain speaks to the relevance of the event for past, present, and future generations. Hiroshima carries, in Spanish media, a double significance. On the one hand, it's a powerful synonym with tragedy, horror, massacre, annihilation, holocaust, death, pain, disease, terror, and apocalypse. On the other, it bears a critical message of peace and forgiveness. Twenty-five years from now, the world may or may not look familiar to us. But if the past and present are good indicators of the things to come, Hiroshima's message will still resonate in Spanish society, reflecting in collective memories, and echoing in the media.

5. China, Taiwan, and Hong Kong

This section analyzes and discusses articles on the Hiroshima atomic bombing in Chinese language newspapers: national newspapers such as *The People's Daily*, *The Guangming Daily*, *Reference News*, and *Global Times*; local newspapers such as *Shanghai Daily*, *Yangtse Evening Post*, and *Southern Metropolis Daily*; and Taiwanese and Hong Kong newspapers.

5.1. Reflecting the Chinese Government's Opinion
The year 2020 marks the 75th anniversary of the atomic bombings of Hiroshima and Nagasaki, but there were only a limited number of articles

related to them. Chinese national newspapers reported more on the bombing than local newspapers did, but the overall number of articles was small. *The People's Daily*, China's largest national newspaper published no articles at all. Meanwhile, *People's Daily Online* (the online version of the paper) carried an article[7] on August 7: "Hiroshima, Japan marks 75 anniversary of the atomic bombing."

The article reports on the Peace Memorial Ceremony held on the anniversary day in Hiroshima, the number of participants, and the speeches by Mayor Matsui and Prime Minister Abe. However, the article ends with the statement, "Japan has positioned itself as a 'victim' of World War II, especially the atomic bombing, but has rarely touched on the historical background that led to the atomic bombings."

Since China and Japan were on opposite sides in World War II, China's view is that the tragedies of Hiroshima and Nagasaki caused by the atomic bombs must not be repeated, but at the same time, the crimes committed by Japan should not be forgotten. The article does not directly state that Japan was responsible for the atomic bombings. However, it suggests that the historical background of the bombings is related to Japan's aggression during World War II.

From the editorial stance, we can learn about the opinions of the Chinese government about Hiroshima and other related issues. In addition, national newspapers' and news agencies' articles are often reprinted in other newspapers in China. Since this article was distributed by *Xinhua*, China's news agency, it was reprinted and carried by many other Chinese newspaper websites.

5.2. Editorial Stances

Each newspaper covers news according to its characteristics, i.e., editorial stances. For example, *The Guangming Daily* focused on the theme of "anti-Japanese" rather than the Hiroshima atomic bombing; *Reference News* translated foreign media news stories into Chinese and reprinted them; *Shanghai Daily* did not report on the Hiroshima atomic bombing, but on the impact of the bomb on Japanese animation and manga.

The Guangming Daily, like *The People's Daily*, did not publish any article on the Hiroshima atomic bombing. However, on August 13 and 15 it carried full-page reports on the "War of Resistance against Japan." The articles were not ordinary newspaper articles, but research papers: "International Significance of Research on the Chinese Anti-Japanese War and Anti-Japanese War history" (16), "New Developments and New Trends in Research on the Backwardness of the Anti-Japanese War" (16), "Research on the Northeast China Anti-Japanese League from an International Perspective" (16) and "Victory in the Anti-Japanese War and the Brilliance of Scientific Theory" (7).

Reference News, which mainly focuses on international news, reprinted all articles (translated into Chinese) on the Hiroshima atomic bombing from foreign media: the online editions of *Kyodo News Agency* and *the Asahi Shimbun* in Japan; *Newsweek* online and *The New York Times* online in the US; *El País* and *El Mundo* online in Spain; and *Buenos Aires Economic News* online in Argentina.

Shanghai Daily published only one photo and a brief description of the Peace Memorial Ceremony held in Hiroshima on August 7. The article on the 9th was not about the atomic bombing itself, but a full-page feature on the impact of the atomic bomb on Japanese animation and manga (10). Combining the rather dark topic of the atomic bomb with subcultures would allow readers to gain more knowledge about the atomic bomb and pay more attention to Japanese animation and manga. This is a very interesting style of coverage that was not found in other newspapers.

Yangtse Evening News and *Southern Metropolis Daily* did not have any articles on the issue at all. This may be due to the fact that local newspapers focus on regional and domestic news coverage.

5.3. Lesser Coverage: Taiwan and Hong Kong

Taiwan's *United Daily News* published two articles on the atomic bombing on August 10: "Nagasaki mayor calls for signature and ratification of the Treaty on the Prohibition of Nuclear Weapons, Abe handles it cold" (12) and "US 'nuclear umbrella' requested, even though Japan calls for 'abolition of nuclear weapons'" (12). Both articles covered the Treaty on the Prohibition of Nuclear Weapons and reported that although the mayor of Nagasaki and the victims of the atomic bombing called on the Japanese government to sign and ratify the treaty, their appeals were ignored, and ultimately the Japanese government "would not sign" it.

The China Times had two articles on August 7: "Hiroshima atomic bombing memorial: Abe avoids the Treaty on the Prohibition of Nuclear Weapons" (7) and "Tragic recollections of survivors" (7). The former covered the Hiroshima peace memorial ceremony and reported that Mayor Matsui had called for "signing and ratifying the Treaty on the Prohibition of Nuclear Weapons," but Prime Minister Abe avoided the topic. The latter focused on survivors' recollections of the aftermath of the atomic bombing and their misery during that time. One of the major newspapers, The Liberty Times, did not report on the atomic bombing.

In Taiwan, former President Lee Teng-hui died on July 30 of that year. All three newspapers examined for this study filled their pages with articles related to Lee almost every day. "Zero coverage" of the atomic bombing in The Liberty Times, and the minor treatment in The United Daily News and The China Times (two articles each) could be due partly to the extraordinarily big news of Lee's death.

The Hong Kong edition of the China Daily, an English-language newspaper, published a contribution by UN Secretary-General António Guterres on August 7 (9). The article, which was carried in some newspapers around the world, highlighted the dangers of nuclear weapons and concerns about the nuclear threat. It also referred to the Nuclear Weapons Non-Proliferation Treaty and the Treaty on the Prohibition of Nuclear Weapons. To indicate that this was not an original report by the newspaper, a disclaimer was added at the end of the article, "(It) does not necessarily reflect the views of the China Daily." The main content of the article is consistent with the Chinese government's stated nuclear policy. However, there are differences between them, such as their views on the Treaty on the Prohibition of Nuclear Weapons.

Unfortunately, Ming Pao, one of the major newspapers in Hong Kong, could not be obtained. *The South China Morning Post*, an English-language newspaper, was not obtained either (two articles were confirmed to have appeared on the inside pages). In 2005, the paper reported the issue and carried a total of nine articles, including front-page headlines and editorials (Inoue and Rinnert 2007). The number of articles on the 75th anniversary of the atomic bombing significantly decreased. It is thought that the weakening of its editorial resource and the situation in Hong Kong in 2020 may have had an impact.

6. South Korea: Conflicting Views between Conservative and Progressive

South Korea's Newspapers reported only a little on Hiroshima and Nagasaki even on the 75th anniversary of the atomic bombing. Out of the six major newspapers, from August 1 to 16 in 2020, one conservative paper published two articles regarding the atomic bombing, and one progressive paper published three. Four other newspapers did not carry any items about the atomic bombing during the same period.

Donga Ilbo, a conservative paper, published two articles on August 7. One of them was related to Korean *hibakusha* and second generation A-bomb survivors (23). Researchers found that 70,000 people from the Korean Peninsula were living in Hiroshima and Nagasaki when the bombs were dropped and 40,000 of them were killed. The article reflects on the special law for Korean *hibakusha* Support established in 2016 and reports on the government's survey about the victims' current health conditions. The other article covers a regrettable situation that nuclear tests and nuclear development were not banned yet regardless of the suffering of many *hibakusha* (23).

In addition to these two articles, a news story on its website titled "*Abe* insisting that [Japan is] the only country which experienced atomic bombing while ignoring her war responsibility again this year," refers to Japanese Prime Minister Shinzo Abe's remarks at the Peace Memorial Ceremony on August 6 in Hiroshima, and criticizes him for never acknowledging the

Japanese war responsibility which led to the atomic bombing.

Hankyoreh, a progressive paper, published three articles. The first one on August 5 reported on the A-bomb aftereffects, especially hereditary effects caused by the atomic bombing (14). The second was an essay on August 14 by a correspondent in Japan about the Japanese artists Iri and Toshi Maruki who collaborated on a masterpiece "The Hiroshima Panels," consisting of 15 folding panels, some of which depict Korean victims killed by the atomic bomb (22).

The third was a long article by a professor, titled "Why Korea was divided instead of Japan" (August 13, 20). It discusses a historical analysis of the Japanese war, A-bombing by the US, the Soviet Union's entry into the war, Japan's surrender, and the Korean Peninsula's division. The author carries an argument about Japan's delayed surrender to preserve the national polity, *Kokutai,* and to avoid the occupation of Hokkaido by the Soviet Union. In conclusion, the author argues that the A-bombing by the US demonstrated the new weapon's power and consolidated the US hegemony after the war. Because of such power politics, it was liberated Korea that was divided, not defeated Japan.

Common tendencies as well as a sharp contrast can be found between the conservative and the progressive media's framings of the atomic bombing of Hiroshima and Nagasaki. On the one hand, both the conservative and the progressive media often point out Japan's war crimes in contrast to the Japanese government's appeals for peace and the abolition of nuclear weapons. On the other hand, the conservative media often state that the atomic bombing led to Japan's surrender, the end of the war, and the liberation of Korea from Japanese colonial rule while the progressive media sometimes maintain that the atomic bombing of Hiroshima and Nagasaki was a war crime by the US as well as a strategic operation aimed at the Soviet Union.

There is less newspaper coverage of the atomic bombing in South Korea than in the other countries examined in this chapter. This is partly because the South Korean media often emphasize Japan's war crime which brought about the A-bombing, and partly because North Korea's nuclear issues have been attracting much more attention from policymakers, mass and social media, researchers, and ordinary people than the atomic bombing. Indeed, South Korea's newspapers are sharply divided into conservative and progressive papers, and they are often opposed to each other over the problems of North Korea.

It seems to be true that each newspaper's views of North Korea's nuclear development influence not only its views of the alliance with the US and the extended nuclear deterrence by the US (the so-called "nuclear umbrella") but also its views of the atomic bombing of Hiroshima and Nagasaki. In other words, the news media's framings of North Korea's nuclear issues and those of the atomic bombing of Japan influence each other, but in an opposite way.

The conservative media tend to imply that they should enforce sanctions and provide deterrence *against* North Korea. Therefore, they have a fear of being abandoned by the US and state clearly that the alliance between South Korea and the US is crucial. In contrast, the progressive media tend to hold that they need common security *with* North Korea. Therefore, they have a fear of a US military attack on North Korea and keep their distance from the alliance with the US.

US President Barack Obama's visit to Hiroshima in 2016 attracted much more attention among the South Korean media than any other event. At that time, editorials in both the conservative and the progressive newspapers criticized that Obama's visit might obscure Japan's responsibility for the war. However, both parties showed contrasting attitudes over the US atomic bombing of Hiroshima and Nagasaki. The conservatives advocated that the atomic bombing resulted in Japan's surrender and the liberation of its colonies, while the progressives criticized Obama for failing to apologize for the indiscriminate massacre of civilians.

7. Latin America's Nuclear-Free Zone and Atomic Bomb News Reports

Fifty-three newspapers in 16 countries and regions in Latin America were surveyed, and it was found that 36 newspapers featured news coverage about the Hiroshima atomic bombing. In other words, nearly 70 percent of all newspapers reported on Hiroshima in some way. It can be said that these data clearly show the high level of interest in Latin America for news coverage about Hiroshima. On the other hand, looking at the content of the articles published in each newspaper, I found a certain tendency in the tones of Hiroshima coverage in Latin America, which reflect a skeptical and negative view of the legitimacy of the atomic bombings and a critical attitude toward the development and possession of nuclear weapons.

For example, an Argentinian newspaper *Clarín* published an interview with Professor Peter Kuznick of American University, who is well versed in the atomic bombing issues (8/7: 28). The interview reveals the falsity of claims that suggest the use of the atomic bombs hastened the end of the war and saved lives, an assertion the US government has long used to justify its dropping of the atomic bombs. In the same interview, when asked about President Truman, who decided to use the atomic bombs, Professor Kuznick said, "He [Truman] said at the time that half a million young Americans would die if the United States invaded Japan." However, the fact is that "[Truman] himself knew the words were not true," Professor Kuznick added. Moreover, regarding the official view that dropping the atomic bombs hastened the end of the war and saved lives, he said that the president himself was aware at the time that this view was nothing more than a deception.

In addition, a Mexican newspaper *El Universal*, assuming that an atomic bomb was dropped on Mexico City, describes the extent of the damage, illustrates it on a map of the city, and communicates the nuclear threat as a familiar issue to readers (8/6: A15). For example, if Little Boy, the atomic bomb dropped on Hiroshima, were dropped on Mexico City, the report says that it would "cause catastrophic damage within a radius of 340 meters from the blast center, and would even completely destroy concrete buildings." It further explains that "within a radius of 1.67 km . . . most houses would be destroyed and only the most robust structures would remain." By presenting the damage caused by nuclear weapons as a present and realistic risk, the newspaper tried to sound the alarm about the nuclear weapon development.

In the Latin American newspaper reports, no articles were found that openly accepted the American atomic bomb myths, supported the legitimacy of dropping the atomic bombs, defended nuclear deterrence, or recommended the development and possession (or use) of nuclear weapons. Rather, the articles described the atomic bombings with negative expressions such as "evil," "holocaust," "horror," "atrocity" and "war crime." The majority of the articles pointed to the "destructive power," "danger," "catastrophe," "tragedy" and the possibility of "human extinction" that nuclear weapons pose. In this respect, there was little difference between countries and newspapers in terms of attitudes toward the atomic bombing. In fact, this view seems to broadly represent public opinions in Latin America. Why is such a view prevalent in Latin America? There are a number of factors. The most influential one is the concept of military denuclearization in the Latin American region and the history of the Treaty of Tlatelolco.

While not well known in Japan, Latin America promoted the concept of military denuclearization for the entire region ahead of the other countries and regions, and then realized it. The driving force behind this effort was the "Treaty for the Prohibition of Nuclear Weapons in Latin America and the Caribbean," commonly known as the Treaty of Tlatelolco, a regional agreement signed in 1967. For countries in Latin America and the Caribbean, while recognizing their right to peaceful use of nuclear energy, this treaty stipulates a total ban on the testing, use, production, importation, purchase, stockpiling, and deployment of nuclear weapons. It became effective in 1968 with the signatures of 21 Latin American countries. Cuba, the last participating country, ratified it in 2002. As of today, the nuclear-weapon-free zone treaty has been ratified by all the 33 Latin American countries.

The Treaty of Tlatelolco was prompted by the Cuban Missile Crisis that occurred in October 1962. The 1959 Cuban Revolution sparked a military conflict between the United States and the Soviet Union, and the world was pushed to the brink of full-scale nuclear war. It was a major crisis in the twentieth century. This incident became a turning point that changed the perception of nuclear issues in Latin American countries. One of the reasons for this change is that for Latin American countries with close political, economic, and military ties to the US to the extent that they were taunted as being the "backyard" of the US, the threat of a nuclear war involving Cuba created a concern among the countries in the region. In addition to the possibility that the US and the Soviet Union could bring nuclear weapons into the region, Latin American countries that have the technical and economic capability to develop and possess nuclear weapons (such as Brazil and Argentina) could promote their own nuclear weapon development. This fact raised awareness of the possibility that Latin American region could be placed directly under the nuclear umbrella of these countries.

Among the Latin American countries worried by the threat of nuclear war as a result of the Cuban Missile Crisis in 1962, four countries, Brazil, Bolivia, Chile, and Ecuador, took the lead in submitting a non-nuclear resolution to the United Nations General Assembly after the crisis was resolved. In 1967, 14 Latin American countries signed the Treaty of Tlatelolco, which stipulates a total ban on nuclear weapons within the region, then in 1968, the world's first nuclear-weapon-free zone treaty came into effect.[8]

As explained above, the entire region shares the history of being driven to the brink of nuclear war. For the people of Latin America, who perceive the threat of nuclear weapons as being close to them, the growing interest in news coverage about the atomic bombing issue and nuclear weapons can be seen as a logical consequence. Such public awareness is also reflected in the attitudes of Latin American countries toward the Treaty on the Prohibition of Nuclear Weapons, which took effect in January 2021. Of the 86 countries that have signed or ratified the treaty, 27, or more than 30 percent, are Latin American countries. In other words, Latin America has a prominent presence in the treaty.

In this survey, the dominant tone of criticism and skepticism toward the dropping of the atomic bombs and the development of nuclear weapons can be seen as the flip side of the sense of crisis regarding the nuclear issue.

8. The Middle East and the Atomic Bombing of Hiroshima

8.1. Perspective Setting

The world has long seen chaos and turmoil in the Middle East. However, the region has been making progress by the popular movements for reform while it exposes the contradictions of the current world framework and nation-state based capitalism.

As the role of Social Networking Service (SNS) expands globally, in the Middle East particularly, the media situation has changed radically. The Arab Spring was a milestone in which the role played by SNS has been pointed out as significant. Among the traditional media, newspaper essays remain an effective way of expression that can appeal to the emotions of people accustomed to SNS.

For this section, a total of twenty newspapers from six Arab countries (Egypt, Jordan, Palestine, Saudi Arabia, UAE, and Oman), Iran, Turkey, and Israel were examined (August 1 to 16, 2020). First, the author reviews the coverage on the 75th anniversary of the A-bombing of Hiroshima, including commemorative ceremonies, testimonies by A-bomb survivors, and views on the purpose of the bombing. Then, the author explores essays related to the atomic bombing and "Hiroshima reporting in a broader sense." Although there are differences in the coverage of the 75th anniversary, the articles and essays about Hiroshima show unique ways of perceiving the world which can be found only in the Middle East in turmoil.

8.2. Report on the 75th Anniversary of the Hiroshima Atomic Bombing

The discussion of the Middle East and nuclear issues generally bring to mind the subject of Iranian nuclear enrichment. However, it should be noted that the Arab world considers Israel's actual possession of nuclear weapons to be a bigger issue than Iran's. At any rate, the reticence of newspapers in these two countries to cover the 75th anniversary of the bombings cannot be regarded as a coincidence. Newspapers in Turkey, where US strategic nuclear weapons are deployed, also avoided clearly addressing the respective nuclear positions of Japan and Turkey by focusing on the grandiose performance of the Turkish president who delivered a video message at the Hiroshima Peace Memorial Ceremony.

In contrast, Arabic-language newspapers based in the Gulf, including those in UAE and Saudi Arabia, published emphatic feature coverage on the matter. *Emarat Al Youm* (8/6: 26-27) of the UAE ran a double-page spread featuring the testimonies of five survivors of the atomic bomb, one of them was a Korean. The pan-Arab *Asharq Al-Awsat* (8/10: 11) criticized the refusal of the Japanese government to join the Treaty on the Prohibition of Nuclear Weapons.

A Jordanian newspaper, *Al-Ghad* (8/10: 31) and UAE's *Al-Bayan* (8/15: 16), both of which relied on articles distributed by AFP, mention the justification for the atomic bombings but their articles are structured to give a stronger and more convincing impression of the arguments against the bombings. Although there are various nuances, the atomic bombings are generally reported in the Arab media as massacres indiscriminately targeting civilians and war crimes.

A different perspective is reflected in an article published by *the Saudi Al Watan* (8/10: 10). Written by a researcher named Sami Hamad, this piece differs in character from the articles mentioned above. It describes the history of the development of the atomic bomb, contains a matter-of-fact account of the destruction it wrought, and evokes the thinking of a natural scientist with an underlying admiration for science and technology and the power of nuclear weapons. It is interesting to note the discussion of nuclear weapons in the Saudi Arabian newspaper, given that country's interest in the promotion of plans to introduce nuclear power plants.

8.3. Hiroshima Reporting in a Broader Sense

The most prominent subject that falls under Hiroshima reporting in a broader sense is comparing the damage of Hiroshima to that in war-torn areas in the Middle East. In the case of 2020, many newspapers compared the scale of a huge explosion in Beirut, Lebanon (which occurred two days before the anniversary of the Hiroshima bombing) to the impact of the atomic bombing of Hiroshima. Although different from political violence such as war or terrorism, the disaster was partly caused by corrupt politics, which, in turn, results from the colonial history of the country.

In an essay carried by *Alquds Alarabi* (8/10: 23), Haifa Zangana, an Iraqi Kurdish female writer quotes a phrase from "We are the children of Hiroshima," a poem by Sankichi Tōge, which has been translated into Arabic. In the title of her essay, she asks "How many Hiroshimas will we live through?" She does not stop at the devastation of her homeland of Iraq, but names cities throughout the Middle East that have been bombed in recent wars. Then she asks herself, "How many Hiroshimas will we live through?" For Syria, in particular, she gives specific numbers of buildings destroyed in each city to convey the realities of the damage.

A Palestinian journalist Abu Zaina notes (*Al-Quds*, 8/10: 11) that at least 1,500,000 Iraqis have died of disease and malnutrition as a result of sanctions since 1990. This number of victims in Iraq is many times larger than that of Hiroshima and Nagasaki. He also says that the damage Palestinians have suffered over the decades cannot be compared to that of Hiroshima and Nagasaki.

This is not to trivialize the damage caused by the Hiroshima and Nagasaki atomic bombings. In fact, one can naturally notice the writer's frustration at the indifference with which the Palestinian people have been treated across the world over the years, in comparison with the worldwide attention that Hiroshima and Nagasaki receive. It may also be the expression of his frustration with the difficulty in directly linking "Hiroshima and Nagasaki" to the situation in Palestine, where "ethnic cleansing" has been committed against its indigenous people. The frustration seems to be driven by the indifference of the international community to the damage caused by the intervention and domination at the hands of other nations.

Acknowledgments

This chapter is a revised and summarized version of a book edited/written by the first author of this chapter (Inoue 2021). Data collection for this study was partially supported by The Hiroshima Peace Creation Fund's Peace

Grant.

Notes

1. For more information about framing, see Gamson (1989).
2. For detailed data selection/collection methods, and a complete list of the newspapers, refer to Inoue (2021).
3. For detailed investigations of *NYT* coverage, see Inoue (2018), Keever (2004), and Lifton and Mitchell (1995).
4. Further, all the military documents estimated the casualties and fatalities far less than a half million. For detailed information, see Bernstein (1999).
5. For more information, see Harwit (1996).
6. https://yougov.co.uk/topics/politics/articles-reports/2016/05/19/america-was-wrong-drop-bomb-public (accessed on June 15, 2022).
7. *People's Daily Online* (August 7, 2020). http://japan.people.com.cn/n1/2020/0807/c35421-31813950.html.
8. For details on the Treaty of Tlatelolco, see the Agency for the Prohibition of Nuclear Weapons in Latin America and the Caribbean (Organismo para la Proscripción de las Armas Nucleares en la América Latina y el Caribe, http://www.opanal.org/).

References

Bernstein, Barton J. (1999) "Reconsidering Truman's claim of 'Half a million American lives' saved by the Atomic Bomb: The construction and deconstruction of a myth," *Journal of Strategic Studies*, 22 (1), pp. 54-95.

Gamson, William A. (1989) "News as framing: Comments on Graber," *American Behavioral Scientist*, 33 (2), pp. 157-161.

Harwit, Martin (1996) *An Exhibit Denied: Lobbying the History of Enola Gay.* NY: Copernicus.

Herrera Plaza, José, and López Arnal, Salvador (2019) *Silencios y deslealtades: El accidente de Palomares: desde la Guerra Fría hasta hoy.* Laertes Editorial.

Historical Research Project No. 1421. Nuclear Accidents at Palomares, Spain in 1966 and Thule, Greenland in 1968. Office of the Historian. United States Department of State. Bureau of Public Affairs. Declassified on September 4, 2008.

Iglesias, Leyre (2016) "Palomares desclasificado," *El Mundo*, June 26.

Inoue, Yasuhiro, and Rinnert, Carol (2007) "Editorial Reflections on Historical/Diplomatic Relations with Japan and the U.S.: International Newspaper Coverage of the 60th Anniversary of the Hiroshima Bombing," *Keio Communication Review*, 29, pp. 59-83.

Inoue, Yasuhiro and Rinnert, Carol (2010) "International newspaper coverage of the 60th anniversary of the Hiroshima bombing," in Edward Demenchonok (ed.), *After*

Hiroshima: Memory, Warfare, and the Ethics of Peace, UK: Cambridge Scholars, pp. 69-96.

Inoue, Yasuhiro (2018) *Amerika no Genbaku shinwa to jouhou sousa* [Atomic Bomb Myths and Information Manipulation in the US], Tokyo: Asahi Shimbun Publications.

Inoue, Yasuhiro, ed. (2021) *Sekai wa Hiroshima wo dou rikaishiteiruka?* [How the World understands Hiroshima?], Tokyo: Chuokouron Shinsha.

Keever, Beverly Deepe (2004) *News Zero: The New York Times and the Bomb*, Maine: Common Courage Press.

Laynez-Bretones, F. and Lozano-Padilla, C. (2017) "Fifty years since the nuclear accident in Palomares (Almería). Medical repercussions," *Revista Clínica Española,* 217 (5), pp.263-266.

Lifton, Robert Jay, and Mitchell, Greg (1995) *Hiroshima in America: A Half Century of Denial*, NY: Avon Books.

Philipps, Dave (2016, June 19) "Decades Lates, Sickness Among Airmen After a Hydrogen Bomb Accident." *The New York Times*, p.A1.

Stiles, David (2006) "A Fusion Bomb over Andalucía: U.S. Information Policy and the 1966 Palomares Incident," *Journal of Cold War Studies,* 8 (1), pp. 49-67.

Stone, Robert S., Warren, Stafford L., Langham, Wright, Hempelmann, Louis H., Friedell, Hymer, Hamilton, Joseph G., Howland, Joseph, and Bassett, Samuel H. (2017) "Human Radiation Experiments," Atomic Heritage Foundation < https://www.atomicheritage.org/history/human-radiation-experiments>.

Wilson, Ward (2014) *Five Myths about Nuclear Weapons*. Boston: Mariner Books.

Chapter 5
The New York Times: Transition from Accomplice to Questioner of the Atomic Bombing

Yasuhiro Inoue

1. Accomplice and the Government Mouthpiece

One of the most prestigious and trusted newspapers in the world is *The New York Times*. Its fame is widely acknowledged and few would challenge the newspaper's status. However, when it comes to nuclear-related issues in general, and the atomic bombing of Hiroshima and Nagasaki specifically, the newspaper colluded with the United States government and helped to manipulate information and disseminate propaganda in covering up the most distinctive effect of the atomic bomb, i.e., radiation.[1]

The US government and the War Department badly needed the prestige of *The New York Times* (*NYT*) to publicize the no-one-know new weapon, justify the atomic attack, and cover-up "inconvenient" facts such as civilian suffering and lingering effects of radiation. The commander of the Manhattan Project (the atomic bomb development project) approached *NYT* to ask for a Pulitzer-awarded science reporter, William L. Laurence, to cover the atomic bombs. By giving exclusive privilege to Laurence and *NYT*, the War Department was able to establish a "monopoly propaganda" (Keever 2004: 53) through which information manipulation and cover-up were easily conducted. The War Department's goal was accomplished almost perfectly. In other words, the general understandings of the atomic bombing in the minds of the American people have been formed. These points are more specifically described as Atomic Bomb Myths[2]:

1. The atomic bomb was used with prior warnings in order to avoid civilian victims. An important military base was targeted

and destroyed.

2. The atomic bomb (and its psychological shock) forced Japan to surrender and ended the war sooner.

3. Thanks to the bombs, the US was able to avoid the planned invasion of Japan's mainland. Therefore, the atomic bombings saved a half to one million American lives and even more Japanese lives.

4. Americans are a chosen people and "God let us do the merciful act", i.e., atomic bombing. The atomic bombing is salvation for the US as well as for Japan.

5. Most of the radioactive material of the bomb turned into enormous heat and blast. Therefore, there was little residual radiation. Heat and blast, not radiation, killed (military) people.

This chapter examines the role *NYT* played as the government's accomplice to manipulate information and cover-up facts relating to the atomic bombing by using content and frame analysis (see Section 1 in Chapter 4) of the newspaper's coverage from the first year, 1945 to the 75th anniversary of the bombing, 2020. By tracking down its coverage in chronological order, this study reveals (1) *NYT*'s biased and deceptive coverage (or non-coverage) and its collusion with the government, and (2) the transitions of *NYT* coverage and editorial stance on the issue marking its shift from accomplice to questioner.

2. Key Player: Pulitzer Prize Reporter, "Atomic Bill" Laurence

Before tracing the coverage of *NYT*, it will be helpful to present some background information and historical facts. Behind-the-scene contexts, which have been documented in academic books and articles, will be useful to comprehend the analysis.

2.1. Participant, Consultant, and Cheerleader

NYT provided the War Department with the Pulitzer Prize science reporter, William L. Laurence, after the publisher had been requested by the Manhattan Project commander, General Leslie Groves. The government, in return, exclusively privileged the reporter to eyewitness the Manhattan Project: the development, the making and even the use of the atomic bomb in warfare. He was called "Atomic Bill" in the newsroom (see Section 6).

Laurence, exulted at the offer, apparently regarded himself not only as a participant but also as an important member or "(p)rivileged honorable cheerleaders" (Grossman 1997: 170) of the Manhattan Project. As the official public relations consultant and the scribe of the Project, Laurence drafted and wrote the President's first statement about the atomic bomb (see Section 3), most of the press releases, and even "model" articles about the bomb and its development for other newspapers. Keever (2004) describes Laurence's roles and influences:

Often edited by military brass, Laurence's words. . . served as War Department communiques given worldwide distribution. They also provided most of the material reworked for the news columns that *The Times* [*NYT*] used in devoting ten of its 38 pages on August 7, 1945. . . Laurence was thus a major player in providing many text-based images, language and knowledge that first fixed and molded the meanings and perceptions of the emerging atomic age (40).

All other news media reporters, including those at *NYT*, could not help but totally depend on materials that Laurence prepared. The reason is simple: they didn't know anything about the atomic bomb. "[Laurence's] language appeared in newspapers around the world. At first, this was almost the only material available. When other writers began to describe the emergence of nuclear energy, they either followed Laurence's lead or reached into the same stock of familiar images that he had used" (Weart 1988: 104).

2.2. They Knew Radiation Effects from the Start

The Manhattan Project leaders and Laurence were aware of the dangers and the most defining feature of radiation on human health and the environment before the first detonation of the atomic bomb, the top-secret Trinity test in New Mexico on July 16, 1945 (Keever 2004). Therefore, they knew the serious effects of the bombs on the people living in Hiroshima and Nagasaki. Yet the US government ignored and later denied the serious effects. *NYT* toed the government's line, or rather, they helped to inscribe it.

As mentioned above, most of the first words describing the atomic bomb to the world were drafted by Laurence, double-paid by *NYT* and the War Department for his publicity and cover-up mission. He seldom mentioned the word radiation and virtually ignored its effects, even in his Pulitzer Prized ten-article series first published by *NYT* and then reprinted free of charge by many other newspapers.

Radiation was not just unmentioned or ignored. Parroting War Department announcements, he dismissed claims about the existence of radiation in Hiroshima and Nagasaki as Japanese "propaganda. . . attempting to create sympathy for themselves" (9/12/1945: 1-4). He (and of course, most of the reporters) and the War Department portrayed the atomic bomb as a conventional super-bomb by repeatedly mentioning TNT as if it were the explosive material used in the atomic bombs instead of the radioactive matter actually used (uranium for the Hiroshima bomb, Little Boy and plutonium for the Nagasaki bomb, Fat Man). *NYT* continued this omission and the denial of the material facts for readers long after the post-World War II while real facts and scientific experts' comments were demoted to short items and inconspicuously buried inside pages (Keever 2004).

NYT committed sins of omission and deception to dismiss concerns about radiation. The prestige of *NYT* played a decisive role in perpetuating Atomic Bomb Myth 5: no radiation.

Now the coverage of *NYT* is to be tracked down in chronological order.

3. The Day of the Atomic Bombing Hiroshima

3.1. President's Atomic Bomb Statement

The world was abruptly informed of the atomic bomb attack on Hiroshima by a statement of US President Truman[3] on August 6, 1945. The news was literally "a tremendous bolt from the blue" and jolted the world. The statement was distributed as a press release to the White House press corps without being read out by Truman because he was crossing the Atlantic Ocean on his way back from the Potsdam Conference. The first part of the statement established the narratives and understandings of the atomic bomb:

> Sixteen hours ago an American airplane dropped one bomb on Hiroshima, an important Japanese Army base. That bomb had more power than 20,000 tons of TNT. . . . The Japanese began the war from the air at Pearl Harbor. They have been repaid many fold. . . . It is an atomic bomb. It is a harnessing of the basic power of the universe.

Without mentioning the defining feature of the atomic bomb that most distinguishes it from conventional weapons, the statement framed the atomic bomb as "targeting at an important military base," "the bomb as a super-blockbuster but a conventional weapon," and "justifying [the atomic bombing as] a retaliatory act of Pearl Harbor" (Lifton and Mitchell 1995: 5-6). Both this president's statement and other press releases (most drafted by Laurence) did not mention its most distinctive new feature: radiation. What was emphasized (falsely): A military base was the target of the bomb.

Although "the official narrative was built on a lie, or at best a half-truth" (Mitchell 2013), the framings of the Truman statement echoed "long afterward in official and unofficial rhetoric. . . (T)hese themes have continued to dominate peacetime discourse about Hiroshima and the bomb" (Lifton and Mitchell 1995: 7). In other words, the framings of the atomic bomb presented in the statement (and other materials) formed the basis for the atomic bomb narratives and understandings in the American people's minds.

3.2. *NYT*'s Mouthpiece Coverage on the First Day

All the news media including *NYT* had no other choice but to depend solely on the Truman announcement and other press releases. Many newspapers on August 7 gave huge front-page headlines to the president's claim of an explosive force equivalent to 20,000 tons of TNT. This framing of the atomic bomb as a super conventional bomb is manifested in *NYT*'s front page with a three-line headline across all eight columns:

FIRST ATOMIC BOMB DROPPED ON JAPAN;

MISSILE IS EQUAL TO 20,000 TONS OF TNT;

TRUMAN WARNS FOE OF A 'RAIN OF RUIN'

The first sentence of the news article highlights the destructiveness framing of the president's statement: "The White House and War Department announced today that an atomic bomb, possessing more power than 20,000 tons of TNT, a destructive force equal to the load of 2,000 B-29's and more than 2,000 times the blast power of what previously was the world's most devastating bomb." Then, the third paragraph echoes the statement again by framing Hiroshima as a military target, "an important army center."

This sentence of "military target framing" is followed and reinforced by a sub-headline, "Japanese Solemnly Warned" without clearly saying that the US warned the Japanese of the atomic bomb. This headline would give readers the false impression that the Japanese had been warned of the bomb and had ignored it. This is not the case. In fact, (1) leaders of the US government had decided not to give any prior warning and the military abided by the decision; (2) warning leaflets were dropped in Japan meaninglessly after Nagasaki was bombed, four days after the Hiroshima atomic bombing.

Even though the actual aiming point was the center (a commercial and residential area) of Hiroshima with a population of more than 300,000, the civilian population in Hiroshima was almost unmentioned. Another front page article, "War News Summarized" mentions the city's population but highlights the military aspects of Hiroshima: "Hiroshima was a major military target, a city of 318,00 persons thickly settled around a quartermaster's depot, an embarkation port, armament and airplane parts plants." In fact, *NYT* did not raise or even imply any questions about the indiscriminate nature of the atomic bomb which caused the mass killing of civilians.

As for Myth 5, *NYT* did not address the distinguishing feature of the atomic weapon, radiation. This is again no wonder because *NYT* and all the news media relied totally upon the War Department press releases which did not touch on the issue. The omission has a power: radiation wouldn't come to people's minds.

General Groves later reflected, with satisfaction, that "most newspapers published our releases in their entirety. This is one of the few times since government releases have become so common that this has been done."[4] As a reminder: most of the first day articles had been drafted and written by Laurence even though the article bylines were other reporters' names.

4. Cover-up of Radiation in Jacobson and Nakashima Stories

4.1. Denial of 70 Years Radiation Effects

On August 7 and 8, many newspapers in the US, but not *NYT*, printed a shocking news story about the radiation effects of the atomic bomb. Dr. Harold Jacobson of Columbia University, a Manhattan Project scientist, declared the bomb's 70-year effects: "Any Japanese who try to ascertain the extent of damage caused by the atomic bomb in Hiroshima are committing suicide. . . radiation in an area exposed to the force of an atomic bomb will not be dissipated for approximately 70 years" (*The Atlanta Constitution*, 8/8/1945: 1). This article was distributed throughout the country (and relayed to the world) by International News Service, which was one of the major news agencies at that time. Although its assertion was found false eventually, the story caused a sensation across the world.

NYT did not publish the exclusive story. The government counterattack was swift and effective; on August 9, *NYT* joined the counter information as the government's mouthpiece by publishing an article titled "70-YEAR EFFECT OF BOMBS DENIED" (8). The article repudiates Jacobson's claims with a statement from Dr. J. Robert Oppenheimer, director of the Manhattan Project: "Based on all our experimental work and study and on the results of the test in New Mexico. . . there is every reason to believe that there was no appreciable radioactivity on the ground at Hiroshima and what little there was decayed very rapidly." It also quotes the War Department: "in the opinion of 'qualified experts' who had been studying the bomb from all phases, no such thing would happen."

This is the first *NYT* article that mentioned the words "radiation" or "radioactivity" and discussed (actually denied) its effects after Day One of the paper's Hiroshima and Nagasaki coverage (Keever 2004).

4.2. The First Hiroshima Report by a Western Reporter: Nakashima

It is commonly and falsely believed that the first Western reporter who entered Hiroshima and reported the aftermath was an Australian reporter (the following section deals with this topic). In fact, a Japanese American, Leslie Nakashima of United Press (UP), was the first Western journalist who cracked the information wall.[5]

US-born Nakashima was in Japan working for UP's Tokyo bureau, which was closed at the outbreak of the war. He moved to a Japanese news agency during the war. After the war, he returned to UP. Thus, he was able to visit Hiroshima on August 22 before the US Occupation implemented control over the city (his mother was in Hiroshima).

On August 31, 1945, *NYT* published Nakashima's exclusive account distributed by UP four days earlier. Even though it was the first story of its kind, *NYT* buried the article on page 4 inconspicuously. Moreover, the newspaper grossly cut down and omitted almost all Nakashima's descriptions of radiation's acute and lingering effects. In addition, an editor's note, "United States scientists say the atomic bomb will not have any lingering after-effects in the devastated areas," was inserted immediately after a sentence that implies lingering effects: "The death toll is expected to reach 100,000 with people continuing to die daily from burns suffered from the bomb's ultra-violet rays."

The heavily edited version of Nakashima's article gives a false impression that people were dying solely from burns and injuries by the bomb rather than radiation sickness. Here are some critical parts *NYT* slashed off from Nakashima's original piece:

> Miraculously he suffered no burns but he became sick from inhalation of the bomb's gas, for which he is still taking treatment. . . . Warnings that people would take sick from the effects of uranium, which had seeped into the ground, kept people away from the destroyed area. . . . From such developments a fear has risen among Japanese authorities that reports from American sources that such bombed areas will be impossible for human habitation for 75 years may well be true. . . . (I)t is likely that I inhaled uranium because I'm still troubled with a loss of appetite and the least little exertion finds me tired.

These are not the all *NYT* did to undermine Nakashima's. Right after this heavily edited article, *NYT* ran an item headlined "Japanese Reports Doubted" in which General Groves was quoted as saying, "Japanese reports of death from radioactive effects of atomic bombing are pure propaganda."

5. Burchett's Scoop: Warning to the World "Atomic Plague"

The first Allied journalist to enter Hiroshima "independently" (braved the off-limit) was Wilfred Burchett, an Australian working for the UK's largest circulation newspaper at that time, *The London Daily Express*.[6] There were a number of Allied reporters in Japan after Japan surrendered on August 15, 1945. But they were not allowed or brave enough to go into either Hiroshima or Nagasaki.

With his great determination, help from a Japanese news agency, and sheer luck, Burchett conquered many hurdles and managed to make it to Hiroshima. He walked around the devastated city and visited a hospital on September 3. That made him write an article titled, "THE ATOMIC PLAGUE" with headlines "a warning to the world" "Doctors fall as they work" "Poison gas fear" which was miraculously cabled to London and published by *The Daily* on September 5. The opening paragraph states:

> In Hiroshima, 30 days after the first atomic bomb destroyed the city and shook the world, people are still dying, mysteriously and horribly—people who were uninjured by the cataclysm—from an unknown something which I can only describe as atomic plague.

The newspaper gave free rights to reprint Burchett's report to other newspapers around the world. However, so far as it is known, no US newspapers reprinted the historical article, for some reasons.

Burchett came across a group tour of American journalists, who had been handpicked in Washington, D.C., as they were shepherded around Hiroshima by Army public relations officers. While Burchett made his own way by a grueling 24-hour train ride without any transmission equipment, the junket was flown in a shining B-17 specially equipped with state-of-the-art devices. The members of the junket, according to Burchett, were upset because they thought they were the first and the only non-Japanese journalists who would be able to write exclusive stories.

He alerted them: "The real story is in the hospitals" (Burchett 1983: 41). But the junket, which stayed in Hiroshima only a few hours, ignored or were not given a tour of the hospitals. During the short and hasty visit to Hiroshima, journalists were fed with sanitized information by the military. Most wrote reports about the destroyed city by characterizing the atomic bomb as vastly more powerful than conventional ones.

6. The Government's Counter Publicity and Docile News Media

6.1. *NYT* Backed off and Turned around

In fact, there was a *NYT* correspondent among the junket: William H. Lawrence. He is not "Atomic Bill" <u>Laurence</u>, but "Non-Atomic Bill" <u>Lawrence</u> (in order to distinguish the two, they were differently called in the newsroom).

On the same day that Burchett's "warning to the world" was published, *NYT* published an article by Lawrence headlined "Visit to Hiroshima Proves It World's Most-Damaged City—Four Square Miles Leveled by the Atomic Bomb. People Reported Dying at Rate of 100 a Day" on page one. To some degree, the article contains eyewitness accounts not only about the destruction of buildings but also about human suffering as the headline indicates. It is assumed that he held a bit of journalistic faith or one of the principles in *NYT*, "Give the news impartially, without fear or favor," at that point. Although this eyewitness account does not mention radiation or uranium at all, the article implies the lingering effects of radiation as follows:

> Japanese doctors told us they were helpless to deal with burns caused by the bomb's great flash or with the other physical ailments caused by the bomb. Some said they thought that all who had been in Hiroshima that day would die as a result of the bomb's lingering effects. They told us that person who had been only slightly injured on the day of the blast lost 86 per cent of their white blood corpuscles, developed temperatures of 104 degrees Fahrenheit, their hair began to drop out, they lost their appetites, vomited blood and finally died (1-4).

General MacArthur, the Supreme Commander for the Allied Powers, was outraged not only by Burchett's story but also by some of the junketeers' reports including this *NYT* story by "Non-Atomic Bill." On the same day, those eyewitness stories were published, the US Occupation Forces in Japan rushed into counter publicity operations, declaring the atomic cities fully off-limits to reporters and imposed strict press restrictions. The Allied reporters were confined to a "press ghetto" (Burchett 1983: 24) in Yokohama.[7] The strict press control and obedience of the news media soon became manifest in coverage about the atomic-bombed cities.

Less than a week after publishing the "Dying at Rate of 100 a Day" account, *NYT* and the reporter ("Non-Atomic Bill" Lawrence) suddenly backed away from the somewhat neutral position evident in the earlier piece. As if docilely obeyed, Lawrence then turned 180 degrees by writing an article dispatched from Nagasaki (9/10: 1-5). With the section header "Foe Seeks to Win Sympathy," his Nagasaki dateline story reports:

> We now have visited both Hiroshima and Nagasaki. . . . I am convinced that, horrible as the bomb undoubtedly is, the Japanese are exaggerating its effects in an effort to win sympathy for themselves in an attempt to make the American people forget the long record of cold-blooded Japanese bestiality.

Were the attitude change of *NYT* and the publication of Burchett's "Atomic Plague" coincidence or the result of the counter information/publicity efforts by the US government?

6.2. Toughening Counter Information and Denial of Radiation

NYT's "Foe Seeks to Win Sympathy" on September 10 was just the start. After this piece, a barrage of counter-information articles was published by *NYT*. The reports denied (residual) radiation and regarded Japanese claims about radiation as attempts to seek sympathy.

On September 9, the Manhattan Project leaders General Groves and Dr. Oppenheimer gave a tour of the Trinity Test Site in New Mexico to a group of around thirty journalists. The purpose of the tour was apparent: to demonstrate how safe the Trinity test site was from radioactivity and to counter reports about radiation deaths in Hiroshima.[8] The attending journalists fell in line as expected. Among the shepherded journalists, there was only one reporter who eye-witnessed the first detonation and the atomic bombing of Nagasaki: "Atomic Bill" Laurence. He wrote a stronger counter information story than the one written by "Non-Atomic Bill" Lawrence a couple days before. The article by "Atomic Bill" was published on September 12 on the front page:

U.S. ATOM BOMB SITE BELIES TOKYO TALES
Tests on New Mexico Range Confirm That Blast, and Not Radiation, Took Toll
This historic ground in New Mexico . . . gave the most effective answer today to Japanese propaganda that radiations were responsible for deaths even after the day of the explosion. . . and that persons entering Hiroshima had contracted mysterious maladies due to persistent radioactivity.

This front page story was accompanied by an item sub-headed "Foe's Propaganda at Work" (4). It reports as follows:

"The Japanese claims," General Groves added, "that people died from radiations. If this is true, the number was very small. . . While many people were killed, many lives were saved, particularly American lives. It ended the war sooner. . ." . . . The Japanese are still continuing their propaganda aimed at creating the impression that we won the war unfairly, and thus attempting to create sympathy for themselves and milder terms, an examination of their present statement reveals.

On the following day, *NYT* reinforced the government's "no radiation" policy by carrying a more straightforward-headlined story datelined in Tokyo: NO RADIOACTIVITY IN HIROSHIMA RUIN (9/13: 4). This was written by "Non-Atomic" Lawrence, who visited Hiroshima as a member of the junket and ran into Burchett in the ruins.

(C)hief of the War Department's atomic bomb mission, reported tonight after a survey of blasted Hiroshima. . . he [General Farrell] denied categorically that it produced a dangerous, lingering radioactivity in the ruins of the town or caused a form of poison gas at the moment of explosion.

The article emphasized the destruction of military buildings by saying, "the area including the Japanese military headquarters was completely demolished." Under a sub-heading "Blast Is Chief Effect," it repeats the government line:

General Farrell . . . made it clear that the weapon's chief effect was blast, and that only in a limited area whose geographical extent he would not estimate was there any radioactivity and this exclusively at the moment of the explosion. He said his group of scientists found no evidence of continuing radioactivity in the blasted area on Sept. 9.

One fact should be noted here. Burchett was refused to take a flight back to Tokyo, so he had to make his way back from Hiroshima, again by train. He made it back by himself and unexpectedly attended *the* press briefing by General Farrell. He first asked whether the briefing officer had been to Hiroshima. Then, he described what he saw in Hiroshima, "any who had not been in the city at the time of the blast were later affected" and "the fish still dying when they entered a stream running through the centre of the city." According to Burchett (1983: 22-23), Farrell bluntly refuted Burchett's claims: "I'm afraid you've fallen victim to Japanese propaganda." Lawrence of *NYT* was there, but did not report the exchange.

"NO RADIOACTIVITY" was not the only story on the day bolstering the US government's position. An editorial titled "AFTER-EFFECTS OF THE BOMB" (22) added support by stating:

The measurements of residual radioactivity which were made in

New Mexico, over the area where the first atomic bomb was exploded in a test made nearly two months ago, do not support the reports that have come from Hiroshima and Nagasaki of lingering death caused by powerful radiations from contaminated soil and buildings.

It would take forever to point out all of *NYT*'s radiation denial articles. As a final example in the newspaper, "SCIENCE IN REVIEW" article published on September 16 (E9) is mentioned. Titled "Radiologists Determine the After-Effects of Explosions of Atomic Bombs," this review states, "Japanese tales of hundreds who died weeks after the explosions . . . and of lowered white-corpuscle blood counts were largely refuted."

With such highly orchestrated news management, the word "radiation" scarcely filtered through to the American people's understandings of the atomic bombings (Blume 2020). American news media did not dare to report on the issue. Instead, reporting Hiroshima focused on the city's recovery and the near normal lives of the people in Hiroshima. For example, *NYT*'s report on the first anniversary (8/7/1946: 13) flatly states:

> The soil of Hiroshima remains fruitful, as the hundreds of tiny gardens attest. . . The scientists' conclusion. . . that the atomic bomb has a fairly limited range of effectiveness in both time and space. . . few signs have as yet been found of permanent injury caused by rays to those who survived.

7. Two Major Stories and Contrasting Coverage by *NYT*

7.1. Hersey's *HIROSHIMA*

The New Yorker, an urban monthly magazine, devoted the entire August issue in 1946 to a single story: *HIROSHIMA*. It was written by a renowned Pulitzer-winning journalist, John Hersey. The magazine quickly sold out. *HIROSHIMA* was later republished as a book and became a run-away best-seller.[9] When Hersey's story first hit the store shelves, the media coverage was sensational (except for *NYT*). *HIROSHIMA* made front-page news around the world (except for Japan due to the restrictive press code). The entire story was read and broadcast four consecutive nights by more than five hundred radio stations in the US alone. Hersey's work, which described the lingering effects of radiation, had an immediate and profound impact on American understandings of the atomic bombing.

NYT ran a tiny filler buried inside about *HIROSHIMA* on the day it was published (8/29: 37). The next day, however, the paper changed its editorial tone, considering the past coverage on the atomic bomb issues. The editorial titled "TIME FROM LAUGHER" raises a question about the legitimacy of the atomic bombing (8/30: 13). In the first paragraph, it warns know-it-alls: "Every American who has permitted himself to make jokes about atom bombs. . . ought to read Mr. Hersey." Although in a gentle way, it went as far as taking issue with the decision of the atomic bombing:

> The disasters at Hiroshima and Nagasaki . . . were defended then, and are defended now, by the argument that they saved more lives than they took—more lives of Japanese as well as more lives of Americans. The argument may be sound or it may be unsound. One may think it sound when he recalls Tarawa, Iwo Jima, or Okinawa. One may think it unsound when he reads Mr. Hersey.

NYT, up to that time, was a reliable partner and even a confederate in the US government propaganda operation. Did the paper convert from collabolator to critic? No. While the editorial jolted the government and the military public relations officers who had been successful in characterizing the atomic bomb as humane and life-saving, it was the only major item the newspaper published about *HIROSHIMA* for decades to come.

Aside from *NYT* coverage, *HIROSHIMA* itself was a nightmare and embarrassed the government. Hersey's story definitely became a trigger for doubting and criticizing the atomic bombings. Some well-known persons including war leaders openly voiced uneasiness and doubts about the decision of the bombing. No wonder it disturbed the leaders of the Manhattan

Project, especially James B. Conant, president of Harvard University. He was an important member of the Interim Committee that decided every policy regarding the atomic bomb. And it was he who advocated that the atomic bomb should target populated areas without any warning.[10]

7.2. Stimson's "The Decision to Use the Atomic Bomb"

Conant was deeply concerned that HIROSHIMA could turn public opinions against the bombing and the future nuclear programs. He approached former Secretary of War Henry L. Stimson who retired weeks after the surrender ceremony on September 2, 1945. Conant persuaded Stimson, who was greatly respected by Americans, to write, actually allow to ghost-write, an article to counter the bad publicity caused by Hersey.

Stimson's article titled "The Decision to Use the Atomic Bomb" was published by *Harper's* Magazine in the February issue of 1947. Its primary contentions are the government's official justifications: the atomic bombings ended the war and saved lives:

> Such an effective shock would save many times the number of lives, both American and Japanese, that it would cost.
> We estimated that if we should be forced to carry this plan [invasion of Japan's mainland] to its conclusion, the major fighting would not end until the latter part of 1946, at the earliest.[11]
> I was informed that such operations might be expected to cost over a million casualties, to American forces alone[12]. . .
> All of the evidence I have seen indicates that the controlling factor in the final Japanese decision to accept our terms of surrender was the atomic bomb.
> My chief purpose was to end the war in victory with the least possible cost in the lives of the men in the armies which I had helped to raise. . .
> The bombs dropped on Hiroshima and Nagasaki ended a war.[13]

On the day the Stimson article hit the shelves, *NYT* published a front-page story written by "Atomic" Laurence (1/28). Titled "Truman Used Atom Bomb To Halt War, Stimson Says," Laurence praised and supported what was written in the Stimson article by quoting the President's letter: "The Japanese were given fair warning. . . well in advance of the dropping of the bomb. I imagine the bomb caused them to accept the terms."

Further, not surprisingly, the paper's editorial board blatantly and uncritically repeated Stimson's assertion in the same day's editorial titled "WAR AND THE BOMB" (22):

> Replying to many misgivings and some open criticism aroused by this country's use of the atomic bomb against Japan, both President Truman and . . . Stimson . . . have now published statements of the reasons which prompted them to introduce this dread weapon to modern warfare. By coincidence, these statements appear simultaneously."[14]
>
> . . . The best American estimates were that it would cost at least a million American—and many more Japanese casualties . . . as President Truman . . . gave them "fair warning" that continued resistance would mean the "utter devastation of the Japanese homeland." . . . this notice was adequate . . . the psychological impact of the new weapon, and the dread of more to come, put an end to the war, and sacrificing thousands of lives, saved millions. That is the justification for the bomb's use.

7.3. The Orchestrated Coverage Framed and Set the Understandings

The impact of the Stimson article was tremendous. It became the Hiroshima narrative and the basic text for journalists and even historians. "[The article] would reassert the official narrative so effectively it would remain virtually unchallenged for decades. . . . Indeed, its influence endures to this day" (Lifton and Mitchell 1995: 93-94). The framings of the atomic bombings were deep inset as the American understandings of Hiroshima.

NYT had maintained its editorial stance for decades to follow: no report or underreport of the atomic bombing; trivialization or denial of radiation and; justification of the decision of the bombing. The overall editorial stance continued up until the 60th anniversary (Inoue and Rinnert 2010). In 2005, the newspaper framed Hiroshima as a past event, particularly represented by an opinion article titled "An Anniversary to Forget" (8/7: 12).

As its headline indicates, this article frames the Hiroshima atomic bombing as a past event that should be forgotten by saying, "(T)he bombings don't really matter to me. . . the horror of that war and its nuclear evils feel distant, even foreign." Other framing exemplars of the atomic bombings were "pop culture," "elevator music" and "the equivalent of a cultural 'game over' or 'reset' button."

8. Shifting Editorial Stance: Questioning the Atomic Bombing

8.1. Trivialization to Recognition of the Importance

A decade later, editorial stance shifts were observed in the *NYT* coverage of the 2015 anniversary. The changes were represented by publishing (1) a questioning "Editorial Observer" (a bylined opinion article that follows regular editorials) by a *NYT* editorial board writer, (2) a critical opinion article by a historian, and (3) a feature of readers' debate about the bombing and the decision to use atomic weapons. Considering the newspaper's long history of trivialization and utter justification of the bombing, the stance shifts are noteworthy.

The Editorial Observer titled "Remembering Hiroshima, and How It Changed the World" (8/8: A18) raises a question by stating, "whether the bombings were necessary or moral. . . The debates and questioning will continue, and they should." While avoiding outright condemnation, the editorial writer recognizes the bombings as an important present issue by stating, "The world has not been the same since those bombs fell on Hiroshima and Nagasaki. . . the threat of the doomsday weapon is very much with us."

The opinion item by a historian, Susan Southard, titled "Nagasaki, the Forgotten City" (8/8: 19) goes far beyond questioning into criticizing the bombing. *The Washington Post* in 2020 published the same historian's commentary which harshly condemned the atomic bombings and provided graphic descriptions of the victims and plenty of historical evidence (see Section 2.4 in Chapter 4). Her commentary carried by *NYT*, on the other hand, is not as relentless or graphic as that of *The Post*. However, it is significant that *NYT* decided to publish such a critical commentary that denounces the US suppression of radiation sufferings and denies the Atomic Bomb Myths:

> Initially, purple spots appeared on their bodies, their hair fell out, and they developed high fevers, infections, and swollen and bleeding gums. Later, cancer rates surged. The survivors, known as hibakusha, lived in constant fear of illness and death. The United States suppressed this part of the story. . . . To counter growing criticism of the bombings, American leaders established a narrative that the bombings had ended the war and saved up to 1 million American lives by preventing an invasion of Japan. . . . Most Americans accepted this narrative.

This level of condemnation is not uncommon, often found in newspapers in Europe and Latin America (see Sections 3 and 6 in Chapter 4; Inoue, 2021). But, as far as the author can tell, the commentary is probably the first case that has gone this far in *NYT*'s atomic bomb coverage.

The feature of the readers' debate (8/9: 10) looks balanced at first glance of the title, "Evaluating Military and Moral Fallout of Atomic Bomb" and the opening sentence, "Did the United States have to drop the bomb?" In fact, it presents both sides of the argument. However, its overall tone is definitely biased for the justification of the bombing by presenting more supporting and praising comments such as "Truman did the right thing. . . it was politically correct and saved American lives and ended the war," and "I am here, no doubt, because the bomb was dropped."

While the coverage of 2015 obviously (and finally) became more balanced, the shifts in the editorial stance are mixed and differ in degree.

8.2. Hibakusha on the Front Page and Photograph of Injured Infant

On the day after the 75th anniversary of the Hiroshima bombing in 2020, *NYT* published a hibakusha family photograph on the front page. In addition, it ran a double-page feature (A14-15) with a photograph that shows a badly injured infant by the atomic bomb. In the author's examination,[15] it was the first time for *NYT* to run a photo of hibakusha on page one and a graphic picture of a child victim. In particular, the photograph of an infant whose face was seemingly burnt must be a good indicator of the editorial attitude change on the bombing because almost all the photographs *NYT* previously published in its reports on the atomic bomb were rubbles and ruins, such as the Atomic Bomb Dome, and/or recovered adults.

The trivialization of the bombing, which was the consistent stance of *NYT*, seems to have changed. An editorial titled "Into a New Arms Race" (8/7: A26) appreciates the importance of Hiroshima lessons in the present time by saying, "the wrenching images of scorched rubble where Hiroshima had stood ought to be cause for serious reflection on what nuclear weapons do—and what they cannot do."

The coverage of the 75th anniversary year, however, did not have any castigating articles about the bombing. The depth of questioning and criticism of *NYT* coverage is pale compared to the opinion articles published by *The Washington Post* and *Los Angeles Times* (see Chapter 4, Section 2.4 & 2.5). Further, it is absolutely beyond comparison with those by some newspapers in Europe and Latin America which severely denounce the bombing with words like "crime against humanity," "genocide," and "holocaust."[16] But *NYT* is definitely moving away from the perennial cold attitudes and adopting a more balanced, somewhat critical, position about the atomic bombing.

As for the reasons underlying the changes, the author deduces several causal factors in *NYT* newsroom: (1) generational turnover, i.e., more young reporters, (2) overall editorial stance shift toward a more liberal and international-minded approach as global readership increases due to Internet subscription, and (3) one of the pioneers and the leading news media in data journalism and evidence-based reporting differ drastically from old-fashioned reporting which is dependent on the establishments. Of course, various social changes impacting public opinion and the political environment are certainly important factors, too.

Such social changes helped make it possible for President Obama to visit Hiroshima in 2016 as the first sitting president of the US. It is assumed that the changes are also making the American people face (or feel less burdened to face) a difficult historical fact: the United States remains the only country to have deployed nuclear weapons in combat targeting the densely populated cities of Hiroshima and Nagasaki.

The New York Times has changed the editorial stance from being an accomplice in the US government's manipulation of information to a questioner of the atomic bombing.

Acknowledgments

Data collection of this study was partially supported by The Hiroshima Peace Creation Fund's "Peace Grant."

Notes

1. This chapter about *The New York Times* and the coverage of the atomic bombing is dependent upon Berger (1951), Blume (2020), Boyer (1985), Grossman (1997), Inoue (2018), Keever (2004), Lifton and Mitchell (1995), Salisbury (1980), and Weart (1988).
2. For an overall examination of historical evidence that disproves the Myths, see Inoue (2018). As for "the number saved," Chapter 3 and Bernstein (1986), (1999); "ended war," Chapter 3 and Hasegawa (2005).
3. This section about the statement and the reporting draws on Lifton and Mitchell (1995) and Mitchell (2013).
4. Cited in Lifton and Mitchell (1995: 10).
5. This section draws from Blume (2020) and Inoue (2018). Nakashima's original article is available at www.upi.com/Archives/1945/08/27/Hiroshima-as-I-saw-it/8051438702501/

6. This section draws from Blume (2020), Burchett (1983), and Keever (2004).
7. Press restrictions is dependent on Blume (2020: 31) and Braw (1991).
8. All of them wore special white protective shoe covers. This section draws on Blume (2020) and Keever (2004).
9. This section about Hersey and *HIROSHIMA* draws on Blume (2020), Keever (2004), and Yavenditti (1974).
10. For detailed information about Conant, see Hershberg (1993).
11. The official government document, *The United States Strategic Bombing Survey*, clearly states, "it is the Survey's opinion that certainly prior to December 31, 1945, and in all probability prior to November 1, 1945, Japan would have surrendered even if the atomic bombs had not been dropped, even if Russia had not entered the war, and even if no invasion had been planned or contemplated." This official survey was conducted by the order of President Truman, and published a half year prior to Stimson's article.
12. No official records which support this assertion have yet been found.
13. Chapter 3 rebuts Myth 2 and 3: ended war, saved lives.
14. The simultaneous publications were thought to be coordinated primarily by Conant and his partners.
15. The author collected almost all the articles about Hiroshima published by *NYT* from 1945 to 2020.
16. For international coverage, see Chapter 4 and Inoue (2021).

References

Berger, Meyer (1951) *The Story of The New York Times, 1851- 1951*. NY: Simon and Schuster.

Bernstein, Barton J. (1986) "A Postwar Myth: 500,000 U.S. Lives Saved," *Bulletin of the Atomic Scientists*, 42, pp.38-41.

Bernstein, Barton J. (1999) "Reconsidering Truman's Claim of 'Half a Million American Lives' Saved by the Atomic Bomb: The Construction and Deconstruction of a Myth," *Journal of Strategic Studies*, 22 (1), pp.54-95.

Blume, Lesley M.M. (2020) *Fallout: The Hiroshima Cover-up and the Reporter Who Revealed It to the World*. NY: Simon & Schuster.

Boyer, Paul (1985) *By the Bomb's Early Light: American Thought and Culture at the Dawn of the Atomic Age*. NY: Pantheon Books.

Braw, Monica (1991) *Atomic Bomb Suppressed: American Censorship in Occupied Japan*. Armonk, NY: M. E. Sharpe.

Burchett, Wilfred (1983) *Shadows of Hiroshima*. London: Verso.

Grossman, Karl (1997) *The Wrong Stuff: The Space Program's Nuclear Threat to Our Planet*. Maine: Common Courage Press.

Hasegawa, Tsuyoshi (2005) *Racing the Enemy: Stalin, Truman, and the Surrender of Japan*. Cambridge, MA: Harvard University Press.

Hershberg, James G. (1993) *James B. Conant: Harvard to Hiroshima and the Making of the Nuclear Age*. NY: Alfred A. Knopf.

Inoue, Yasuhiro and Rinnert, Carol (2010) "International newspaper coverage of the 60th anniversary of the Hiroshima bombing," in Edward Demenchonok, (ed.), *After Hiroshima: Memory, Warfare, and the Ethics of Peace*, UK: Cambridge Scholars, pp. 69-96.

Inoue, Yasuhiro (2018) *Amerika no Genbaku shinwa to jouhou sousa* [Atomic Bomb Myths and Information Manipulation in the US: NY Times Reporter and Harvard University President who Distorted Hiroshima], Tokyo: Asahi Shimbun Publications.

Inoue, Yasuhiro, ed. (2021) *Sekai wa Hiroshima wo dou rikaishiteiruka? Genbaku 75-shunen no 55 kakoku chiiki no houdou* [How the World understands Hiroshima?—The Coverage of the 75th Anniversary of the Atomic Bombing in 55 Countries and Regions]. Tokyo: Chuokouron Shinsha.

Keever, Beverly Deepe (2004) *News Zero: The New York Times and the Bomb*. Monroe, Maine: Common Courage Press.

Lifton, Robert Jay and Mitchell, Greg (1995) *Hiroshima in America: Fifty Years of Denial*. NY: A Grosset/Putnam Book.

Mitchell, Greg (2013) "68 Years Ago: Truman Opened the Nuclear Era—With a Lie About Hiroshima." *Huffpost*. <www.huffpost.com/entry/68-years-ago-truman-opene_b_3713210>

Salisbury, Harrison E. (1980) *Without Fear or Favor: The New York Times and its Times*. NY: Times Books.

Weart, Spencer R. (1988) *Nuclear Fear: A History of Images*. Cambridge, MA: Harvard University Press.

Yavenditti, Michael J. (1974) "John Hersey and the American Conscience: The Reception of 'Hiroshima,'" *Pacific Historical Review*, 43 (1), pp.24-49.

PART II
Hiroshima and Its Various Narratives

Chapter 6
What We Talk About When We Talk About Hiroshima

Mariko Nagai

We talk about the trams that snail through the city, even now, 77 years later, that made their ways through the city *that* day. A young woman was driving the tram because all able-bodied men had been drafted already, and Hiroshima was a naval town, an army town, so even ones who didn't fight were working for the war effort. One minute, women and men and children

Sunset Over the Hiroshima Peace Memorial Park

crammed together in the car as they had always done every morning—
through the war years and before—their destinations firm in their mind.
Then, a second later, the flash. Then the shock. Then the darkness. Then the
silence. Then the roaring of fire. Then the screams. Then the calling. Then
. . . 77 years later, I step down from the tram and stand on the bridge, looking
down at the river and the Atomic Dome.

We talk about Sadako Sasaki of the paper cranes, the girl who became a
representation of innocent victims of atomic bombs. When her parents took
her to the Red Cross Hospital after she developed swellings, the doctors
there diagnosed Sadako with leukemia. *A-bomb disease*. Just as they had
feared. Ten years previously, Sadako was there on that day, 1.6 km away
from the epicenter, but her mother wondered, "Was it the bomb itself, or
was it the black rain as we fled the damaged neighborhood? Was it all the

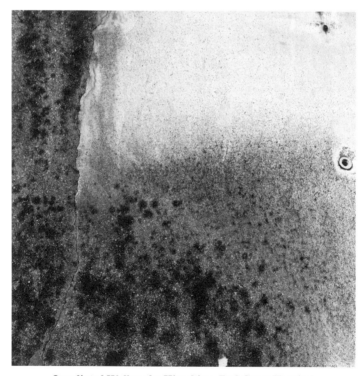

Irradiated Wall at the Hiroshima Red Cross Hospital

food I cooked for her after the war? Was it my fault?" For ten years, her parents wondered and feared over each nose bleed, each cough, each fever, just like they watched over their own symptoms as harbingers of something darker, and something made normal on that day. So, on the hospital bed, she folded her wishes into the paper cranes, one thousand cranes carrying the same wish, "Let me be well." She died and became a legend, and her stories have been written, statues built, fictionalized, revised, rewritten, retold.

When we talk about Sadako Sasaki, we don't talk about how her body was taken away by the ABCC, Atomic Bomb Casualty Commission, whose black American cars were seen driving around all over Hiroshima and Nagasaki during the Occupation Era. People whispered about whenever someone died, how these black American cars would drive up to their homes and pay the families to examine the corpses. Families often handed

Sky Over the Peace Museum

over the still-warm bodies—three thousand yen bought them food and overdue rent and other things to keep them alive. What the families didn't know was that even now, 77 years later, there are shelves and shelves of specimen jars that line the basement rooms—organs and skin and, rumor has it, deformed aborted fetuses.

When we talk about ABCC—or RERF—we don't talk about all the footage in the National Archives of the living, all ages, with various scars both visible and invisible, standing in front of the cameras. Nameless, coded by numbers. Or sometimes, just one-dimensional descriptions: a mother, a boy, an old man, a girl. Girls—old women now, 77 years later—whisper of being asked intimate questions they didn't even tell each other: When did you start your menstruation? When was your last menstruation? Have you ever had sexual intercourse? They remember the shame. They remember

ABCC or RERF

male doctors coercing them to answer prying questions they didn't know how to answer. They remember standing topless, sometimes completely naked, as male doctors looked at their pubic area to see whether they had hair. They are made anonymous, even though celluloids captured their most naked, most intimate selves. Naked.

When we talk about Hiroshima, we talk about the *before* and the *after*, and the moment on *that* day: I was a kilometer from the epicenter; I was at school playing with my friends by the window; I was standing outside, getting ready to go to the ammunition factory; I was on the tram; I was at home 4 kilometers away; I was . . . I was . . . They all saw the white flash. And, at the few seconds after the impact, they found themselves somewhere other than where they'd been: I was trapped under a beam; I was blown against the other wall; I was lying on the ground; I was lying on the hallway

Tissue and Histopathology Department

with glass shards all over me; I was . . . I was . . . These memories are as real as when they are retelling them, the past and the present folding like corners of the origami paper that Sadako folded on her hospital bed. *I was* slips into *I am*. And before is always painted in the perfect present and the after in the imperfect. *Before,* my mother was kind, my father strong. *Before,* we were a complete family. *Before,* I didn't really think about war. *After* is about fragmentation, something scarred and scared and sacred, a lost home, a lost family, a lost past, something no one can be critical of.

When we talk about Hiroshima, we talk about the brutal symmetry of the Peace Park, the meticulously sculpted space that is meant to awe and provoke. And silence the critics. It is beautiful in its minimalist grief. When we take a step into the park, a quietude descends on us, and we are hushed into the belated mourning, 77 years later. And during the annual memorial

Twilight at the Peace Museum

day, the streets are swamped with people who want to remember, though they weren't there that day. Tourists pose in front of the Dome, their fingers holding up peace signs, with big smiles, leaning against the railing so easily and nonchalantly. They bring their beliefs with them—against war, against government, against the Japanese government, against the governmental denial of Fukushima, against China, against revisionists, against the radical left, against communism, against nuclear power plants, against . . . but all united in their stance against nuclear bombs. And when the sun starts to set, the lit lanterns make their ways south down the river, just like the bodies did that day, though now, men in canoes stop their journey south. It is a beautiful space, giving an illusion that we "know" Hiroshima.

We don't talk about the residents of this city. We don't talk about the people who used to live where the Peace Park is now, driven out and told to make their way north up the river. They called it the Atomic Slum: people living in shacks huddling the river, huddling each other. Too sick to rebuild their lives. Too old to start all over again. Not Japanese enough to find a job, but their home in Korea has been divided in two, and they've made this city their home for the last 30 years. As the rest of Japan seems to go on, they were left behind in history. Then the people of the Atomic Slum were driven out, just like when they built the Park, and in its place, public housings. Brutal concrete public housings shadow their steps. Fear rises every time their noses bleed, or they cough, or they have fever—the bomb that took away the most important things that day keeps them company even after all these years.

And we don't talk about *hibakusha* who do not have Japanese citizenship, because it's complicated, because it brings out the inevitable questions: What were Koreans doing in Hiroshima and Nagasaki? What were Americans doing in Japan? What were British soldiers doing in Japan? Why were some people not considered hibakusha? It's complicated. You see, to talk about Koreans in Japan in 1945, you have to talk about colonialism. You have to talk about the Japanese government's policy of stripping Koreans of their names and mother tongue, of denying them basic rights as Japanese, because they weren't quite Japanese and they were no longer

Korean because Korea had been annexed into the Empire of Japan. They were the people from the peninsula, and they had been working in Japan as cheap labor, or as labor disguised as patriotism. And what were Americans doing in Japan? If Koreans were cheap labor in Japan, Japanese men crossed the sea to America in the late 19th century and early 20th century as exports, just like silk reels and coals and tea, and when they settled in towns and farms in California, Washington, Utah, Colorado, and Mexico, they called for wives. And they started families. But they always remembered Japan: that's where they were from, and their children couldn't quite be Americans, no matter what the passports said and no matter if it was their birthright. Sending them to an American university sent them back to the farms and family grocery shops and maybe, just maybe as doctors, but their skin and their last names just couldn't fit into white America, so they sent their children back to Japan as kibei—maybe to try their luck or to learn enough Japanese to come back into the Japanese community in America. And the war started, and the border closed, and so did most of the news from America. But these are anomalies, history says, and can only be found in a footnotes, or a small article in the corner of the newspaper. Relegated to the side, just like the Korean victims' monument standing on the very edge of the Peace Memorial Park.

When we talk about hibakusha, we talk about people who were there on that day, within a few kilometers of the epicenter. The ones who survived, somehow. The ones who survived despite the fact that so many died around them. That's how it was for a very long time—people who were there in Hiroshima (or Nagasaki) that day. Then, as the radius slowly opened up to include those who came the next day or a few hours after the bomb, who rode bicycles and walked to get to the city center looking for their family members who had left that morning to go to work, to shop, to visit a relative, to work at the ammunition factory. As soon as they heard about a bomb that was dropped on Hiroshima, they started walking to the city. They might have come looking for their loved ones each and every day, walking from one destroyed school to another where they knew injured and the dying were carried to; they might have gone to the neighborhood where the missing might have gone that morning. They left messages on the wall of schools; they read messages on the wall: "We are safe," "Looking for Nephew," messages scrawled in desperation and in hope. Then there are so many who were there on that day, and they refused to carry the hibakusha card. They refused to be defined by one day. Or they refused to be defined by what people fear. They never talk about that day, even after all these years.

What we don't talk about is that doctors and nurses, if they survived that day, had to choose—triage. Who is worth saving? Who isn't? And the visibly injured were the easiest. It was the ones who seemed to have gotten through that day unscathed that started dying minute by minute, their bodies covered in purple spots, bruised, sudden hair loss and bleeding gums. Those were the ones that seemed hard to detect, that died so quickly and so

Hiroshima Shirt

mysteriously.

What we don't talk about when we talk about Hiroshima is that, on that day, the residents have mixed feelings. Some say that the outsiders have taken over the memorial, making it into a political festival. Some don't want all these people gathering at the Memorial Peace Park, not talking about who did it, only that they vow never to make that mistake again. But the subject of who made the mistake is missing. A taxi driver asks whether I am here for the annual memorial, and when I tell him, "No, I am here to give a talk," he relaxes and says that he makes a lot of money that day; you can even say that he makes a month's worth just in 18 hours, but how he hates it. He hates people coming to take away his personal grief. Then he talks of the lack of rain, and I answer that my green peas have died because of dryness. He says that his tomatoes cracked. He says that the streets we are

Wall at Fukuromachi Elementary School

driving now get so congested on that day. I tell him that I reserved the hotel room a year in advance because the year before, I was invited at the last minute, and I couldn't find an available hotel room, except two—one that was ten times more than its regular price and another about two hours away. He clicks his tongue. See how the city makes so much money on people's trauma? He talks tomatoes, and I think of a girl from *Machinto*, a picture book about a girl who died wishing for tomatoes after *that* day. And I wonder whether I am remembering the wrong story; and I also think of my mother in the hospital, folding paper cranes, as she undergoes radiotherapy for her cancer. And tomatoes she had planted in spring dying in my absence. We get to the hotel. I thank him. He drives away.

When we talk about Hiroshima, we talk about this dress, or that pair of charred bento boxes, or this shirt, worn on that day that loved ones kept in

Hiroshima on that Day

their homes because they could not find the ones who wore them, who carried them that morning. This dress was made by her mother, the dress made from old dresses they could no longer wear because of the war, because the world changed when the war started and women could no longer wear dresses or even dress up: luxury is our enemy; we shall not want until we win the war. That morning, a mother packed the aluminum bento box with what little they had—not enough white rice, not enough egg, not enough seaweeds, but she packed her love because love could have been enough to make her child full. There was a war. There was a bomb, but people that morning went about their day as normally as possible. That's what people do, each with their individual stories and sorrows and small moments of joy.

When we talk about Hiroshima, we hardly ever talk about pumpkin

A Fragment from Trinity

bombs that were dropped before and after August 6. Shaped similar to Little Boy and Fat Man, B-29s that were part of those days in Hiroshima and Nagasaki carried them, taking off from Tinian, taking the Hirohito Route, and veering to cities like Toyama, Ogaki, Nagoya, Tokyo, Kobe, Koriyama, killing civilians. Practice run. Enola Gay and Necessary Evil had practice runs on July 24 and 26, dropping pumpkin bombs just like they would on August 6. They were ready for Hiroshima. They were ready for Nagasaki. We don't talk about the pride Paul Tibbits had until the day he died on ending the war, saving lives. For him, it was his job. His duty. He was of the Greatest Generation, and he was doing his duty to the United States of America. He said he felt sorry for these people, but this was a mission, just like any other, a step toward peace. He climbed into his plane early in the morning in Tinian, took off from Runway A, and followed the Hirohito

Tinian Runways

Road, just like he had imagined many, many times. He did not tell his crews that he had cyanide capsules—just in case. His men ate sandwiches and listened to music. As he neared Iwo Jima, the other two planes rendezvoused and they headed out as one. They looked for the five-fingered rivers in the bay. There. It took 59 seconds for Little Boy to explode. And just like that, nearly 80,000 people died. Paul Tibbits felt sorry for them, but until the day he died, he did not repent.

We talk about the importance of keeping the memory of that day alive. We talk about the need to document, to bear witness. Never again. We talk in whispers of the hibakusha who are dying, one by one, in the way we talk about animals being the last of their species. We don't talk about how old the ones who are still alive were on that day: they were young, and their memories might not be as vivid as those of the adults. How do we talk about

Sunset in Hiroshima

Hiroshima now, those of us who weren't there? Who has the right to talk about that day? Now, it's their children who are talking. It's their children, or their grandchildren, who can talk about it because they are from there; there is a connection. If there is no connection to that day, one has to be careful, being mindful that all corners are lined, all folds are straight, just as one has to be when folding a paper crane. There is no space for error when talking about that day, and the thousands of days that followed.

What we don't talk about is when we step into the city, we can't help but see everything with the filter of that day: trees, buildings that are no longer there, streets, old walls, rivers, bridges, trams, people. We are told that this bridge, the same one, stood here that day, people throwing themselves into the river, or people trying to flee the city, the bridge that withstood the weight of confusion and fear and blood and wounds and dying and death. I

Trees and the Atomic Dome

see an elderly woman dressed in a thin black dress, and wonder whether she was here that day, though she must have been a small girl that day. A man with keloid on his arm, and I assume that he is a hibakusha: "My arm? I had an accident at work. I burned my arm," laughing at me for my presumption, my naivety. The epicenter is a clinic. The building across is a mirrored building. The clinic is discreet in its atomic history. Across from the Atomic Dome, a cafe with outdoor tables, with nicely dressed women and men sitting around with their dogs. On the other side of the Atomic Dome street, a high-end tourist shop that sells crafts made in Hiroshima: sewing needles handcrafted individually by craftsmen, clay figurines with bells in shapes of animals; lemon jams and lemon soaps; canned oysters and marinated oysters in jars; goods with the word Peace; earrings and necklaces with folded cranes. I buy a tote bag with a picture of a folded crane. There goes the tram that ran that day, and it's still running. And the sun is setting, and the clouds look as if there should be a meaning in their shapes. The Atomic Dome is beautiful, though it shouldn't be.

References

Agawa, Hiroyuki (2002) *Ma no Isan (An Evil Inheritance)*. Tokyo: PHP Bunko.

Boyer, Paul (1994) *By the Bomb's Early Light: American Thought and Culture at the Dawn of the Atomic Age*. Chapel Hill: University of North Carolina Press.

Caufield, Catherine (1989) *Multiple Exposures: Chronicles of the Radiation Age*. NY: Harper and Row.

Chisholm, Anne (1985) *Faces of Hiroshima*. London: Jonathan Cape.

Chujo, Kazuo (1986) *Genbaku to Sabetsu (Atomic Bombs and Prejudice)*. Tokyo: Asahi Shinbunsha.

Collie, Craig (2011) *Nagasaki*. NY: Allen and Unwin.

Cooke, Stephanie (2009) *In Mortal Hands: A Cautionary History of the Nuclear Age*. NY: Bloomsbury.

Committee on Damage Caused by the Atomic Bombs, (ed.), (1981) *Hiroshima and Nagasaki: The Physical, Medical, and Social Effects of the Atomic Bombings*. NY: Basic Books.

Committee of Japanese Citizens to Send Gift Copies of a Photographic & Pictorial Record of the Atomic Bombing to Our Children, and Fellow Human Beings of the World (1975) *Hiroshima-Nagasaki*. Tokyo: *Hiroshima-Nagasaki* Publishing Committee.

De Groot, Gerard (2006) *Bomb: The Biography*. Cambridge: Harvard University Press.

Fradkin, Philip (1988) *Fallout: An American Nuclear Tragedy*. University of Arizona Press.

Fukushima, Kikujiro (2003) *Hiroshima no Uso: Utsuranakatta Sengo* (*Lies of Hiroshima: Unphotographed Postwar*). Tokyo: Gendai Jinbunsha.

Genbaku Iseki Hozon Undou Kondankai (1996) *Guidebook: Hiroshima Hibaku no Ato o Aruku* (*Guidebook: Hiroshima Atomic Bomb Walking Tour*). Tokyo: Shinnihon Shuppansha.

Genbakukorou Kankou Iinkai, ed. (1980) *Genbaku Korou* (*Atomic Bomb Victims Aging Alone*). Tokyo: Roudou Kyouiku Center.

Goin, Peter (1991) *Nuclear Landscapes*. Baltimore, MD: Johns Hopkins University Press.

Hachiya, Michihiko (1955) *Hiroshima Diary: The Journal of a Japanese Physician, August 6 – September 30*. Chapel Hill: University of North Carolina.

Hayashi, Shigeo (1993) *Bakushinchi Hiroshima ni Hairu Kameraman wa nani o mitaka* (*Entering Hiroshima: What the Cameraman Saw*). Tokyo: Iwanami Junior Shinsho.

Henriksen, Margot (1997) *Dr. Strangelove's America: Society and Culture in the Atomic Age*. Berkely: University of California Press.

Herbaut, Guillaume (2004) *Urakami: Memoire de L'Impact de la Bombe Atomique*. Paris: Anabet Editions.

Hiraoka, Takashi (1983) *Muen no Kaikyo Hiroshima no Koe Hibaku Chousenjin no Koe* (*The Straight of No Help: Voices of Hiroshima, Voices of Korean Hibakusha*). Tokyo: Kageshobou.

Hodge, Nathan and Weinberger, Sharon (2008) *A Nuclear Family Vacation: Travels in the World of Atomic Weaponry*. NY: Bloomsbury.

Inoue, Kyosuke (2003) *Hiroshima Kabe ni Nokosareta Dengon* (*Hiroshima: Messages on the Wall*). Tokyo: Shueishinsho.

Jacobs, Robert (2010) *The Dragon's Tail: Americans Face the Atomic Age*. Amherst: University of Massachusetts Press.

Jenkins, Rupert, ed. (1995) *Nagasaki Journey: The Photographs of Yosuke Yamahata, August 10, 1945*. SF: Pomegranate Artbooks.

Johnson, Robert R. (2012) *Romancing the Atom: Nuclear Infatuation from the Radium Girls to Fukushima*. Westport, CT: Praeger.

Lifton, Betty Jean and Hosoe, Eikoh (1985) *A Place Called Hiroshima*. Tokyo and NY: Kodansha International.

Lifton, Robert Jay (1991) *Death in Life: Survivors of Hiroshima*. Chapel Hill: University of North Carolina Press.

Light, Michael (2003) *100 Suns: 1945-1962*. NY: Alfred Knopf.

Lindee, M. Susan (1997) *Suffering Made Real: American Science and Survivors at*

Hiroshima. University of Chicago Press.

Linner, Rachelle (1995) *City of Silence: Listening to Hiroshima.* Maryknoll, NY: Orbis Books.

Malloy, Sean L. (2012) "'A Very Pleasant Way to Die': Radiation Effects and the Decision to Use the Atomic Bomb Against Japan," *Diplomatic History,* 36(3), pp. 515-545.

Nagasaki Heiwa Kenkyujyo, ed. (200) *Guidebook Nagasaki Genbaku Iseki to Senseki o Meguru* (*Guidebook Nagasaki Atomic Bomb and War Ruins*). Tokyo: Shinnihon Shuppansha.

Nagasakiken Burakushi Kenkyujo, ed. (1995) *1945.8.9 Nagasaki Furusato ha Isshun ni Kieta* (*August 9, 1945 Nagasaki: Our Home Perished in an Instant*). Nagasaki: Kaihou Shuppansha.

Nagasaki Yugaku, ed. (2004) *Genbaku Hisaichi ato ni Heiwa wo Manabu* (*Learning About Peace from the Ruins of the Atomic Bomb*). Nagasaki: Nagasaki Bunkeisha.

Nakazawa, Keiji (2012) *Watashi no Isho* (*My Last Will*). Tokyo: Asahi Gakusei Shinbunsha.

Neel, James V., and Schull, W.J. (1956) *The Effect of Exposure to the Atomic Bombs on Pregnancy Termination in Hiroshima and Nagasaki.* Washington D.C.: National Research Council.

Neel, James V., and Schull, William J, eds. (1991) *The Children of Atomic Bomb Survivors: A Genetic Study.* Washington D.C.: National Academy Press.

Nihon Gensuibaku Higaisha Dantai Kyougikai, ed. (1994) *Hiroshima Nagasaki Shi to Sei no Shougen.* Tokyo: Shinnihon Shuppansha.

Nogi, Kyoko (2010) *Sora o Nagareru Kawa: Hiroshima Genshiko* (*River Running Through the Sky: Imaginary Trip to Hiroshima*). Tokyo: Furansudo.

O'Donnell, Joe (2005) *Japan: 1945: A US Marine's Photographs from Ground Zero.* Nashville: Vanderbilt University Press.

Oughterson, Ashley W. and Warren, Shields, eds. (1956) *Medical Effects of the Atomic Bomb in Japan.* NY: McGraw-Hill.

Ooura, Fumiko (2011) *Yugamerareta Doushinen* (*The Unaccounted Hibakusha*). Tokyo: Kinoizumisha.

Palevsky, Mary (2000) *Atomic Fragments: A Daughter's Questions.* Berkeley, CA: University of California Press.

Peterson, Leif E., and Abrahamson, Seymour (1998) *Effects of Ionizing Radiation: Atomic Bomb Survivors and Their Children (1945-1995).* Joseph Henry Press.

Rhodes, Richard (2012) *The Making of the Atomic Bomb.* NY: Simon and Schuster.

Roff, Sue Rabbitt (1995) *Hotspots: The Legacy of Hiroshima and Nagasaki.* Cassell.

Saviano, Paul (2011) *From Above.* Tokyo: Contents Factory.

Schull, William J. (1995) *Effects of Atomic Radiation: A Half-Century of Studies from Hiroshima and Nagasaki.* NY: Wiley-Liss.

Shindo, Kaneto (2005) *Genbaku to Toru (Filming Atomic Bomb)*. Tokyo: Shinnihon Shuppansha.

Seldon, Mark, and Seldon, Kyoko (1997) *The Atomic Bomb: Voices from Hiroshima and Nagasaki*. Armonk, NY: ME Sharpe.

Swedin, Eric G. (2011) *Survive the Bomb: The Radioactive Citizen's Guide to Nuclear Survival*. Zenith Press.

Vanderbilt, Tom (2010) *Survival City: Adventures Among the Ruins of Atomic America*. Chicago: University of Chicago Press.

Watanabe, Chieko (1973) *Nagasaki ni Ikiru*. Tokyo: Nihonshinsho.

Weller, George, and Weller, Anthony, eds. (2006) *First Into Nagasaki: The Censored Eyewitness Dispatches on Post-Atomic Japan and Its Prisoners of War*. NY: Crown.

Welsome, Eileen (2000) *Plutonium File America's Secret Medical Experiments in the Cold War*. NY: Random House.

Yamashiro, Tomoe, ed. (1965) *Konosekai no Katasumide (At the Corner of This World)*. Tokyo: Iwanami Shinsho.

Yamashita, Kazuo, Kano, Masaki, and Ide, Michio (2006) *Hiroshima o Sagasou Genbaku o Mita Tatemono (Looking for Hiroshima: Buildings that Witnessed the Atomic Bomb)*. Tokyo: Nishida Shoten.

Yamazaki, James N., and Fleming, Louis B. (1995) *Children of the Atomic Bomb: An American Physician's Memoir of Nagasaki, Hiroshima, and the Marshall Islands*. Durham, NC: Duke University Press.

Zinn, Howard (2010) *The Bomb*. City Lights Publishers.

Zoellner, Tom (2010) *Uranium: War, Energy, and the Rock that Shaped the World*. NY: Penguin.

Chapter 7
Inheriting "Hiroshima Heart": Imaginary and Institution in Cornelius Castoriadis' Social Theory

Masae Yuasa

I was born and brought up in Hiroshima. It is my hometown, but I did not like the city because I thought Hiroshima is only special in a negative way, a city attacked by an atomic bomb. However, abroad, I was surprised to find some people welcomed me and showed me special affection because of the city's negative history. When I was in Palestine, a female high school teacher came up to me and told me cheerfully that her students knew Hiroshima very well and their eyes shone when they heard the name of "Hiroshima." It was nice to see such friendly reactions. However, I felt a bit guilty because I had done nothing to make Palestinian kids' eyes shine. On those occasions, the term "Hiroshima Heart" (ヒロシマの心) popped up in my mind.[1]

To me, the definition of Hiroshima Heart seemed be based on a mixture of facts, beliefs, and expectations. I understood the term as follows:

- Hiroshima people, along with Nagasaki people, are the only people who were targeted by the atomic bombs and experienced a resulting hell beyond human imagination.
- Therefore, they are people who know the very nature of nuclear weapons, the absolute evil, more than anyone else.
- Because of this unique experience, they have an unshaken desire for abolishing nuclear weapons and achieving world peace. This desire is called Hiroshima Heart.

Hiroshima Heart was said to be a survivor's heart. Survivors' relentless activism for abolishing nuclear weapons was explained by this concept.

However, at the same time, it was expected to be shared by Hiroshima citizens, who were also expected to send Hiroshima Heart to the outside. Some Hiroshima activists used the term in their speeches or writings. Mayors of Hiroshima spoke about Hiroshima Heart as if it was shared by all citizens. I took it for granted and felt ashamed that I could not fulfill it, but at the same time I was very pessimistic toward Hiroshima Heart. When I was nine, my mother brought me to the Hiroshima Peace Memorial Museum. I was shocked by the atrocities. Since then, I have feared a third bombing. I felt helplessness and learned that the violence was mighty and the weak could only be subjugated to it. I felt sorry for elderly hibakusha whose earnest desires could not be realized. Hiroshima Heart sounded sad, hollow, and bitter to me.

This chapter explores the norm of "inheriting atomic-bomb experiences" in Hiroshima. The term "Hiroshima Heart" was used in this mission and made up a part of this norm. It was institutionalized as a core policy of Hiroshima City's peace administration in the late 1970s and has continued encouraging hibakusha and citizens to take action. Satoru Ubuki, a historian, says the national anti-nuclear movement, Gensuikin, identified the atomic bomb experiences as social experiences, but its disintegration in the 60s allowed individual hibakusha to explore a new meaning of their experiences (Ubuki 2014: vii). It was the time when the city government set up the policy, authorizing hibakusha's experiences as the basis of the city's peace mission.

The city government has continued the policy for more than a half century, while it has kept lamenting "hibaku taiken no fuuka [weathering or fading memories of atomic-bomb experiences]" despite its continuous political efforts. The effectiveness of fulfilling "Hiroshima Heart" has been questioned by researchers. Masashi Nemoto argued that the normalization of "inheriting experiences" deprived us of the chance to think about the reasons why we should inherit and what exactly we need to inherit (Nemoto 2018:16). Lisa Yoneyama (1999:144) said the inherited "experiences" have been constructed by legal, political, economic, and academic discourses in postwar Japan and are not simple "facts" or authentic "realities." Akiko

Naono developed Yoneyama's point and argued that we should inherit not the experiences per se but the basic principle (理念) of never creating a hibakusha again (Naono 2015: 221). Nemoto, on the other hand, states our task is not "inheriting" but questioning our own position and taking action against the continuing violence the atomic bomb has inflicted on hibakusha (Nemoto 2018: 267). Despite those critical evaluations, the determination of the city government to stick to the policy has seemingly never been swayed. Faced with decreasing numbers of hibakusha, it started a new system, bringing up "memory keepers," to continue to inherit the experiences. Ubuki, however, argues it is now time for making "history," beyond "inheriting" experiences (Ubuki 2014: ix). It might require a new policy, based on proper evaluation of the past practices of inheriting and sharing.

There is no doubt the global and national discursive powers have intervened in the practices and helped their normalization.[2] I also agree with Nemoto (2018), who saw the significant role of the local government in making it a norm. But I would like to introduce here the concept of social imaginary to shed a new light on the process. According to Cornelius Castoriadis, the imaginary is not simply someone's idea in his/her head but a way to produce, reproduce, and transform social institutions. Survivors, who were the main agents inheriting and sharing their primordial experiences, did not simply follow the norm; nor were they manipulated by the ideology. They actively committed to the mission and sustained the institution based on their imaginaries, although they have been the minority of the whole survivors' population.[3] In order to discuss it, I firstly describe the policy of inheriting experiences in the city's consecutive governments and secondly introduce Castoriadis's social theory on the imaginary; and lastly, I will apply the theory to examine the role of the social imaginary and Hiroshima Heart in practice. I hope that this examination will contribute to the discussion of what we should inherit for the future by regaining and reimagining survivors' his-stories and her-stories.

1. Policy of Inheriting Atomic Bomb Experiences in Hiroshima City's Peace Administration

The Local Autonomy Act in 1969 stipulated that local governments were to make the Basic Vision and Plan through the resolution of the local council in order to establish comprehensive local governance. The first Basic Vision and Plan of Hiroshima City was created under Mayor Yamada in 1970. Since then, the city has recreated visions and plans almost every ten years until today. Takeshi Araki became Mayor when his predecessor, Mayor Yamada, suddenly passed away in 1975. Although the term of Yamada's vision and plan was to last until 1985, Araki created a new one in 1978 in which the policy of "inheriting atomic-bomb experiences" first appeared.

The plan has three pillars based on the city's ultimate objective/ identity as "International Peace Cultural City" (Hiroshima City 1978). The first pillar was developing a town aiming for "peace"; the second was building an economically active town open to the "international" arena; and the third was cultivating rich "culture." The first pillar consisted of three policy categories: 1) uplifting peace consciousness, 2) promoting domestic and international exchange, and 3) managing peace memorial facilities (Hiroshima City 1978: 38). "Inheriting atomic bomb experiences" was the first agenda of the policy of uplifting peace consciousness.

Hiroshima's earnest desire and mission of realizing lasting world peace starts from people's hearts [心] loving peace and seeking peace. Therefore, we, Hiroshima citizens, rightly grasp and inherit the realities [実相] of atomic bomb experiences and telling many people. Also we should raise international peace consciousness, cultivating our own heart seeking peace, sharing our heart with people all over the world (Hiroshima City 1978: 39, translated by the author).

However, the city continued to argue that the atomic bomb experiences were fading because the survivors were no longer the majority, science had not yet clarified the realities of the atomic bomb, and precious documents were scattered and lost. Thus, the city government needed to "inherit the experiences" by discovering and preserving documents, conducting scientific research, and disseminating the results, while promoting civic activities related to peace issues and encouraging peace education (Hiroshima City 1978: 38-9). This agenda also directed the other two policy categories in the first pillar. The inherited experiences must be shared domestically and internationally (the second policy category) and kept, preserved, and opened to the public in the peace facilities (the third policy category).

Mayor Araki also reorganized the Hiroshima Peace Cultural Center created by Mayor Yamada as a city department in 1978. It was the first city organization specializing in peace issues set by a local government in Japan. Araki made it a foundation, as an external body of the city government, and set a new objective to "disseminate thoughts promoting peace to citizens from the pan-human perspective and contribute to world peace and human happiness by inheriting Hiroshima (ヒロシマ),[4] collaborating with peace research institutions and related organizations in Japan and abroad" (Hiroshima Peace Cultural Center 1997: 342).

The term "Hiroshima Heart" gained its central significance during Mayor Araki's term. The local newspaper *Chugoku Shimbun* summed up Mayor Araki's 14-year peace policy as "celebrating the internationalization of 'Hiroshima Heart'" while repeating Japan to be "the only country to have suffered atomic bombs" without mentioning hibakusha outside Japan, including those from nuclear accidents or nuclear tests, by analyzing his fourteen Peace Declarations, issued on the Peace Memorial Day every year (Chugoku Shinbun-sha 1995: 220). His 1977 Peace Declaration, for example, started with the sentence, "Peace is Hiroshima Heart," and set the mission of Hiroshima as to "let the world know about the realities of the damage caused by the atomic bomb in order to abolish nuclear weapons and realize everlasting peace." Although there was no official definition of "Hiroshima Heart," Araki repeated the term, for example, in a 1986 speech for university students:

It is Hiroshima's mission to continue to work for internationalization of Hiroshima Heart, that is, seeking the abolition of nuclear weapons and lasting world peace by telling the realities of atomic-bomb experiences (Araki 1986: 78, translated by the author).

Since Araki's 1978 Basic Vision and Plan, city administrations have up until now kept the policy of inheriting atomic-bomb experiences as the core policy of its peace administration with some minor changes. The fourth and fifth plans covering the period from 1999 to 2020, created under the Akiba government, emphasized "realities" of the experiences, and the term "heart" disappeared (Hiroshima City 1999, Hiroshima City 2009). Mayor Akiba also came up with a new initiative, the Hiroshima-Nagasaki Protocol, a strategic plan for abolishing nuclear weapons by 2020. He actively worked, aiming for its adoption at the NPT conference in 2010, using the network of Mayors for Peace,[5] but failed to realize his goal (Mayors for Peace 2010). Kazumi Matsui become the new Hiroshima Mayor in 2011 and again situated the policy of "inheriting the experiences" and "Hiroshima Heart" at the center of his peace administration.

In the Sixth Hiroshima Basic Vision and Plan from 2020 to 2030, the Matsui administration set one of three pillars of the Basic policies as creating "a town spreading 'Desire for Peace' to the world." The city promised to share and send "Hiroshima Heart" by means of the network of Mayors for Peace to cultivate an international opinion for "abolishing nuclear weapons and realizing lasting peace" (Hiroshima City 2020: 30). Also, the city aimed to share "Hiroshima Heart" with policy makers around the world by inviting them to visit. This is termed a policy of "Welcoming Peace," aiming to let world leaders "touch realities of atomic bombing and share the desire for peace" (Hiroshima City 2020: 31). The city also set a new policy of cultivating atomic-bomb "memory keepers" "inheriting hibakusha's experiences and their thinking/desire (Omoi 思い)," while strengthening the messages sent from the Peace Memorial Museum (Hiroshima City 2020: 31).

This shows that inheriting Hiroshima's atomic-bomb experiences and

Hiroshima Heart has been firmly institutionalized in Hiroshima City policy since Araki's administration. It should be noted, however, that the city's policy objective was not originally one of abolishing nuclear weapons, but of achieving "lasting peace" based on the Hiroshima Peace Memorial City Construction Law.

2. Hiroshima Peace Memorial City Construction Law and Anti-war Pacifism of the International Peace Cultural City

The second Basic Vision and Plan issued in 1978 under the Araki government was radically different from the first one created by Mayor Yamada in 1970. Yamada was the mayor who first set "International Peace Cultural City" as the supreme objective of its administration and stipulated it in the City's first Basic Vision and Plan in 1970 (Hiroshima City 1970). It soon became the identity of the city and has been the objective of its whole administration until today. This objective had the legal foundation of the Hiroshima Peace Memorial City Construction Law, set by the national Diet and approved by local referendum in 1949. The law stated its aim in Article One as "to provide for the construction of the City of Hiroshima as a peace memorial city to symbolize the human ideal of sincere pursuit of genuine and lasting peace." The term, "sincere pursuit of genuine and lasting peace," originated from the Preamble and Article Nine of the Japanese Constitution, which symbolized the anti-war pacifism of the nation (Chugoku Shinbun-sha 1995: 24). In Article Six of the law, the mayor's responsibility is specified as follows:

> The Mayor of Hiroshima shall, with the cooperation of residents and support from relevant organizations, establish a program of continuous activity toward completion of the Hiroshima Peace Memorial City (Hiroshima City 1949).

It must have been more than natural for Yamada to embed this mission into the City's vision and plan. Yamada was one of the main contributors to making the law. He was a Diet member from Hiroshima and negotiated with the GHQ to create the draft (Reminiscence Publication Committee 1976: 127). Also, Mayor Yamada was a well-known world federalist and worked as a Vice President of the World Federalist World Council and Japan's Alliance for Constructing World Federation. He organized their national and international conferences and set up an office and headquarters of related organizations in the City government (Hiroshima Peace Cultural Center 1997: 8). The world-federalist vision helped him to envisage policies leading to a "lasting peace" and encouraged him to incorporate the Constitutional anti-war mission deeply into the city's administration even in a situation where the Constitutional no-war pacifism had been the anti-reality under the Japan-US Security Treaty. Masayuki Tsuda, the then Deputy Mayor of Hiroshima City, said that it was Yamada's "landmarking achievement" which all his predecessors had failed to realize (Reminiscence Publication Committee 1976: 124).

Yamada's 1970 Basic Plan listed its policy of "establishing citizens' peace spirit (精神) by teaching the democratic principles of justice, freedom, and peace, enhancing understanding of international affairs, and disseminating high culture by cultivating strong awareness of citizens' autonomy and self-governance" (Hiroshima City 1970: 20). Yamada regarded democracy and individual autonomy as the foundation for peace, realizing his federalist vision by transforming "state sovereignty to human sovereignty" (Hiroshima Peace Cultural Center 1977: 340, Yuasa 2019: 8). Yamada, of course, identified Hiroshima as a city which experienced the tragedies of the atomic bomb, but his primary mission was realizing world peace, that is, his legal obligation as stated in the Hiroshima Peace Memorial City Construction Law.

Yamada's federalist vision and policies of cultivating democracy in order to cultivate citizens' peace sprit had disappeared in Araki's 1978 Vision and Plan. Instead, the new policy of inheriting and sharing atomic bomb experiences and Hiroshima Heart filled the void. It was a fundamental change in philosophy, policy, and grounding (Hiroshima City 1978). The mission was transformed from an anti-war peace based on democracy, grounded in legal obligation, to an anti-nuclear peace by inheriting experiences based on hibakusha's heart. Ubuki (2017) saw a clear demarcation between Yamada's and Araki's administrations when he periodized the city's peace administrations based on foundational ideas.

The transition can also be traced in the consecutive Basic Vision and Plans. The 1978 second Basic Plan stated only realizing "lasting world peace" (Hiroshima City 1978: 39-40) as the policy objective of inheriting atomic-bomb experiences. But the 1989 Basic Plan added "abolishing nuclear weapons" (Hiroshima City 1978, 39-40; 1989: 31). In the 1999 Basic Plan, the order of the two objectives had been inverted, with "abolishing nuclear weapons" coming first and "lasting peace" being second, and it newly listed a policy of "realizing a world without nuclear weapons" as an independent category (Hiroshima City 1999: 77). Since then, until the latest plan, the policy objectives were stated as "abolishing nuclear weapons and everlasting world peace" (Hiroshima City 2020: 30). It scarcely explained the meaning of "lasting peace" in relation to the Constitution.

Hiroshima Heart, hibakusha's desire, appealed to ethical duty, not legal obligation. It justified the policy of inheriting atomic-bomb experiences by setting a new objective, the abolition of nuclear weapons. On the other hand, the anti-war mission symbolized by the term "lasting peace," the legal duty of Hiroshima's mayor and citizens, was losing substance in the city's peace administration.[6] I would argue that Hiroshima Heart was more than a political slogan. It was a social imaginary which maintained the institution while socializing people. I will explain it, using the social theory of Cornelius Castoriadis.

3. The Imaginary in Castoriadis's Social Theory

Cornelius Castoriadis is a Greek philosopher, economist, psychiatrist, and social theorist. In his main work, *The Imaginary Institution of Society*, he argues that the imaginary creates a perspective through which people see, think, and represent the world and themselves (Castoriadis 1987). But by doing so, more importantly for him, the imaginary constructs, reproduces and transforms society. However, we are born in society and socialized by the imaginary and mostly cannot question our own imagery, ideal, norms, and institutions. Castoriadis, as a post-Marxist revolutionary, encourages us to examine existing institutions and social imaginary in order to realize autonomy and democracy (Adams 2014: 1-2).

Social-Historical

Castoriadis prefers to use the term "social-historical" rather than simple "society." He aims in this manner to overcome a fallacious distinction between society and history (Mouzakitis 2014: 90). History is not a dimension of society, nor "external" to society, but the "self-development society." Castoriadis sees we are creating the social-historical every moment regardless of the political system, be it monarchy or democracy (Adams 2014: 1). The mode of human societies cannot be either static or dynamic, but both. He conceptualizes the social-historical as "the union and the tension of instituting society and of instituted society, of history made and history in the making" (Castoriadis 1987: 108).

Institution

The Institution is the central concept of Durkheimian sociology. However, the vital feature of Castoriadis's concept owes much to Marx and his concept of alienation. With critical examination, he contrasts the institution against creative and autonomous actions and understands it as loss of autonomy, as exemplified by "discourse of the other" that structures the unconscious (Arnason 2014: 102). The social-historical institution is thus regarded as the socio-historical patterns of action and thought, imposed on the human psyche as a complex of relations irreducible to shared norms or intersubjective understanding (Arnason 2014: 102). The concept is further enriched by his appreciation of the idea of Marcel Mauss, who argues that institutions, as they emerge, function and transform themselves (Arnason 2014: 103). The key to this dynamism is the psyche.

Psyche as Magma and Creative/Radical Imagination

"Psyche" is a Greek term for soul. Castoriadis sometimes writes psyche/ soma in order to remind his readers that psyche is somatic, as soma is psychical (Smith 2014: 278). He also emphasizes that psyche is not determined by mere biological imperatives, as Freud claims, but de-functioned such that "representational pleasure" become dominant over organ pleasures. Psyche is irreducible to any rationality or end-means logic (Smith 2014: 77). Although a living being must fulfill self-preservation functions, psyche disconnects pleasure principle from self-serving instinct.

Psyche is unlimited and unmasterable flux, and this feature is metaphorically illustrated as "magma," which is another key term for Castoriadis (Rosengren 2014: 65). Magma is originally a geological term which describes a blend of molten or semi-molten rock, volatiles, and solids beneath the surface of the earth. It only extrudes onto the surface as lava or in explosive ejections. For Castoriadis, those are all important characteristics of his concept of psyche (Rosengren 2014: 65). Institutions never completely contain the magma by socialization (Smith 78-79). This psyche is the energy for creative imagination, both at a personal (radical imaginary) and a collective (social imagery) level (Ablett 2016).

> Psyche is a *forming*, which exists in and through *what* it forms and *how* it forms; it is *Bildung* and *Einbildung*—formation and imagination—it is the radical imagination that makes a "first" representation arise out of a nothingness of representation, that is to say, *out of nothing* (Castoriadis 1987: 283).

The human psyche, as creative/radical imagination, must create a world, making sense of chaos, constructing a world of its own with, from, and in the flux of representation, affects, and intentions (Castoriadis 1987: 149, 300). Those need to be done in the tension between self and other, between opening and closure (Smith 2014: 83-4). The new psyche enters the world as a chaotic psychic flux of indistinct representations and as a drive towards closure. But to satisfy its demand for meaning, the psyche needs resources which the radical imagination cannot supply for itself. This paradoxically directs its openness to constructing its own closure. It is a productive union of the self and the other (Castoriadis 1987: 105). Through this process, radical imagination produces social imaginaries and institutions.

Social Imaginary Significations

The social imaginary significations (SIS) make up the key concept bridging magmatic psyche and social-historical institutions in Castoriadis's social theory. The significations work on both institutions and individuals. Castoriadis writes:

> The imaginary significations construct (organize, articulate, vest with meaning) the world of the society considered (and lean each time on the "intrinsic" ensidic organization of the first natural stratum). Yet in the same stroke and indissociably, they also do much more than that. To borrow metaphorically the distinctions correctly made by ancient psychology, they determine at the same time the representations, the affects, and the intentions dominant in society (Castoriadis 2007: 231).

Every individual is born in the socio-historical and needs to be socialized from the very beginning of the individual's life.

> Society socializes (humanizes) the wild, raw, antifunctional mad psyche of the newborn and imposes on it a formidable complex of constraints and limitations (the psyche must renounce absolute egocentricity and omnipotence of imagination, recognize "reality and existing others," subordinate desires to rules of behavior, and accept sublimated satisfactions and even death for the sake of "social" ends). Society thereby succeeds to an unbelievable degree (though never exhaustively) in diverting, orienting, and channeling the psyche's egoistic asocial (and, of course, fully "a-rational") drives and impulses into coherent social activities,

more or less "logical" everyday thinking (Castoriadis 2007: 230-1).

From the view of the psyche, this process whereby the psyche abandons (not fully though) its initial ways and objects—and invests in (cathects) socially meaningful ways of behaving, motives, and objects—is a kind of sublimation. The psyche, "in exchange," as it were, imposes on the social institution an essential requirement: "the social institution has to provide the psyche with meaning" (Castoriadis 2007: 231).

The Social-historical Change, Shock, or Project of Autonomy

The psychic flow may be seen as internally generated, but it must also be seen to be externally stimulated by the shock (Anstoss) at the point of the subject's encounter with the external world (Smith 2014: 81). The imaginary is flexible and good at synthesizing different elements, but it has a certain limitation to accommodate new stimuli. If the social imaginary cannot absorb the shock into the existing network of symbols, its world of meaning is destabilized. The psyche starts to extrude or erupt violently. This "shock" thus creates or recreates social imaginaries and institutions which bring social changes.

Castoriadis, however, does not mean that everyone participates equally in this creation. On the contrary, in most societies the imaginary of the dominant group is instituted as natural and inevitable, thus justifying the institution by concealing its socially-constructed nature (Castoriadis 1987: 155, Ablett 2016: 2). Therefore, we firstly need to recognize that we are the source of our own forms, customs, meanings, and institutions, which we unintentionally and even unconsciously reproduce. Castoriadis, as a post-Marxist revolutionary, encourages us to examine and interrogate existing institutions and social imaginary significations, then work collectively to alter them, using radical creative imagination. This project of autonomy is central to his intellectual and political work (Adams 2014: 1-2).

Based on this Castoriadis's social theory, the atomic-bomb experience for Hiroshima is nothing but the shock (Anstoss) which could not be absorbed in the existing institutions, or the network of symbols, such as that of "Japan as a divine land." The psyche of survivors started to extrude or erupt violently and sought to make sense of the chaos, constructing a world of its own with, from, and in the flux of representation, affects, and intentions (Castoriadis, 1987: 149, 300). I would argue this is the origin and the power of Hiroshima Heart, the desire of survivors. However, in the case of atomic-bomb survivors, the press code under the Allied Occupation of Japan prevented their experiences from becoming public knowledge until the mid 1950s. Then the rise and fall of the national Gensuikin movement, triggered by the Bikini incident, further tripped up the psychic movement, containing it along with the narrow objective of party politics until the mid 60s. Their radical imagination has at last been gradually forming its social imaginary and became institutionalized in the 70s as the city's policy of inheriting survivors' experiences.

4. The Social Imaginary of Survivors

Robert Lifton, a psychiatrist, was one of few researchers who examined the psychic "magma" of Hiroshima survivors (Nakazawa 2007: 179). His research, based on the psychoanalytic tradition, developed a "psychoformative" perspective with symbolic and thematic emphasis. He tried to examine the psychic rebuilding or "formulation" of Hiroshima survivors who experienced psychic disintegration caused by their atomic-bomb experiences (Lifton [1968] 1991: 3). It was the process which Castoriadis sees as the work of "radical imagination" seeking meaning. Lifton interviewed 73 survivors in 1962 including influential hibakusha opinion leaders and activists and examined their "formulation," which he sometimes called "A-bomb philosophie."

By formulation, I do not mean detached theories about the atomic bomb, but rather the process by which the hibakusha re-create [themselves]—establish[ing] those inner forms which can serve as a bridge between self and world. Ideology and "world view"

167

—often in their unconscious components—are central to the process, and by studying their relationship to A-bomb mastery, we gain a sense of their significance for mental life in general. Formulation includes efforts to re-establish three essential elements of psychic function: the sense of connection..., the sense of symbolic integrity..., and [the] sense of movement... (Lifton [1968] 1991: 367).

Lifton concluded that overcoming their own atomic-bomb experiences was not easy for the majority of his interviewees, even after almost two decades had passed since the experience. The predicament for the survivors related to the unique features of the nuclear damage which their psyche/soma received. They needed not only to overcome the fear of the past but also to deal with the fear of death from the aftereffects of the radiation, such as leukemia or various cancers, and the future danger of a possible nuclear war, living in a world with piled nuclear warheads. The sudden death of their acquaintances, news on nuclear testing in the Pacific, or a politician's statement threatening nuclear attacks, those all trigger them to recall the past fear and future anxiety. Also, survivors were suffering from a sense of guilt about what they did or did not do, such as leaving their own mother in the fire or failing to give a drop of water to those dying.

Lifton, however, observed two predominant emerging patterns of formulation among his interviewees in the 60s. They were: 1) psychological non-resistance or resignation, and 2) survivors' sense of mission. The former is a protective blunting of emotions in continuous fear and anxiety. The latter gives form to guilt feelings, and at the same time, goes beyond them. Without psychological non-resistance, for example, accepting the experience as destiny or fate, survivors would be unable to absorb their losses and continuing anxiety. Without a sense of special mission, they would be unable to justify their continuing life (Lifton [1968] 1991: 385). Any survivor needs both, he argues. Without them, survivors had a negative formulation, one of breakdown, such as dreaming of the end of the world (Lifton [1968] 1991: 387).

The City's policy of "inheriting and sharing the experience" for the goal of abolishing nuclear weapons could be a model formulation for survivors, combining non-resistance and special mission. It provided the survivors a special mission of abolishing nuclear weapons to save the world and humankind. Committing to it, they could ease their own sense of guilt towards the dead and also gain meaning for their survival, which was often painful and full of anxiety. However, in order to fulfill this mission, they have to face and accept their own horrible experiences as a part of their lives. It is a painful act of non-resistance which has never been easy for any survivor. It is, nevertheless, also an act of overcoming the past. The recent research on trauma survivors talking about their own experiences with others is one of three effective ways to improve the situation (van der Kolk 2015: 3). It reconnects survivors to others and helps them to objectify what has happened and is happening to them. Also, the sympathetic reactions from their audience give them a special experience which deeply contradicts the helplessness, rage, or collapse that results from trauma, which is the second effective way to alleviate the damage. Those body experiences gradually let survivors regain self-mastery, the confidence to live their own lives again (van der Kolk 2015: 4). The city's policy possibly had a great therapeutic effect on hibakusha who could not get any professional psychiatric treatment, especially the third treatment option, a medicine controlling the brain's mechanisms, which had not become available until quite recently.

The special mission of inheriting and sharing one's own experiences to abolish nuclear weapons could provide resources to the radical imagination of survivors and channel the energy of their volatile psyches and socialize them. In this way, survivors have gained meaning in their life by making sense of the chaotic world, simultaneously legitimizing and justifying the city's policy. Their acceptance and behavioral commitment to this policy might have convinced non-hibakusha citizens to share the imagery. On a side note, Mayor Araki, who implemented the policy by emphasizing Hiroshima Heart, was also hibakusha.

Other than these therapeutic effects, the survivors in the 1980s had more reasons to inherit their own atomic-bomb experiences (Yoneyama 1999: 142-152). The average age of hibakusha was well over the "retirement age," so they no longer had to be concerned about discrimination at the workplace, and they needed a new target of commitment after their retirement. It was also a time when they were free from concern about marriage discrimination against their children. They were, as well, reaching the "cancer age" that increased death anxiety and pushed them to reflect more about the meaning of their lives. Since the late 70s, the demands for testimony of hibakusha were dramatically expanded by an increase in grassroot anti-nuclear movements in Europe and North America and by increasing numbers of school study trips to Hiroshima, which needed hibakusha testimonies. This was a great interest of the city's sightseeing industry.

However, the social imaginary was not a political theory that was created or examined scientifically or objectively. There was no reason to believe or predict that sharing experiences could have an impact on global nuclear disarmament. Therefore, its political outcome could not be assured.

5. Is the Policy of Inheriting and Sharing Experiences Effective?

Kazumi Mizumoto, a professor at the Hiroshima Peace Research Institute, examined the following eight propositions in his article titled "Have Appeals from Atomic-bombed Cities Promoted Nuclear Disarmament?" (Mizumoto 2018). The propositions were: 1) the cities actively appealed for nuclear disarmament, 2) their appeal of "never use nuclear weapons" had reached the world, 3) their appeal for "abolishment of nuclear weapons" had reached the world, 4) their appeal of "banning nuclear tests" had reached the world, 5) their appeal of "banning nuclear weapons" had reached the world, 6) their appeal to "change the nuclear deterrence policy" had reached the world, 7) their appeal of "listening to atomic bomb experiences" had reached the world, and 8) their appeal for nuclear disarmament had reached the Japanese government. The result showed the only verified proposition was the first one, cities actively appealed for nuclear disarmament.

Propositions 2 and 5 could not be denied, but could not be proved. Propositions 3, 4, and 7 were denied, but with some exceptions. Propositions 6 and 8 were totally rejected. This examination indicated the cities' policy of sharing the experiences was not very effective in terms of not only abolishing nuclear weapons, but also promoting nuclear disarmament.

Shiro Sato (2021) examined the well-known aporia that widely-shared atomic bomb experiences could result in more dependence on nuclear weapons in order to avoid inhuman consequences. He concluded that he could not verify the aporia because the voice of hibakusha who appealed against the inhuman consequence of the atomic bomb had still been weak and failed to widely spread a "nuclear taboo." Moreover, he even argued that a widespread "nuclear taboo" would not undermine theories of nuclear arming and nuclear deterrence as long as nation-states kept the concepts of state sovereignty and national security (Sato 2021: 163-165). Sato's examination indicated the city's policy of sharing and inheriting atomic-bomb experiences had not been and will not be an effective means of realizing the "abolishment of nuclear weapons."

The conclusions drawn by of these two academic works are not new or surprising in Hiroshima. Increasing numbers of nuclear countries, continuing nuclear tests, and the presence of 13,000 nuclear warheads in the world have all indicated no tangible result of their political endeavor in terms of "abolishing nuclear weapons" or even nuclear disarmament. Furthermore, the adoption of the Treaty on the Prohibition of Nuclear Weapons in the UN clearly showed that a concrete step toward abolishing nuclear weapons required something more than inheriting and sharing experiences.

Furthermore, the practices also seemingly had some detrimental effects on the outcome of inheriting and sharing. The narrow set objective of abolishing nuclear "weapons" has excluded the issue of nuclear technology and its civilian usage from the policy agenda, which was another side of the coin of nuclear weapons. This exclusion also significantly obstructed the understanding of radiation damage caused by internal exposure, which was a dominant form of exposure to radiation fallout widely observed in nuclear accidents, nuclear mining, and tests sites.[7] Furthermore, to reach the goal of "abolishing weapons," the targeted experiences and stories tended to focus on shocking and cruel experiences which could impress the audience with the destructive power of the "evil" and "inhuman" weapon. This often cut off the atomic-bomb experiences from the context of the Pacific War and from current international relations, especially Japanese foreign policies based on its nuclear alliance with the US. All are vital issues for abolishing nuclear weapons. These exclusions and the narrow focus of the policy have certainly decreased the power of the "realities" of these experiences and Hiroshima Heart, and prevented them from reaching a wider audience beyond the group sharing the imaginary. It has in turn possibly exacerbated the "weathering" experiences. I would argue that the policy should be examined now. In order to do this, we should reexamine the "deep desire" of hibakusha beyond the current social imaginary, or simple political slogan.

Conclusion: Various Hiroshima Hearts

Hiroshima Prefectural Gensuikin published a booklet titled "50 Years Footsteps of Gensuikin Movement" in 2004 (Hiroshima Prefectural Gensuikin 2004). In its introduction, it carries an article, "Questioning Hiroshima Heart," which introduces public statements about Hiroshima Heart, made by thirteen famous Hiroshima activists, hibakusha, novelists, academics, and mayors. Their definitions of Hiroshima Hearts were all different and indicated great variety of Hiroshima Hearts even among just 13 people. Gensuikin Hiroshima also asks readers to reflect on their own "inner Hiroshima" and "Hiroshima Heart." I will introduce some of them.

Tomin Harada, a doctor who devoted himself to hibakusha treatment, understood Hiroshima Heart as an apology and promise not to repeat the act again to the dead killed by the atomic bomb. It was written on the cenotaph at the Hiroshima Peace Memorial Park as "Let all the souls here rest in peace; For we shall not repeat the evil." A poem created by Dr. Harada has become a choral work titled "Life of the World is Hiroshima Heart." Ichiro Moritaki, an iconic leader of the Hiroshima anti-nuclear movement, used the term "Hiroshima Heart" as his life principle (Moritaki 1976: 89, 105-6,

122, NHK 1994). He philosophically declared it as "value life," "mankind must live," therefore, "absolute rejection of the nuclear" because "the human and the nuclear are mutually exclusive." Akira Ishida, a hibakusha teacher and activist, defined it as a wakened human love, love of mother and desire for peace, dignity of life, and the future of humanity full of dreams. A Korean pastor, Kim Shinfan, defined it as "commitment to the oppressed with responsibility of the victimizer." For Mayor Tadatoshi Akiba, it was "reconciliation," starting from cooperation in order to make a future together beyond simple compromise or restoration of friendship. Sunao Tsuboi, the chair of Hiroshima Prefectural Hidankyo, saw Hiroshima Heart as existing beyond the reported "tragedies" and tested "realities," and it could be sensed through intelligent and heartfelt conversation. Among the thirteen people, Kenzaburo Oe, a Nobel laureate, talked about Hiroshima Heart in quite a comprehensive manner.

> Heart or soul is an important word, as well as those of sensitivity, imagination, will, prayer, and love. We might can call them all together unified as heart. It means humanity differentiates humans from animals… It will be clearer when we say Hiroshima Heart. Humans have suffered huge agony and kept memories and anxiety until now. Humans bring up babies. They have a desire to hand over this world to babies as a place where humans can live and heart can exist, along with a desire to harness human sensitivity, imagination, and opinions and prayer for the new world, which all together will become "Hiroshima Heart" (Hiroshima Prefectural Gensuikin 2004; Akiba 1988: 190, translated by the author).

However, we also cannot forget about desperate Hiroshima Heart full of resentment, anger, hate, and distrust (Lifton [1968] 1991). Survivors were not "sages" but human beings who have struggled for survival. We can learn more about asocial and antisocial Hiroshima Heart and its complexities in literature and artworks, which are also powerful "realities" we should inherit.

In this chapter, I have argued the role of the social imaginary in the city's policy and practices of inheriting and sharing atomic bomb experiences. Although I discussed the ineffectiveness and negative aspects of the policy, I have no intention of rejecting or suggesting the scrapping of the whole policy altogether. Instead, I would like to propose reexamining the practices from the perspective of rethinking Hiroshima Heart beyond a simple political slogan. We need a new social imaginary of Hiroshima Heart to create a renewed vision for the future based on atomic-bomb experiences.

Notes

[1]   The city government's official translation is "Hiroshima Spirit," but I choose to use "heart," another connotation for the Japanese term kokoro (心), to differentiating it from seishin (精神), which is normally translated as spirit.

[2]   This has already been pointed out by many, but there is much more to be examined, and a detailed discussion is beyond the scope of this chapter. I am preparing a book on this issue with new discoveries.

[3]   Matsumoto (1995: 130) argued there are two types of hibakusha, one is "overcoming" and the other is "escaping." The latter comprise the majority.

[4]   Writing Hiroshima in katakana, ヒロシマ often indicates Hiroshima after the atomic bomb.

[5]   Mayors for Peace is an international organization of cities dedicated to the promotion of peace that was established in 1982 at the initiative of then Mayor of Hiroshima Takeshi Araki.

[6]   It could be convenient for the city's administration to cooperate with the central government whose defense or security policy has always been controversial with respect to the Constitution (Yuasa 2019: 14-16).

[7]   The Japanese government has kept rejecting acknowledgement of the damage caused by this internal exposure until now (Yuasa forthcoming).

References

Ablett, Phillip (2016) "Castoriadis, Cornelius," in *Wiley Blackwell Encyclopedia of Sociology Online*. https://onlinelibrary.wiley.com/doi/10.1002/9781405165518. wbeosc010.pub2.

Adams, Suzi (2014) "Autonomy," in Suzi Adams (ed.), *Cornelius Castoriadis Key Concepts*. London/ New York: Bloomsbury. pp. 1-12.

Akiba, Tadatoshi (1988) *Ningen no kokoro Hiroshima no kokoro* (*Human Heart and Hiroshima Heart*). Tokyo: Sanyusha shuppan.

Araki, Takeshi (1986) *Hiroshima wo sekai e* (*Sending Hiroshima to the World*). Tokyo: Gyousei.

Arnason, Johann (2014) "Institution," in Suzi Adams (ed.), *Cornelius Castoriadis Key Concepts*. London/ New York: Bloomsbury. pp. 101-106.

Castoriadis, Cornelius (1987) *The Imaginary Institution of Society*. Cambridge: Polity Press.

Castoriadis, Cornelius (2007) *Figures of the Thinkable*. CA: Stanford University Press.

Chugoku Shinbun-sha (1995) *Kenshō Hiroshima 1945-1995* (*Examining Hiroshima 1945-1995*). Hiroshima: Chugoku Shinbun-sha.

Hiroshima City (1949) "Hiroshima Peace Memorial City Construction Law" (Accessed on October 20, 2022), https://www.city.hiroshima.lg.jp/www/contents/1391050531094/html/common/5d775774011.htm

Hiroshima City (1970) *Hiroshima-shi sougou keikaku syo* (*Hiroshima City Comprehensive Plan*). Hiroshima: Hiroshima City.

Hiroshima City (1978) *Hiroshima-shi shin kihon keikaku* (*Hiroshima City New Basic Plan*). Hiroshima: Hiroshima City.

Hiroshima City (1989) Dai Sanji Hiroshima-shi kihon keikaku (The Third Hiroshima City Basic Plan). Hiroshima: Hiroshima City.

Hiroshima City (1999) *Hiroshima-shi sougou keikaku* (*Hiroshima City Comprehensive Plan*). Hiroshima: Hiroshima City.

Hiroshima City (2009) *Hiroshima-shi kihon kousou daigoji kihon keikaku* (*Hiroshima City Basic Vision and 5th Basic Plan*). Hiroshima: Hiroshima City.

Hiroshima City (2020) *Hiroshima-shi sougou keikaku* (*Hiroshima City Comprehensive Plan*). (Retrieved October 20, 2020), https://www.city.hiroshima.lg.jp/uploaded/life/213450_320878_misc.pdf

Hiroshima Peace Cultural Center (1997) *Hiroshima heiwa bunka senta 20-nen shi* (*20-Year History of Hiroshima Peace Cultural Center*). Hiroshima Peace Cultural Center.

Hiroshima Peace Cultural Center (2010) "Hiroshima Nagasaki Giteisho no naiyou to koremade no torikumi [Summary of Hiroshima/ Nagasaki Protocol and Endeavors Undertaken thus far]" (Accessed on October 20, 2022), https://www.city.funabashi.lg.jp/shisei/shoukai/002/p046555_d/fil/hiroshima_nagasaki.pdf

Hiroshima Prefectural Gensuikin (2004) *Gensuibaku kinshi undo 50 nen no ayumi* (*50 years Footsteps of Gensuikin Movement*). Hiroshima: Hiroshima Prefectural Gensuikin.

Lifton, Robert ([1968] 1991) *Death in Life: Survivors of Hiroshima*. Chapel Hill/ London: The University of North Carolina Press.

Matsumoto, Hiroshi (1995) *Hiroshima toiu shisou* (*Thought as Hiroshima*). Tokyo: Tokyo Sougensha.

Mizumoto, Kazumi (2018) "Hibakuchi no uttae ha kaku gunshuku wo sokushin shitaka [Has Appeals from Atomic-bombed Cities Promoted Nuclear Disarmament?]," in Peace Studies Association of Japan, (ed.), *Heiwa wo Meguru 14 no Ronten* (*Fourteen Issues Concerning Peace*). Tokyo: Horitu Bunka Sha.

Moritaki, Ichiro (1976) *Hankaku 30 nen* (*30 Years for the Anti-Nuclear*). Tokyo: Nihon Hyouronsha.

Mouzakitis, Angelos (2014) "Social-Historical," in Suzi Adams, (ed.), *Cornelius Castoriadis Key Concepts*. London/ New York: Bloomsbury, pp.89-100.

Nakazawa, Masao (2007) *Hibakusha no kokoro no kizu wo otte* (*Pursuing Broken Hearts of Hibakusha*). Tokyo: Iwanami.

Naono, Akiko (2015) *Genbaku taiken to sengo nihon* (*Atomic-bomb Experiences and Post-War Japan*). Tokyo: Iwanami.

Nemoto, Masashi (2018) *Hiroshima paradokusu* (*Hiroshima Paradox*). Tokyo: Bensei Shuppan.

NHK (Japan Broadcasting Corporation) (1994) *Hiroshima no kokoro wasuremaji* (*Never forget Hiroshima Heart*). Broadcasted on February 3, 1994. https://www.nhk.or.jp/archives/shogenarchives/no-more-hibakusha/library/bangumi/ja/80/

Reminiscence Publication Committee (1976) *Yamada Setsuo tsuisou roku* (*Reminiscences of Setsuo Yamada*). Hiroshima: Reminiscences Publication Committee.

Rosengren, Mats (2014) "Magma," in Suzi Adam, (ed.), *Cornelius Castoriadis Key Concepts*. London/ New York: Bloomsbury, pp. 65-74.

Sato, Shiro (2021) *Kaku to hibakusha no kokusai seiji gaku* (*International Politics of Nuclear Weapons and Hibakusha*). Tokyo: Akashi Shoten.

Smith, Karl (2014) "Psyche," in Suzi Adam, (ed.), *Cornelius Castoriadis Key Concepts*. London/ New York: Bloomsbury, pp. 75-88.

Ubuki, Satoru (2014) *Hiroshima sengo shi* (*Post-war History of Hiroshima*). Tokyo: Iwanami.

Ubuki, Satoru (2017) "Hiroshima sengo shi kara [From Post-war History of Hiroshima]," (Accessed on October 20, 2022), https://hiroshima-ibun.com/lec/20171202.pdf.

van der Kolk, Bessel (2015) *The Body Keeps the Score: Mind, Brain, and Body in the Transformation of Trauma*. London: Penguin.

Yuasa, Masae (2019) "Imajinari toshiteno sengo nihon no heiwa shugi to Hiroshima [Pacifism as Imaginary of Post War Japan and Hiroshima]," presented at the Spring Research Conference of Peace Study Association of Japan on May 30.

Yuasa, Masae (forthcoming) *Challenging Nuclear Pacifism in Japan: Hiroshima's Anti-nuclear Social Movements after Fukushima*. London: Routledge.

Yoneyama, Lisa (1999) *Hiroshima Traces: Time, Space, and the Dialectics of Memory*. Berkeley: University of California Press.

Chapter 8
Hiroshima, Nagasaki, and the Environmental Age

Toshihiro Higuchi

The atomic bombings of Hiroshima and Nagasaki are typically remembered as a human tragedy. The first and only use of nuclear weapons in warfare, however, was also an environmental disaster. The attacks on the two Japanese cities not only killed and wounded hundreds of thousands of people, they also destroyed and scarred countless numbers of plants and animals, with some notable genetic mutations found in their posterity. In addition, the mass fires ignited by the nuclear explosions created their own weather, giving rise to a severe thunderstorm resulting in "black rain," which washed radioactive ashes and dust over large areas beyond the bombed site. The firestorms observed in Hiroshima and Nagasaki provided rare empirical evidence to the nuclear winter theory, which predicted that the smoke and soot arising from mass fires would block out sunlight and cool the Earth's surface, resulting in crop failure and mass starvation around the world. The environmental consequences of the first nuclear war, however, have been conspicuously absent in historiography. The existing literature on the effects of the atomic bombings focuses primarily on the human casualties and survivors (Beatty 1993; Hatakeyama 2021; Lindee 1994, 2006; Sasamoto 1995; Takahashi 2009). Those who have examined the contribution of atomic energy to environmental knowledge and consciousness also tend to ignore Hiroshima and Nagasaki and investigate other topics instead, such as reactor-produced radioisotopes, nuclear weapons testing, radioactive waste disposal, the nuclear winter theory, and nuclear accidents (Badash 2009; Bocking 1995; Brown 2019; Bruno 2003; Creager 2013; DeLoughrey 2013; Dörries 2011; Edwards 2012; Hamblin 2008, 2013; Higuchi 2020; Jessee 2014, 2022; Kwa 1993; Masco 2010; Lutts 1985; Martin 2018; Rainger 2004; Rothschild 2013, 2017). To fill this notable gap in the extant scholarship on the historical connections between the nuclear age and the environmental age, this essay will examine how the Hiroshima and Nagasaki bombings changed the ways we think about nature and its relationship to humans in the nuclear age.

The atomic bomb surveys on plants, animals, and weather conducted in the aftermath of nuclear destruction revealed that the bombed cities were teeming with life and subject to various forces of nature, which shaped the effects of the atomic bomb in ways that radically differed from those observed in a controlled test explosion. Scientists, citizens, and atomic bomb survivors also frequently observed, recorded, and remembered environmental changes following the bombing to make sense of nuclear destruction and foresee the possibility of survival and recovery in its aftermath. The scientific knowledge and lived experience of the human-made environmental catastrophes in Hiroshima and Nagasaki thus suggest that humans and non-humans were inseparable in the atomic bombings of the biologically diverse and meteorologically dynamic cities. This more-than-human and multispecies perspective (Bennett 2010; Tsing 2015) is crucial to understanding not only the true magnitude of the nuclear destruction but also the post-attack identity and agency of the atomic bomb survivors.

1. Plants and Animals

In his pathbreaking study on the end of World War II in the Pacific, historian Tsuyoshi Hasegawa has explained the atomic bombings of Hiroshima and Nagasaki as part of a geopolitical race, where Harry Truman and Josef Stalin tried to outmaneuver each other to force Japan's surrender (Hasegawa 2005). The bombings, however, sparked another race, this time to find out what happened to the bombed cities. The Japanese Army and the Japanese Navy were the first to send fact-finding missions to Hiroshima and Nagasaki immediately after the attacks. Although Japan's surrender briefly interrupted the investigations, the Japanese government reconstituted them under the Japan Science Council (JSC) in September. Meanwhile, the survey parties organized by the US Army, the US Navy, and the Manhattan

Project arrived in Hiroshima and Nagasaki. The US Strategic Bombing Survey conducted a separate inquiry into the atomic bombings as part of its investigation on the effectiveness of aerial attacks on Japan in general (Kesaris 1977). Not to be outdone by the Americans, the British and Soviet missions to Japan respectively dispatched their staff members to Hiroshima and Nagasaki to report their findings back to London and Moscow.

Although the initial surveys conducted by these countries covered a wide range of the effects of the atomic bombings, only the Japanese systematically studied their impact on plants and animals rather than solely humans. This divergence between the Allied Powers and Japan resulted from the different purposes of their surveys. On the one hand, the military's needs dictated the Allied research in Hiroshima and Nagasaki. Indeed, one of the major objectives for the American investigations was to check radioactive contamination for the occupying forces before their entry into the bombed cities. More importantly, the Allied forces desperately needed information about the effects of the atomic bombings to prepare for future major conflicts involving the use of nuclear weapons. The focus of the Allied investigations was therefore almost exclusively on humans and structures that constituted a country's war-making capabilities. A directive issued by the occupation authorities in October 1945 to establish a joint commission for coordination between the American surveys illustrates this human-centered orientation, declaring that the tasks for the commission was to ascertain the nature of the casualties, determine the number of each type of casualty in relation to distance from the bomb, and establish factors of protection (Oughterson et al. 1951: 18-19).

To some extent, the research priorities of the Allied Powers affected the postwar Japanese bombing survey. The occupation authorities included the investigators appointed by the Japanese government in the Joint Commission for coordination and data sharing (Sasamoto 1995). The Japanese scientific community, however, also had its own agenda. When Japan surrendered, many scientists were left without funds, personnel, and facilities to continue their work. Notably, the lack of access to radiation sources in the war-torn country held the Japanese researchers back from conducting advanced research in not only physics and material science but also biology and medicine (Itō 2021; Low 2005). For instance, Yō Okada, a leading experimental biologist appointed as the chief of the bombing survey's biology section, once used uranium in his study of sea urchins during his prewar research sojourn in Europe (Hao 1974: 118). The wide-ranging and lasting effects of the atomic bombings, including environmental ones, thus offered a golden opportunity for these struggling scientists to launch what became one of Japan's first large-scale, multidisciplinary "big science" projects after the war. The directive issued by the Ministry of Education to the Japan Science Council stressed the novelty and inclusivity of the reconstituted civilian survey, declaring that it aimed to "explore all aspects of this unprecedented world event" (Sasamoto 1995: 56-57).

Opportunism, however, was not the only reason for Japan's unusual interest in the multispecies consequences of the atomic bombings. On August 8, 1945, two days after the destruction of Hiroshima, an American news story quoted Harold Jacobson, a staff physicist for the Manhattan Project, as saying that the bomb would not only kill many people but also leave the entire area inhospitable to life due to residual contamination, "not unlike our conception of the moon for nearly three-quarters of a century" (Jacobson 1945: 1). His casual comment caused much sensation around the world. US officials and senior scientists scrambled to deny the allegations, and Jacobson immediately retracted his statement as a groundless speculation. When the war was over, however, the Japanese media picked up the claim about lethal contamination, declaring that the American news story "has thus truly dealt a major blow against Hiroshima's hopes for postwar reconstruction and rehabilitation" ("Hiroshima ni toritsuita 'akuryō'" 1945: 2). According to a later account, such an allegation was devastating to many atomic bomb survivors who still lived in the ruins (Hiroshima Shiyakusho 1971: 598-599). The survey of plants and animals was thus deemed essential not only to promote biological research but also to ascertain the very possibility of the reconstruction of Hiroshima and Nagasaki. Indeed, the Ministry of Education specifically ordered the Japan Science Council to ensure that the investigations "assist in the stability of local public welfare" (Sasamoto 1995: 56-57). The disciplines represented in the Japanese bombing surveys reflected this important social mission, including not only basic sciences and medicine necessary to determine the effects of the nuclear explosion but also civil engineering, agriculture, forestry, and veterinary medicine.

The field surveys in Hiroshima and Nagasaki initially appeared to confirm the rumor that the atomic bomb instantly turned the lively cities into lifeless "atomic desert" (*genshi sabaku*). The plant researchers reported that grass and foliage within a radius of three to four kilometers from the hypocenter were almost completely scorched. Many trees were uprooted or burnt down, and some types, especially pines and cedars, also succumbed to radiation damage. Within a month after the bombing, however, the investigators discovered that weeds and legumes sprang up from the ground, eventually covering much of the ruined city center. The trees that withstood the bomb also leafed out again (Nihon Gakujutsu Kaigi Genshi Bakudan Saigai Chōsa Hōkoku Kankō Iinkai 2011 [1953], vol. 2: 231). The remarkable re-greening of the bombed cities showed some worrisome signs, as the surveyors frequently encountered many unusual types of malformations and discoloration among almost all species observed (Nihon Gakujutsu Kaigi Genshi Bakudan Saigai Chōsa Hōkoku Kankō Iinkai 2011 [1953], vol. 2: 233). In 1947 and onwards, however, the survey could no longer find abnormalities in local flora, presumably because heavy rains and flooding in the intervening time had sped up vegetation renewal in the bombed area (Nihon Gakujutsu Kaigi Genshi Bakudan Saigai Chōsa Hōkoku Kankō Iinkai 2011 [1953], vol. 2: 226, 233). There were even some reports of bountiful wheat and soybean harvest from the bombed area that exceeded the yields in the unaffected neighboring villages (Nihon Gakujutsu Kaigi Genshi Bakudan Saigai Chōsa Hōkoku Kankō Iinkai 2011 [1953], vol. 2: 234).

The animal experts also reported mixed results. On the one hand, birds and large mammals were just as devastated as humans. Almost all of them were found dead within one kilometer, only half of them surviving at a distance of one and a half kilometers, and some severely damaged even two kilometers away. Although cattle and swine were typically penned outside the city center and therefore spared from the bombing, horses suffered the most due to their deep integration into modern transportation. In Hiroshima, for instance, approximately 60 percent of nearly a thousand military and civilian horses died (Itikawa et al 1956). On the other hand, small mammals apparently fared better. Many rabbits kept in cages for research were dead, but most guinea pigs survived. Stray cats and rodents in the bombed area were reportedly as ubiquitous as ever (Nihon Gakujutsu Kaigi Genshi Bakudan Saigai Chōsa Hōkoku Kankō Iinkai 2011 [1953], vol. 2: 219-220). The rest of the animal kingdom seemed hardly disturbed by the bomb. The researchers reported no noticeable change regarding the insects and other invertebrates. The subsurface soil collected from the area near the hypocenter contained earthworms that appeared just as abundant and normal as anywhere else (Nihon Gakujutsu Kaigi Genshi Bakudan Saigai Chōsa Hōkoku Kankō Iinkai 2011 [1953], vol. 2: 222-223, 246).

While the field surveys yielded mixed results about the extent of damage by the bomb, some researchers pinned their hopes on genetic studies. It was well known that radiation could cause chromosomal mutations in the reproductive cells of exposed plants and animals. As biophysicist Kōichi Murachi and geneticist Daigorō Moriwaki, both involved in the bombing survey, explained, however, few genetic studies using radiation had been carried out in Japan until then. The disasters at Hiroshima and Nagasaki thus served to "spur Japanese geneticists to pursue studies on the genetic effects of nuclear detonations" (Murati and Moriwaki 1956: 615). A variety of seeds from local plants such as Asian rice, Chinese cassia, tradescantia, and Persian speedwell were collected around the hypocenter (except Persian speedwell) and cultured in nurseries for genetic and cytological analysis. In the case of the so-called "atomic bomb rice" collected from Nagasaki, for instance, a group of Kyūshū University researchers led by Tsutsumi Nagamatsu raised 20,000 to 50,000 individual plants from 200-500 pedigrees each year through the early 1950s (Iwata 1970). As expected, abnormal traits and partial sterility were often found in the offspring of these cultivated plants (Murati and Moriwaki 1956). Although none of the observed abnormalities seemed to threaten the plant's viability as a species, Nagamatsu and his collaborator concluded that "atomic bomb energy may produce genetic disturbances in the plant world" (Nagamatsu and Katayama 1956: 626). When it came to the fruit fly *Drosophila melanogaster*, a model organism to study radiogenic mutations, however, the results proved inconclusive. Some of the flies collected in the area near ground zero exhibited mutations in hair and eye color. The appearance of such abnormalities, however, seemed to follow no clear pattern. A different type of fruit fly collected from the same location, *Drosophila repleta*, showed no abnormalities, whereas *D. virilis* gathered as far as two and a half kilometers away from the hypocenter produced some mutants. The randomness of the results led the research team to conclude that the observed defects in some fruit flies were highly unlikely to result from the atomic bomb (Nihon Gakujutsu Kaigi Genshi Bakudan Saigai Chōsa Hōkoku Kankō Iinkai 2011 [1953], vol. 2: 222).

Despite the conflicting and inconclusive results of the plant and animal survey, the Japanese researchers consistently interpreted their implications in the best possible light. Some tried to draw practical lessons for survival in nuclear disasters. When a plant researcher saw sprouts coming out of the ground, he noted his astonishment about "not only the resilience of life but also the effectiveness of soil cover against the atomic bomb" (Hiroshima Daigaku Genshi Bakudan Saigai Chōsa Hōkoku Kankō Iinkai 2012 [1972]: 15). Others were eager to find practical applications. In his report on the possible combined genetic effects of radiation and heat in the A-bombed plants, geneticist Nobuhide Suita expressed his hope that "if such a method makes it easy to produce a novel mutant, it will serve some practical purposes" (Nihon Gakujutsu Kaigi Genshi Bakudan Saigai Chōsa Hōkoku Kankō Iinkai 2011 [1953], vol. 2: 238). Most importantly, the Japanese seized on the rapid revegetation of the bombed area as a sign of resilience and hope. In his essay published in 1946, Hiroshima poet Kazuo Yuhki mentioned over 40 kinds of weed that he discovered near ground zero, declaring that "their undaunted and robust growth offers an unspoken lesson to people who have not recovered from war fatigue" (Yuhki 1946: 149). In

1958, when the Hiroshima Recovery Exhibition was held, botanist Yoshio Horikawa and his colleagues prepared the specimen samples of nineteen types of weeds collected near the hypocenter in order to "arouse people's interest and inspire hopes for revival." The completed collection was displayed in the newly opened Hiroshima Atomic Bomb Museum until its removal in 1975 (Hiroshima Daigaku Genshi Bakudan Saigai Chōsa Hōkoku Kankō Iinkai 2012 [1972]: 16). A singular emphasis on the vitality and resilience of the surviving plants, however, played into the American official discourse of the atomic bombings that dismissed allegations about their long-term biological effects. The report of the US Strategic Bombing Survey cited the Japanese findings as concluding: "The radiation apparently had no lasting effects on the soil or vegetation" (United States Strategic Bombing Survey 1946: 28). By the time some Japanese botanists returned to Hiroshima in 1950 to investigate the frequency distribution of Persian speedwell mutants as a possible sign of the long-term impact of the bomb, however, major construction projects had already started across the city (Nihon Gakujutsu Kaigi Genshi Bakudan Saigai Chōsa Hōkoku Kankō Iinkai 2011 [1953], vol. 2: 234). The subsequent destruction of the original post-attack vegetation made a comprehensive follow-up flora survey no longer possible.

The early postwar Japanese biological surveys conducted in Hiroshima and Nagasaki, then, both reflected and reinforced the seemingly conflicting views of nature at the dawn of the nuclear age. One was romantic, celebrating the resilience of nature even in the face of the most extreme form of human-caused disaster. The other was instrumental, seeking to control nature through atomic energy for human betterment. The survey showed that both attitudes came together fueling, materially and spiritually, Japan's single-minded drive for "reconstruction." While the Japanese seemed ready to move on, however, some observers, including those from outside Japan, continued to ponder on the implications of the atomic bombings for the human-nature relationship. One such person was American biologist Rachel Carson, whose 1962 book, *Silent Spring*, published shortly before her untimely death, has been widely credited as a catalyst for the rise of modern environmentalism in the United States and beyond. Historians have pointed out that the contemporary controversy over radioactive contamination due to nuclear weapons testing helped Carson effectively communicate the principles of ecology to a wider audience and arouse popular concerns about the persistence and accumulation of pesticides and other harmful substances in the environment (Lutts 1985). What is less known, however, is that the atomic bombings also played an important role in Carson's thinking. In her speech delivered in 1962, Carson said that, before Hiroshima, she believed that there were untouchable areas of nature that could not be impacted by man. She had since then changed this opinion, she said, declaring that all of nature was "not only threatened but [had] already felt the destroying hand of man" (Hynes 1989: 181). In many ways, her critical reflections prompted by Hiroshima heralded the subsequent rise of Anthropocene consciousness about the unexpected and potentially catastrophic consequences of humanity's domination of nature.

2. Black Rain and Nuclear Winter

Plants and animals were by no means the only nonhumans studied during the early postwar Japanese atomic bombing survey. Another environmental factor of interest was the impact of the nuclear explosion on weather and climate. A series of violent meteorological phenomena following the bombing happened due to the unusual flammability of a modern Japanese city. In Japan, wood was the material of choice for not only houses and buildings but also those which supported urban infrastructure, such as bridges, electronic poles, and railroad ties. In this sense, a modern Japanese city was not unlike a forest. The mixing of highly combustible materials and ignition sources in a crowded area, however, rendered the metropolis a tinderbox. Indeed, during World War II, the US military deliberately chose incendiary bombing as the preferred method of air raids in Japan to maximize the destruction of urban areas (Selden 2009; Ralph 2006). Likewise, the nuclear explosions over Hiroshima and Nagasaki both ignited massive conflagrations. The bomb light instantly caused numerous small flaming and smoldering fires over a large area. Then, the blast wave extinguished some of these primary fires but also ignited secondary fires by spilling fuels and causing sparks. While Nagasaki's irregular terrain somewhat inhibited fires, Hiroshima, located on a flat river delta, proved especially vulnerable. One estimate showed that a heat pulse in the magnitude of 7 calories per square centimeter was sufficient to start mass fires in Hiroshima, as compared to the standard assumption of 20 calories (Ehrlich, Sagan, Kennedy, and Roberts 1984: 85). The nuclear fireballs and mass fires, in turn, created their own weather. As a plume of hot air and smoke mixed with cooler air, a thunderstorm arose and caused heavy downpours that washed down dust and soot in the air to the ground. Although there was not much rain in Nagasaki following the bombing due to the modest scale of fires and the absence of a weather front, the so-called "black rains" fell widely in Hiroshima, leaving a large area contaminated with radioactive substances (Nihon Gakujutsu Kaigi Genshi Bakudan Saigai Chōsa Hōkoku Kankō Iinkai 2011 [1953], vol. 2: 105-106).

When the JSC committee that oversaw the Japanese bombing survey launched a study of the post-attack extreme weather, however, the project leaders had no reliable data on the black rain because there was no meteorological observatory located inside the precipitation area. To overcome this methodological challenge, a group of meteorologists in Hiroshima led by Michitaka Uda decided to rely on the memory of local residents (Nihon Gakujutsu Kaigi Genshi Bakudan Saigai Chōsa Hōkoku Kankō Iinkai 2011 [1953], vol. 2: 102). Their testimonies led the team to conclude that the black rain fell in an oval-shaped area that stretched northwest from ground zero (Nihon Gakujutsu Kaigi Genshi Bakudan Saigai Chōsa Hōkoku Kankō Iinkai 2011 [1953], vol. 1: 117). Instead of considering the potential implications of their research findings for the health of the atomic bomb survivors affected by the black rain, however, the Japanese meteorologists were eager to find the practical applications of their discovery for weather control. Indeed, the final report of the bombing survey published in 1951 included a chapter on the amount of energy added by the atomic bomb to the atmosphere, as "our foremost interest lies in the question of whether or not it is possible to artificially modify the weather by means of atomic energy" (Nihon Gakujutsu Kaigi Genshi Bakudan Saigai Chōsa Hōkoku Kankō Iinkai 2011 [1953], vol. 2: 136). The chapter written by Uda and his associates strongly echoed such a statement, declaring that "studying the precipitation caused by the bombing, especially its climatic conditions, is also extremely important from the point of view of artificial rain" (Nihon Gakujutsu Kaigi Genshi Bakudan Saigai Chōsa Hōkoku Kankō Iinkai 2011 [1953], vol. 2: 106). Similar to their colleagues who studied plants and animals in the bombed cities, the Japanese meteorologists were keen to embrace the promise of the nuclear age to realize human control of nature for social progress. The dream of nuclear-powered weather modification soon dissipated, however, and the data compiled by the Japanese meteorologists was left withering with little use for a long time.

Nearly 40 years later, in the early 1980s, the documentation of mass fires and extreme weathers in Hiroshima and Nagasaki reemerged as key evidence for the nuclear winter theory. Popularized by a group of five American scientists who published some of the earliest findings, the nuclear winter theory posited a drastic decrease in world temperatures following a nuclear war, as a massive amount of smoke arising from mass fires would block the sunlight from reaching the ground for a prolonged period (Badash 2009). Although the hypothesis drew on developments in a variety of scientific disciplines, ranging from atmospheric chemistry to the study of dinosaurs, the nuclear winter researchers still needed empirical information to feed into models. As historian Lynn Eden has noted, part of the uncertainty surrounding mass fires in a nuclear war was the product of organizational bias. To obtain data on various effects of nuclear weapons, the US military conducted nuclear weapons testing in a dry and emptied place free from combustible materials, a setting which produced no information about indirect effects such as mass fires and extreme weather (Eden 2004). The Japanese experience thus offered one of the rare glimpses into the reality of nuclear destruction.

To be sure, some researchers were skeptical about the value of the weather data from Hiroshima and Nagasaki. At an international conference held in

1983 to discuss the nuclear winter theory, Paul Ehrlich, an American biologist best known for his stern warnings about the perils of overpopulation, pointed out that the observations made in Japan following the atomic bombings were not reliable enough to confirm the fact of firestorms, lamenting: "We did not learn anywhere near what we might have, theoretically, from the Hiroshima and Nagasaki events" (Ehrlich, Sagan, Kennedy, and Roberts 1984: 70). Others viewed the successful reconstruction of the Japanese cities as a rebuke to the dire predictions about the climate consequences of nuclear warfare. A conference participant from Indonesia recalled the claim about lethal contamination made by scientists shortly after the attack on Hiroshima. "History proved them wrong because a year later the harvest—melons and other vegetables and other kinds of plants— grew fertile," he said. "So my question is, how accurate are your findings?" (Ehrlich, Sagan, Kennedy, and Roberts 1984: 70). Despite such doubts, many nuclear winter researchers defended the extrapolation of the data from Hiroshima and Nagasaki as reasonable and justifiable. American atmospheric scientist Richard P. Turco, the lead author of a pathbreaking 1983 nuclear winter article in *Science*, asserted that the observations of the nuclear explosions and fires in Japan "reinforce our conceptions of the aftermath of a massive nuclear attack" (Ehrlich, Sagan, Kennedy, and Roberts 1984: 82).

Notably, the nuclear winter debates prompted some Japanese meteorologists to scrutinize the validity of the black rain data in Hiroshima. A key figure in this development was Yoshinobu Masuda of the Meteorological Research Institute. In 1983, the year of his retirement, Masuda learned about the nuclear winter theory and discussed it at an international symposium hosted in the following year by a national nuclear disarmament campaign called Gensuikyō. To rebut a counter-argument in favor of the use of tactical nuclear weapons below the supposed threshold of a climate catastrophe, Masuda gave another talk at Gensuikyō's 1985 World Congress, explaining how even a small-yield nuclear weapon could destroy the livable environment by producing radioactive black rain. Then, Tsuneyuki Murakami, a leader of a mutual-aid group of black rain survivors, stood up complaining about Uda's survey results, as the Japanese government adamantly refused to acknowledge the health effects of the atomic bomb on people located outside of the officially designated rainfall zone. When Murakami asked Masuda if, as a weather expert, he really believed that such a heavy downpour as recorded in Hiroshima after the attack could ever possibly occur only within an oval area, Masuda later recalled, he felt "as if I were punched in the head and was so ashamed that I wanted to crawl under the rug" (Masuda 2012: 72). After many years of research, including an extensive questionnaire survey among the atomic bomb survivors, Masuda determined the rainfall area was four times as large as those identified by Uda (Masuda 1989). His reconstructed precipitation helped to reinvigorate the relief campaign for black rain survivors. In 2020, the Hiroshima district court finally recognized the "black rain" victims outside of the government-designated zone and ordered the city and the prefecture to provide the same medical benefits as given to other survivors (Mukai 2018 for the court case). The shifting meanings of atomic weather thus came full circle, moving away from the earlier, utilitarian view of nature toward its global, catastrophic conception, and finally back to its intimate connections to the atomic bomb survivors.

3. Conclusion

The controversy over the effects of the atomic bombings on plants, animals, and weather in Hiroshima and Nagasaki has demonstrated that the more-than-human perspective powerfully shapes our knowledge of nuclear destruction, both in the past and the future. More recently, such a paradigm has also played an increasingly prominent role in the remembering of the atomic bombings. The story of *hibaku jumoku*, or survivor trees, is a case in point. Trees were among the first nonhuman organisms affected by the bomb that the Japanese researchers studied for damage. Much to their surprise, many trees withstood devastation and leafed out again, and even those which lost trunks were often found regenerating from the base or roots. As urban development in Hiroshima and Nagasaki during the period of economic growth led to the removal of many survivor trees, local communities organized their relocation to schools and parks. A turning point came in 1984, when a typhoon destroyed an atomic-bombed hackberry tree at Motomachi Elementary School in Hiroshima located near ground zero. The local news on this incident aroused much interest among people in Hiroshima, prompting the local authorities to start soliciting information about similar trees across the city. As atomic bomb survivors became older and fewer around to share their stories, the injured trees came to be recognized as "silent witnesses" to the bombings. In 1996, the City of Hiroshima started inspecting and registering trees standing within two kilometers from the hypocenter. As of 2013, 55 such trees were officially certified as *hibaku jumoku* (Tedesco 2020).

Unfortunately, however, survivor trees do not speak for themselves. If the more-than-human history of Hiroshima and Nagasaki shows anything, it is that humans and nonhumans always work together to make sense of a nuclear disaster. As discussed earlier, the revegetation of the bombed cities after the war gave many war-weary Japanese hope for reconstruction. A singular emphasis on resilience, however, has a danger of normalizing nuclear war as if it were no different than a conventional one. A key figure who imbued the survivor trees with a message of peace was Suzuko Numata. Suzuko was a young office worker at the Hiroshima Telecommunication Bureau when the atomic bomb fell less than a mile away. She miraculously survived but lost her left leg and learned about the death of her fiancé who was serving in the military. Numata later recalled: "At the time, people said that no grass and trees would ever grow in Hiroshima for 70 years. I was like that Hiroshima: I loved no one and lived in hatred" (Kawara and Yamada 1994: 105-106). A year later, when Numata walked by her old office building, she noticed fresh sprouts coming out of a charred Phoenix tree, or Aogiri in Japanese, standing in the yard. Deeply touched by the sight, Numata regained her will to live. When she later decided to speak against nuclear weapons and tell her story as a survivor in the 1980s, she did so under the same Phoenix tree, now relocated to Hiroshima Peace Park.

Known as the Aogiri storyteller, Numata inspired many. In 1992, the City of Hiroshima began to grow and distribute seedlings of the Phoenix tree among schools. Six years later, in 1998, school teachers in Hiroshima launched a group to raise awareness of Aogiri's message of peace around the world, with Numata as its chief spokesperson. Established against the backdrop of increasing hostility against peace education in Hiroshima and elsewhere in Japan, the group sought to articulate what to learn from the Aogiri tree, namely the importance of working toward "a peaceful world free from war and nuclear weapons" (Hiroiwa 2013: 211-212).

At the moment the memory of the atomic bombings began to fade away, then, Numata and her supporters successfully forged a symbiotic relationship between humans and trees that resisted the normalizing discourse of nuclear warfare. Numata passed away in 2011, and the average age of hibakushas as of 2022 now stands at 84. It remains to be seen what stories the survivor trees will tell us when a new generation carries the legacy of the atomic bombings into the Anthropocene, where humans are already confronting environmental changes of their own making.

References

Badash, Lawrence (2009) *A Nuclear Winter's Tale: Science and Politics in the 1980s.* Cambridge, MA: MIT Press.

Beatty, John (1993) "Scientific Collaboration, Internationalism, and Diplomacy: The Case of the Atomic Bomb Casualty Commission," *Journal of the History of Biology*, 26(2), pp. 205-231.

Bennett, Jane (2010) *Vibrant Matter: A Political Ecology of Things.* Durham, NC: Duke University Press.

Bocking, Stephen (1995) "Ecosystems, Ecologists, and the Atom: Environmental Research at Oak Ridge National Laboratory," *Journal of the History of Biology*, 28(1), pp. 1-47.

Brown, Kate (2019) *Manual for Survival: An Environmental History of the Chernobyl Disaster.* New York: W. W. Norton.

Bruno, Laura A. (2003) "The Bequest of the Nuclear Battlefield: Science, Nature, and the Atom during the First Decade of the Cold War," *Historical Studies in the Physical and Biological Sciences*, 33(2), pp. 237-260.

Creager, Angela (2013) *Life Atomic: A History of Radioisotopes in Science and Medicine.* Chicago: University of Chicago Press.

DeLoughrey, Elizabeth (2013) "The Myth of Isolates: Ecosystem Ecologies in the

Nuclear Pacific," *Cultural Geographies*, 20(2), pp. 167-184.

Dörries, Matthias (2011) "The Politics of Atmospheric Sciences: 'Nuclear Winter' and Climate Change," *Osiris*, 26(1), pp. 198-223.

Eden, Lynn (2004) *Whole World on Fire: Organizations, Knowledge, and Nuclear Weapons Devastation*. Ithaca, NY: Cornell University Press.

Edwards, Paul N. (2012) "Entangled Histories: Climate Science and Nuclear Weapons Research," *Bulletin of the Atomic Scientists*, 68(4), pp. 28-40.

Ehrlich, Paul R., Carl Sagan, Donald Kennedy, and Walter Orr Roberts (1984) *The Cold and the Dark: The World After Nuclear War*. New York: Norton.

Hamblin, Jacob Darwin (2008) *Poison in the Well: Radioactive Waste in the Oceans at the Dawn of the Nuclear Age*. New Brunswick, NJ: Rutgers University Press.

Hamblin, Jacob Darwin (2013) *Arming Mother Nature: The Birth of Catastrophic Environmentalism*. Oxford; New York: Oxford University Press.

Hao, Tadao (1974) "Meiyo kaiin Okada Yō sensei o shinobu [Remembering Honorary Member Okada Yō]," *Dōbutsugaku zasshi*, 83(1), p. 118.

Hasegawa, Tsuyoshi (2005) *Racing the Enemy: Stalin, Truman, and the Surrender of Japan*. Cambridge, MA: Belknap Press of Harvard University Press.

Hatakeyama, Sumiko (2021) "Let Chromosomes Speak: The Cytogenetics Project at the Atomic Bomb Casualty Commission," *Journal of the History of Biology*, 54(1), pp. 107-126.

Higuchi, Toshihiro (2020) *Political Fallout: Nuclear Weapons Testing and the Making of a Global Environmental Crisis*. Stanford, CA: Stanford University Press.

Hiroiwa, Chikahiro (2013) *Hibaku aogiri to ikiru: Kataribe Numata Suzuko no dengon* [Living with A-Bombed Aogiri: A Message from Storyteller Numata Suzuko]. Tokyo: Iwanami Shoten.

Hiroshima Daigaku Genbaku Shibotsusha Irei Gyōji Iinkai (2012 [1972]) *Genbaku to Hiroshima Daigaku: 'Seishi no hi' gakujutsu hen* [The Atomic Bomb and Hiroshima University: "Fire of Life and Death," the Academic Volume]. Hiroshima: Hiroshima Daigaku Shuppankai.

"Hiroshima ni toritsuita 'akuryō': Ni shukan go niwa shibōsha baizō [An "Evil Spirit" Haunting Hiroshima: The Number of Deaths Doubled in Two Weeks]" (1945) *Asahi Shimbun* (August 25), p. 2.

Hiroshima Shiyakusho, ed. (1971) *Hiroshima genbaku sensaishi* [History of the Atomic-Bomb War Disaster in Hiroshima], vol. 1. Hiroshima: Hiroshima City.

Hynes, Patricia (1989) *The Recurring Silent Spring*. New York: Pergamon Press.

Itikawa, Osamu, et al. (1956) "Studies on the Casualties in Animal Caused by Radioactive Substances," in Committee for Compilation of Report on Research in the Effects of Radioactivity, *Research in the Effects and Influences of the Nuclear Bomb Test Explosions*, vol. 1. Tokyo: Japan Society for the Promotion of Science, 1956, pp.

685-692.

Itō, Kenji (2021) "The Scientific Object and Material Diplomacy: The Shipment of Radioisotopes from the United States to Japan in 1950," *Centaurus*, 63(2), pp. 296-319.

Iwata, Nobuo (1970) "Nagasaki no genbaku hibaku ine no kōdai ni okeru saibō idengakuteki kenkyū [Cellular Genetic Research on the Descendants of the Atomic Bomb Rice from Nagasaki]," *Kyūshū Daigaku nōgakubu gakugei zasshi*, 25(1), pp. 1-53.

Jacobson, Harold (1945) "Death Will Saturate Bomb Targets for 70 Years, Atomic Expert Says," *Atlanta Constitution* (August 8), p. 1.

Jessee, E. Jerry (2014) "A Heightened Controversy: Nuclear Weapons Testing, Radioactive Tracers, and the Dynamic Stratosphere," in James Rodger Fleming and Ann Johnson, (eds), *Toxic Airs: Body, Place, Planet in Historical Perspective*. Pittsburgh, PA: University of Pittsburgh Press, pp. 152-180.

Jessee, E. Jerry (2022) "Radiation and the Environment," *Oxford Research Encyclopedia of Environmental Science* (July 18), https://doi.org/10.1093/acrefore/9780199389414.013.707.

Kawara, Hirokazu, and Yamada, Mariko (1994) *Hiroshima hana ichirin monogatari: Hibakusha Numata Suzuko no owarinaki seishun* [A Tale of a Flower in Hiroshima: A-Bomb Survivor Numata Suzuko's Endless Springtime of Life]. Tokyo: Komichi Shobō.

Kesaris, Paul (1977) *Manhattan Project: Official History and Documents*. Washington, DC: University Publications of America.

Kwa, Chunglin (1993) "Radiation Ecology, Systems Ecology and the Management of the Environment," in Michael Shortland, (ed.), *Science and Nature: Essays in the History of the Environmental Sciences*. London: British Society for the History of Science, pp. 213-249.

Lindee, M. Susan (1994) *Suffering Made Real: American Science and the Survivors at Hiroshima*. Chicago: University of Chicago Press.

Lindee, M. Susan (2016) "Survivors and Scientists: Hiroshima, Fukushima, and the Radiation Effects Research Foundation, 1975-2014," *Social Studies of Science*, 46(2), pp. 184-209.

Low, Morris (2005) *Science and the Building of a New Japan*. New York: Palgrave Macmillan.

Lutts, Ralph H. (1985) "Chemical Fallout: Rachel Carson's Silent Spring, Radioactive Fallout, and the Environmental Movement," *Environmental Review*, 9(3), pp. 211-225.

Martin, Laura J. (2018) "Proving Ground: Ecological Fieldwork in the Pacific and the Materialization of Ecosystems," *Environmental History*, 23(3), pp. 567-592.

Masco, Joseph (2010) "Bad Weather: On Planetary Crisis," *Social Studies of Science*, 40(1), pp. 7-40.

Masuda, Yoshinobu (1989) "Hiroshima genbaku go no 'kuroi ame' wa dokomade futtaka [How Far Did "Black Rain" after the Atomic Bombing of Hiroshima Fall?]," *Tenki*, 36(2), pp. 13-23.

Masuda, Yoshinobu (2012) "'Kuroi ame' kara 'Fukushima' made: Naibu hibaku kenkyū no jūyōsei [From "Black Rain" to Fukushima: The Importance of Internal Exposure Research]," *Hiroshima jānarizumu* (June 15), pp. 70-74.

Mukai, Hitoshi (2018) "'Kuroi ame' higaisha undō to shugo teki aidentitii [The "Black Rain" Victim Movement and Subjective Identity]," *Hiroshima Journal of International Studies*, 24, pp. 95-113.

Murati, K., and D. Moriwaki (1956) "Genetic Effects Induced on Plants," in Committee for Compilation of Report on Research in the Effects of Radioactivity, (ed.), *Research in the Effects and Influences of the Nuclear Bomb Test Explosions*, vol. 1, pp. 615-616.

Nagamatsu, N., and T. Katayama (1956) "Cytogenetical Studies on the Sterile Wild Senna (Cassia Tora L.) Produced by the Atomic Bomb Explosion in Nagasaki," in Committee for Compilation of Report on Research in the Effects of Radioactivity, *Research in the Effects and Influences of the Nuclear Bomb Test Explosions*, vol. 1, pp. 617-628.

Nihon Gakujutsu Kaigi Genshi Bakudan Saigai Chōsa Hōkoku Kankō Iinkai, ed. (2011 [1953]) *Genshi bakudan saigai chōsa hōkoku* [Report on the Investigation of the Atomic Bomb Disaster], vols. 1-2. Tokyo: Fuji Shuppan.

Oughterson, A.W., et al. (1951) *Medical Effects of Atomic Bombs: The Report of the Joint Commission for the Investigation of the Effects of the Atomic Bomb in Japan*, vol. 1. Washington: Army Institute of Pathology.

Rainger, Ronald (2004) "'A Wonderful Oceanographic Tool': The Atomic Bomb, Radioactivity and the Development of American Oceanography," in Helen M. Rozwadowski and David K. van Keuren, (eds.), *The Machine in Neptune's Garden: Historical Perspectives on Technology and the Marine Environment*. Sagamore Beach, MA: Science History Publications/USA, pp. 93-131.

Ralph, William W. (2006) "Improvised Destruction: Arnold, LeMay, and the Firebombing of Japan," *War in History*, 13(4), pp. 495-522.

Rothschild, Rachel (2013) "Environmental Awareness in the Atomic Age: Radioecologists and Nuclear Technology," *Historical Studies in the Natural Sciences*, 43(4), pp. 492-530.

Rothschild, Rachel (2017) "The Environment in the Atomic Age," *Oxford Research Encyclopedia of American History* (November 20), https://doi.org/10.1093/acrefore/9780199329175.013.415.

Sasamoto, Yukuo (1995) *Beigun senryōka no genbaku chōsa: Genbaku kagaikoku ni natta Nihon* [The Atomic Bomb Surveys under U.S. Military Occupation: Japan as an Atomic Bomb Victimizer]. Tokyo: Shinkansha.

Selden, Mark (2009) "A Forgotten Holocaust: US Bombing Strategy, the Destruction of Japanese Cities, and the American Way of War from the Pacific War to Iraq," in Yūki Tanaka and Marilyn B. Young, (eds.), *Bombing Civilians: A Twentieth-Century History*. New York: New Press, pp. 77-96.

Takahashi, Hiroko (2009) "One Minute After the Detonation of the Atomic Bomb: The Erased Effects of Residual Radiation," *Historia Scientiarum*, 19(2), pp. 146-159.

Tedesco, Lianna (2020) "Hibakujumoku: The Trees That Blossomed Through Earthquakes and Hiroshima," *The Travel* (August 5), https://www.thetravel.com/did-ginkgo-trees-survive-hiroshima/.

Tsing, Anna L. (2015) *The Mushroom at the End of the World: On the Possibility of Life in Capitalist Ruins*. Princeton, NJ: Princeton University Press.

United States Strategic Bombing Survey (1946) *The Effects of Atomic Bombs on Hiroshima and Nagasaki*. Washington: U.S.G.P.O.

Yuhki, Kazuo (1946) "Tachiagaru zassō [Rising Weed]," *Saishū to shiiku*, 8(8-9), pp. 148-149.

Chapter 9
Layered Landscapes, Transplanted Tragedies: Kibei Hibakusha Experience in Naomi Hirahara's Mas Arai Mystery Series

Michael Gorman

The Unburied Past—Kibei Hibakusha Experience

When encountering new texts relating to Hiroshima, I often recall Carolyn Forché's haunting poem, "The Garden Shukkei-en," in which a survivor of the atomic bombing of Hiroshima wonders, "Do Americans think of us?" (Forché 1995: 204-205). Forché leaves the seemingly simple question unanswered in her poem, challenging readers to draw their own conclusions. Another American writer, the mystery novelist Naomi Hirahara, takes a decidedly different approach, confronting the issue of what Americans know or think about survivors of the first atomic bombing head on. In *Hiroshima Boy* (HB), the seventh and final book in her Mas Arai mystery series, Hirahara asserts that the suffering experienced by *hibakusha* in Hiroshima and Nagasaki is "swept into corners, known to the intellectually curious but hidden from people who wanted to believe in fairy tale endings" (Hirahara 2018: 147). In other words, the human cost of the production and use of nuclear weapons has been actively concealed from most Americans, so they can conveniently ignore it. Such convenience doesn't seem to sit right with Hirahara, however. By including fictional yet historically-informed survivor narratives into her Mas Arai novels, Hirahara highlights *hibakusha* experience and makes it a little harder for her readers to accept the "fairy tale endings" told about World War II and the Manhattan Project.

While individual novels in the Mas Arai series focus on solving a murder (or a string of related killings), the series accomplishes much more. It educates readers about the bombing of Hiroshima as well as Japanese

American history and the diverse experiences of members in the Japanese American community. Hirahara's novels introduce little-known facts about Japanese American life including details about forced internment during World War II, the heroism of the soldiers in the 442nd Regimental Combat Team, the existence of *kibei hibakusha* living in the United States, and the vital role Japanese Americans have played in the agricultural economy of California. While informed readers will be unsurprised, the lesser-known episodes in Japanese American history and the Second World War to which Hirahara alludes in these novels could strike a lay audience as astonishing. This, on its own, makes the series worthwhile reading.

At the nucleus of Hirahara's mystery series is Masao "Mas" Arai, an elderly Japanese American gardener and accidental detective. Hirahara uses Mas to demystify Japanese American experience and the horrors suffered by *hibakusha* in Hiroshima (and Nagasaki). Mas is *kibei nisei*, an American-born child of Japanese immigrants. Though born in rural California, he was taken to Japan as a toddler when his parents moved the family back to Hiroshima, and he was still living there in his teens when the atomic bomb was dropped on the city.[1] As readers learn in *Summer of the Big Bachi* (BB), Mas survived and made his way back to the United States in 1947 (Hirahara 2004: 184). After returning to California, he "pressed down on his memories so hard that they lay thin and almost invisible. America was again his home. There was no place for Hiroshima anymore" (BB 20). Mas had hoped to make a new start by escaping the scene of so much violence and heartbreak, but even in California the burden of surviving Hiroshima weighs heavily on Mas, just as Robert Jay Lifton reveals it had for thousands of *hibakusha*.[2] In response to trauma, survivor guilt, and the potential for long-term complications relating to his exposure to radiation he buries his memories of the bombing and its aftermath only to have them resurface like shoots of bamboo.

It should come as no surprise that Mas finds himself routinely involved in murder investigations—this is a requirement of the genre after all. Unfortunately for Mas, the untimely deaths of strangers and acquaintances trigger lingering trauma relating to the atomic bombing, the loss of family and friends, and the contradictory aspects of his identity as *kibei* American. Horticulture plays a pivotal role in helping him cope with these psycho-social concerns, yet farming and landscape gardening cannot be reduced to therapeutic instruments for Mas. They are foundational to his sense of self (including his Americanness) and shape the way he sees the world.

Layered Landscapes—Survival, Betrayal, and Belonging in *Summer of the Big Bachi*

The word "bachi" in the title of Hirahara's first Mas Arai mystery suggests that the novel focuses on the theme of comeuppance. Revenge, karma, poetic justice, payback—whatever translation it goes by—bachi is a concern in the book and impacts characters' thinking and actions. The trope is more ornamental than structural, however. The overarching motif of *Summer of the Big Bachi*, particularly as it applies to Hirahara's protagonist, is not retribution but betrayal (in the form of survivor guilt) and belonging.

Notwithstanding a feigned misanthropy that he adopted in response to cruelty witnessed in Hiroshima, Mas frets about not fitting in. In Chapter 2, Hirahara links the horticultural process of grafting to Mas's expectations of being spurned by American society: "Mas was waiting to be tossed out, rejected like those broken branches he tended at one of his longtime customers'. They called it grafting, an attempt to attach something strange and new to an established tree. It usually didn't work, either with plants or with people" (BB 30). Based on what he observed after the atomic bombing Mas pessimistically sees alienation, rather than connection, as inevitable in a crisis. Yet Hirahara casts doubts on Mas's interpretation of the world. In Chapter Three, Mas returns to Mrs. Witt's property where he sees "trees . . . like thin, emaciated bodies. Branches lay on the ground like amputated limbs. Only one tree seemed not to have rejected the grafted branches" (BB 44). The grove is "a killing field" evoking memories of the suffering Mas witnessed in Hiroshima after the bomb.[3] Amid the carnage of Mrs. Witt's fruit trees, however, Hirahara plants hope. Spliced branches have been accepted by one of the trees. The single successful pairing of distinct fruit species is a metaphor for Mas's assimilation into American society. It symbolizes his acculturation to life in the United States.

Hirahara describes Mas as "the ultimate survivor" (BB 5). The epithet links the professional gardener/amateur sleuth to fictional forebears (such as Philip Marlowe, Sam Spade, Mike Hammer, Jake Gittes), case-hardened private detectives whose wits and grit help them escape precarious situations and elude violent death. In Mas's case, however, the chief reason for the sobriquet has less to do with his considerable ingenuity and determination than it does with a single twist of fate. In the morning of August 6, 1945, upon hearing the air raid siren he made his way into the basement of Hiroshima Station (BB 135-136, 257-260), approximately two kilometers from the hypocenter. Had he been above ground when the atomic bomb detonated Mas would have numbered among the dead, which has been estimated to be as high as 140,000 souls by the end of 1945 (Wellerstein 2020).

Events depicted in *Summer of the Big Bachi* take place in the greater Los Angeles area in 1999, 54 years after the bombing of Hiroshima and 52 years after Mas left Japan for the United States, the country of his birth. At 69 years-old and widowed for about ten years, Mas still works as a self-employed gardener, though he has fewer clients than in his heyday. At this point in his life (and in the novel series), Mas has a love-hate relationship with landscape gardening, a profession he has been practicing since he arrived in Los Angeles in 1950 (Hirahara 2013: 193).[4] He is distressed to learn that his daughter, Mari, married a gardener employed by the city of New York. He and his late wife Chizuko did not expect to have a "good-for-nothing gardener" as a son-in-law (BB 61, 63). The dismay Mas feels about his son-in-law's vocation is a projection of his disappointment in himself. In the autumn of his life, he looks back wistfully at roads not taken and regrets settling for being a simple gardener instead of striving to realize earlier ambitions, including a childhood dream to design cars for Ford Motor Company (BB 206) and an intention in the 1970s to purchase a plant nursery in Ventura, California (BB 155-156).

Despite lamenting unfulfilled aspirations and viewing landscape gardening as a trade he fell into rather than a field he purposefully chose, Mas seems well suited to and fulfilled by his work as a gardener. Over the course of the seven novels in the series, his ideas about gardening (and his son-in-law) evolve. Midway through the first novel, in fact, his thoughts about gardening as an occupation shift from viewing it as a source of embarrassment to one of dignity. In Chapter 12, when Yukikazu "Yuki" Kimura, the grandson of a former neighbor from Hiroshima, asks Mas about what he did for employment upon returning to the United States, he explains that he worked as a farm laborer before starting his business as a landscape gardener. In light of Mas's complaints about his son-in-law's job in Chapter 4, the way he describes gardening to Yuki is surprisingly positive: "I'm my own boss. Not too many guys can say that" (BB 207).

Mas characterizes himself as a self-made man. He is exceedingly proud of being self-reliant and values the autonomy that gardening has afforded him over the years. He tells Yuki that he came to the United States and started his gardening business on his own, without any financial support from his parents, and concludes by saying, "I'm an American citizen, after all. I belong here" (BB 208). Moving to America and working as a self-employed landscape gardener is a respectable tale, another episode of the American Dream. Of course that isn't the whole story. Mas fails to tell Yuki that he purchased ship's passage to the United States with money he stole from a criminal acquaintance in Hiroshima (BB 163). Nor does he speak of the guilt that he has been feeling since the war for abandoning Yuki's grandmother, Akemi, and great uncle, Joji, in Hiroshima. Even though he was just a teenager at the time, Mas has not been able to forgive himself. More than 50 years later, he still believes that he had "forsaken" the Hanedas and betrayed their friendship (BB 193).[5]

There's no room in the American Dream for survivor guilt or feelings of betrayal. Mas understands this and modifies his account accordingly. The pride reflected in his abridged version of events echoes J. Hector St. John de Crèvecoeur's description of the transformation emigrants from Europe experience in America: "This great metamorphosis . . . extinguishes all his European prejudices, he forgets that mechanism of subordination, that servility of disposition, which poverty had taught him" (Crèvecoeur 1997: 59). As Crèvecoeur did with European-born immigrant farmers, Hirahara weaves the story of Mas Arai, a *kibei hibakusha* landscape gardener, into the American pastoral tradition and the myth of American Exceptionalism.

Beyond a sense of independence and entrepreneurial standing, a career in landscape gardening has provided Mas a sense of belonging in the Japanese American community. He was born an American citizen to immigrant parents in the agricultural town of Watsonville, California, but was raised in Hiroshima, Japan. As an American citizen living in Japan during World War II, he was viewed with suspicion by neighbors and fellow students. On moving back to California in 1947, he once again felt like an outsider, "a bloody kibei," especially in contrast to Nisei acquaintances such as Tug Yamada—a "red, white, and blue American" who was educated in California and fought with the legendary 442nd Regimental Combat Team during World War II (BB 57).

After returning to the United States, Mas made his way back to Watsonville where he began working as a truck farmer (i.e., migrant laborer) alongside people from Mexican and Filipino backgrounds. In 1950, Mas quit truck farming to become a gardener in Los Angeles. When he informs his cousin Shigeo of the decision, Shigeo replies, "A lot of Nisei are doing that in the big cities" (SY 193). This is quite an understatement. According to "A History of Japanese Americans in California: Patterns of Settlement and Occupational Characteristics," between 1950 and 1960, the Japanese American population of LA more than doubled (increasing from 36,761 to 77,314) and a growing number of Japanese American Nisei were engaged in landscape gardening which had "gained in importance after World War II" (National Park Service 2004). By moving to Los Angeles and becoming a landscape gardener in 1950, Mas had become a resident of the largest Japanese American community in the United States and had entered one of the fastest growing occupations among Japanese Americans. He was no longer an outsider.

Transplanted Tragedies—Trauma and Healing in *Gasa-Gasa Girl* and *Hiroshima Boy*

While classified as a mystery novel, Naomi Hirahara's *Summer of the Big Bachi* goes beyond genre fiction. It's a story of survival and belonging inspired by the author's own father, Isamu Hirahara, an American who survived the atomic bombing of Hiroshima before returning to the United States and staking out a career as a landscape gardener in Southern California. The second and seventh titles in the series, *Gasa-Gasa Girl* and *Hiroshima Boy*, also offer mystery readers more than the typical whodunit. These novels foreground trauma, healing, and the role that landscape gardening plays in helping Mas connect with family and cope with the PTSD plaguing him since Hiroshima.

In *Gasa-Gasa Girl*, Hirahara sends her protagonist across the country to help his daughter, Mari, and son-in-law, Lloyd, restore a private Japanese garden in Brooklyn. Once he arrives there, Mas finds himself in the unsettling, but familiar, role as outsider, and sensing that New York City is "no place for Japanese gardeners and no place for a Kibei" (Hirahara 2005: 4). Nevertheless, during this trip Mas strengthens his connection to family and the larger Japanese American community, deepens his appreciation of the Japanese landscape garden tradition, and, takes a meaningful step towards coming to terms with his own trauma. Landscape gardening plays a key role in this process. As a matter of fact, in *Gasa-Gasa Girl*, Hirahara paradoxically enlists gardens as sites of trauma and healing.

Shortly after arriving in Brooklyn, Mas learns that his infant grandson, Takeo, is suffering from a severe case of jaundice (GG 18-19). Echoing similar concerns that the Nagasaki *hibakusha* writer Hayashi Kyōko has expressed about passing on "*genbaku byō*" to her own son, Mas wonders if his grandson's medical condition is a "legacy of the Bomb pumping through his body, to Mari's, and now the grandson's" (GG 57).[6] Could his exposure to radiation during the atomic bombing of Hiroshima adversely affect the health of his child and grandchild? The answer is immaterial. In terms of traumatic impact, it doesn't matter whether the atomic bomb has physically affected him or altered the genetic material he shares with his descendants. Uncertainty takes a toll on his psyche either way. As nuclear historian Robert Jacobs notes, for *hibakusha* "illness may lurk just ahead, hidden within one's body, a radiogenic time bomb, ticking" (Jacobs 2022: 79). The problem is Mas can never know for sure.

The psychological injury inflicted by the atomic bomb is manifest in bad dreams that have tormented Mas for decades. In *Gasa-Gasa Girl*, Mas's daughter, Mari, and grandson, Takeo, suffer from nightmares, too, and Mas believes that he has passed on the predisposition for having nightmares to his daughter and grandson (GG 21, 213). This suggests a link, in Mas's mind at least, between his persistent nightmares of the atomic bombing and his sustained anxiety about the impact radiation may have had upon him at a genetic level.

While it may seem absurd to think that Mari and Takeo's struggles with bad dreams could be connected to trauma that Mas experienced in Hiroshima long before Mari was even born, scientists and medical professionals recognize that the psychological and biological effects of trauma are indeed heritable. In "Intergenerational Transmission of Trauma Effects" (2018), Rachel Yehuda and Amy Lehrner trace the concept of Intergenerational Trauma to psychiatrist Vivian Rakoff who published a 1966 study suggesting that a significant number of children born after the Holocaust displayed more psychological distress than their parents who experienced it (Yehuda and Lehrner 2018). Clinical psychologists widely believe intergenerational trauma to be a universal phenomenon (Yehuda and Lehrner 2018: 244). Children of *hibakusha*, therefore, could exhibit "anxiety, depression, panic attacks, nightmares, insomnia, ... issues with self-esteem and self-confidence" (Gillespie 2020) and other symptoms first noticed in earlier studies among the children of Holocaust survivors. In other words, there is a psychological explanation for Mari to have inherited her father's propensity for nightmares.

Research into intergenerational trauma goes beyond psychology. Today, scientists in biochemistry, genetics, medicine, and molecular biology have joined psychologists to investigate how trauma is transmitted from one generation to the next.[7] The findings so far are intriguing. Studies with mice, for example, have traced biological and behavioral effects of trauma to the third generation (ETH Zurich 2014), and scientists are optimistic that human studies will reveal similarly meaningful results (Yehuda and Lehrner 2018: 250, 252). In other words, researchers may soon find biological factors confirming Mas's belief that he is the source of his grandson's nightmares.

When Mas makes his first visit to the Waxley House Garden in Brooklyn, it is in a dire condition. Troublemakers have broken the branches of the cherry trees and have filled the dry koi pond with trash (GG 33-34). Despite the vandalism, the garden has potential to be exquisite. Mas is impressed by its expressive landscaping: the course of its path, the placement of stones and lanterns, the outline of a dry pond spanned by a bridge, the arrangement of pines and azaleas and bamboo (GG 35-36). Knowing that it could once again be a living work of art, he immediately sets about nursing it back to health. Like an emergency room doctor, he teaches the property manager, Becca Ouchi, a grafting technique to repair the broken branches and he begins clearing the pond of debris until he discovers a lifeless body (GG 37). Uncovering the corpse at the bottom of the pond stirs up unwelcome memories of people killed during the atomic bombing of Hiroshima. Linked to the Hiroshima dead, the Waxley House Garden has become another traumatic landscape for Mas where "dead bodies, both past and present, would haunt his mind" (GG 40).

The gruesome episode at the Waxley House Garden forces Mas to confront painful memories of Hiroshima. Included among them are the scores of casualties that he encountered in the aftermath of the atomic bombing. An especially heartbreaking recollection is the final moment he spent with Joji Haneda, a close friend who was near death and begging for water (BB 160). Mas was unable to provide Joji relief and is tormented by his failure to save Joji throughout the novel series. The details of this traumatic incident depicted by Hirahara echo accounts in John Hersey's *Hiroshima* of sick and dying people begging the Reverend Kiyoshi Tanimoto and Father Wilhelm Kleinsorge for water within (and in the immediate vicinity of) Asano Park, a Japanese landscape garden known today as Shukkeien (Hersey 2001: 42-43, 48-49, 67-69).[8]

Shukkeien was conceived as the grounds of Asano Nagākira's villa. Commissioned by Lord Asano, Daimyō of Hiroshima, the construction of Shukkeien began in 1620 and was overseen by Ueda Sōko, retired warlord turned landscape architect and tea master.[9] The property remained in the hands of the Asano family until they donated it to Hiroshima Prefecture in 1940 (Hauglann 2021). During WWII, Shukkeien was designated an emergency evacuation site, and until the morning of August 6, 1945, it went untouched by air raids (Hiroshima for Global Peace 2020). As Hersey reports, refugees sought shelter at Shukkeien among "the bamboos, pines, laurel, and maples" that escaped the initial blast (Hersey 47). The garden wasn't spared for long, however. Fires from the atomic bombing eventually reached the area and, after destroying most of its greenery and all of its buildings, turned Shukkeien into a hellscape. Nevertheless, as Hersey and others have documented, great numbers of wounded and dying made their way to Shukkeien in search of medical assistance and drinking water. There was little relief to be found, and "thousands of people lost their lives in and around the garden" (Hiroshima for Global Peace).

In spite of Shukkeien's significance to the history and identity of Hiroshima, the only novel in the Mas Arai series that mentions the site is the final book, *Hiroshima Boy*, in which Hirahara brings her protagonist back to the city where he spent his youth. Mas visits Shukkeien twice in the novel.[10] His initial visit, coming early in the trip to Hiroshima, elicits conflicting sentiments. On one hand, the garden has a spiritual quality reminiscent of Emersonian transcendentalism. Mas deliberately seeks out its verdancy to clarify his thinking (HB 71). A bit later, however, a memorial to the dead alters his mood. He soon has difficulty seeing the garden as anything but a mass grave for victims of the atomic bomb. "New plants . . . could not reverse the damage of radiation and black rain. Architects and workers had restored the garden to what it looked like seventy, a hundred, or even more years ago, but it was like a superficial mask covering the darkness that was below" (HB 72). Overwhelmed by survivor guilt and disturbing memories of the Bomb, Mas cannot see Shukkeien as a hopeful symbol of Hiroshima's perseverance.

**Figure 1: Shukkeien, Kaminobori-cho.
Photo by Kyoko Matsunaga.**

The attitudes Mas holds toward Hiroshima and Shukkeien shift radically after visiting his niece, Shoko, at the Arai family home on August 6, 2015— the 70th anniversary of the atomic bombing of Hiroshima. As the conspicuous date Hirahara selects for the meeting suggests, it is a transformational moment for her 86 year-old protagonist. Upon opening the gate to his childhood home in Kure, he is greeted by familiar sculpted pines and a dry koi pond, elements resembling those of the Waxley House Garden in *Gasa-Gasa Girl* (HB 187). Mas wonders why his father maintained such a fine garden, a seemingly impractical and extravagant feature for a farmer's home, especially during wartime. The answer to the question is irrelevant. What matters is that his father valued having a garden as a source of comfort as well as a token of his existence: "his father . . . had felt one was necessary to make his mark in this world" (HB 187). The meticulously-groomed and cherished space is also a validation of Mas's life, particularly his decision to become a gardener. It signifies his connection to home, not just a bridge between Mas and his birth family but also between his lives in Hiroshima and Los Angeles.

The sense of connection triggered by the garden is deepened inside the house. Shoko invites him into the tatami room, the layout of which Mas can remember "with his eyes closed" (HB 187). There, he sees the family's Buddhist altar (butsudan) sheltering a "lithe standing figure of Buddha," presumably a likeness of Amida Nyorai, the chief object/symbol of veneration to followers of Jōdō Shinshu (True Pure Land Buddhism) (Senshin Buddhist Temple n.d.).[11] The Buddhist statuette in this passage from *Hiroshima Boy* brings to mind an episode in the penultimate chapter of *Gasa-Gasa Girl* in which Hirahara alludes to an intriguing piece of Hiroshima history involving another Buddhist icon. Towards the end of Chapter 14, Tug Yamada takes Mas to the New York Buddhist Church in Manhattan to see a cast bronze sculpture of Shinran Shonin, the founder of Jōdō Shinshu Buddhism. Before being sent to New York, the statue stood watch over Hiroshima from Hijirigaoka, a hill in Mitaki-cho, where it was exposed to the atomic bombing in 1945 (World War II Magazine 2020). Tug likens the image to Mas, saying, "This statue is originally from Hiroshima. Survived the bomb, like you" (GG 275). Mas reacts to Tug's words by staring at the larger-than-life figure of Shinran: "At first the statue looked totally out of place, fenced in behind an iron gate on New York's Riverside Drive. But the longer Mas stared at it, the more at home it seemed to be" (GG 275). As *kibei hibakusha*, Mas has felt like a misfit for much of his life. As an American citizen, he didn't belong in wartime Japan.[12] Nor, unfortunately, did he feel at peace in the United States. After moving back to California, he felt inferior to other Nisei such as Tug who served in the US Armed Forces and went to college. The statue's adaptation to its Manhattan surroundings that Mas visualizes reflects his own desire to feel at home in America and at ease with himself. In this brief but revealing passage from *Gasa-Gasa Girl*, Hirahara suggests that he may eventually.

Five novels later, Hirahara makes good on that suggestion. While talking with his niece beneath portraits of Mas's parents, Mas has a chance to see his life through the eyes of his birth family. Shoko flips through albums full of photographs depicting his Hiroshima and California lives. While he had always considered himself as "the black sheep that had wandered off," the photo album tells the story of a "trailblazer" (HB 189). The family photos and remembered anecdotes reveal that he was admired by his parents and siblings (HB 189, 191). Mas is surprised to hear that his parents respected his decision to build a life in America after they had given up trying and returned to Japan. Even more incredible for Mas was learning that his brothers and sisters viewed him—the only sibling in the city when the Bomb fell—as "one of the lucky ones" (HB 191-192). In combination with his time spent in Hiroshima among other aging *hibakusha*, the conversation with his niece forces Mas to look at his personal history more positively than he previously had. As his thoughts about his own life become less critical, his attitudes toward Shukkeien and the legacy of Hiroshima's atomic bombing become not only more reverential but more hopeful.

Shukkeien—Hopeful and Holy Ground

For 70 years, Mas has been shackled by PTSD forged by the atomic bombing. Trauma from the ordeal has made him wary of others, dismissive of his own worth, and skeptical about the future. He has survived by moving to California and working hard to "remove the sting of deep thoughts, at least for a short time" (BB 20). But Hiroshima provides no refuge from the past. During his visit, he must attend to emotional wounds and graft them to more comforting thoughts and experiences, so he can head into the future unburdened.

Accompanying Mas on his return to Hiroshima are the cremains of his closest friend, Haruo Mukai, a fellow *kibei* gardener from Los Angeles. Like Mas, Haruo survived the bombing of Hiroshima but keloid tissue and a false eye made concealing the experience impracticable for him. Despite living with highly visible reminders of Hiroshima, Haruo was an optimist. Mas understands that for *hibakusha* "to live with hope required the highest level of courage" (HB 46-47), and he had great admiration for Haruo's positive attitude. At the same time, Mas knows that he hasn't exhibited similar courage. Though not visibly disfigured by the atomic bombing, he has been emotionally scarred by the experience, and his first days back in Hiroshima, which included a trip to Shukkeien, were colored by the cynicism and guilt he has been living with since August 6, 1945.

After spending time with his niece in the familiar setting of his parents' home and garden, the "damage" and "darkness" that Mas sensed during his initial visit to Shukkeien (HB 72) have turned to thoughts of survival and beating the odds. In the final pages of the novel, Mas drops by Shukkeien once more. This time, however, he isn't alone. With Haruo's ashes in tow, he walks first to the stone memorial commemorating the victims of the Bomb and, from there, he finds his way to "a low-standing display box" sheltering "a wooden Buddha" (HB 211).

Figure 2: Jyūō-dō at Shukkeien.
Photo by Kyoko Matsunaga.

Like Haruo, Mas, and the statue of Shinran in *Gasa-Gasa Girl*, this wooden sculpture is a survivor. Suspected to have been fashioned around 1100 CE, the carved figure inside the altar has endured flood and the atomic bombing of Hiroshima (HB 212).[13] Although Hirahara makes no mention of the following details in the text, this venerable statue embodies more than just "a" Buddha. The figure represents one of the Ten Kings/Judges in the Afterlife who determine the path to rebirth.[14] Unconcerned with such nuances, Mas views the Jyūō-dō "as good a place as any" and sprinkles some of Haruo's remains at the site before walking to the river's edge to set the rest "free" (HB 212). Haruo isn't the only one released in this moment. Mas, who has always felt the sacred manifest in nature (GG 118), is once again free to appreciate the beauty of Shukkeien and see it as a hopeful and holy space.

Acknowledgements

This chapter is the result of research supported by the Japan Society for the Promotion of Science, Grants-in-Aid for Scientific Research (KAKENHI Grant Number 20H01245). A Japanese version of this article was previously published in *American Studies Now: Crises and Hopes* (Tokyo: Sairyusha, 2023).

Notes

[1]   In *Hiroshima Boy*, the final book of the series, Hirahara reveals that the Arai family lived in Kure, not Hiroshima City. Though the family home is outside the city, at the time of the atomic bombing, Mas was working at Hiroshima Station with a few of his schoolmates.

[2]   Lifton (1991) was originally published by Random House in 1968.

[3]   Mrs. Witt describes the failed grafts as "a damn killing field" (BB 44). Many readers will associate the phrase with the mass graves of the millions executed by Pol Pot's Cambodian government in the 1970s, but when Mas feels sick after seeing "the broken branches jutting out . . . like severed arms and legs" (BB 46), he seems to be recalling Hiroshima.

[4]   Hereafter this novel *Strawberry Yellow* will be cited parenthetically as SY.

[5]   These feelings of betrayal continue to haunt Mas in subsequent novels. In *Gasa-Gasa Girl*, Hirahara writes: "Mas remembered when he abandoned his friends after the Bomb

fell. He felt as though he had killed them, too. And that guilt burned in his gut for close to a lifetime" (266).

[6] For a deeper understanding of Hayashi Kyōko's "radioactive anxiety," see pages 67-71 of Matsunaga (2018).

[7] Transmitted trauma is also known as generational trauma, hereditary trauma, inherited trauma, intergenerational trauma, secondary traumatization, and transgenerational trauma.

[8] Hersey (2001) was originally published as the entire issue of *The New Yorker* on August 31, 1946. <https://www.newyorker.com/magazine/1946/08/31/hiroshima> (accessed on November 30, 2020).

[9] "Beautiful Shukkeien Garden," Shukkeien Garden Brochure; "Shukkeien Garden— An Absolute Must Do in Hiroshima," <www.intrepidscout.com/lost-in-reverie-sublime-shukkeien-garden-hiroshima/> (accessed on February 2, 2022).

[10] Most publications, including the pamphlet produced by the landscape garden itself, romanize the name of the garden as "Shukkeien." Hirahara uses "Shukkei-en" as Carolyn Forché does in the poem cited at the beginning of this chapter.

[11] Hirahara's description of the "Buddha" as "lithe," "dainty," and "almost feminine" (HB 187-188) leaves open the possibility that it is a representation of Kannon Bosatsu (Avalokiteśvara), the Bodhisattva of Compassion, one of Amida Buddha's attendants.

[12] In December 1941 approximately 20,000 "American citizens of Japanese ancestry" were living in Japan, and an estimated 3,000-4,000 of them were living in Hiroshima (Wake 2021: 3-4).

[13] According to the interpretive sign at the site of the Reisekidan (Jyūō-dō) in Shukkeien.

[14] According to Teiser, the kings managed various passages through Hell before rebirth could occur (Teiser 1988: 433-434).

References

Crèvecoeur, J. Hector St. John de (1997) *Letters from an American Farmer.* Oxford: Oxford University Press.

ETH Zurich (2014) "Hereditary Trauma: Inheritance of Traumas and How They may be mediated," *ScienceDaily*, April 13. <www.sciencedaily.com/releases/2014/04/140413135953.htm> (accessed on Feb 2, 2022).

Forché, Carolyn (1995) *Atomic Ghost: Poets Respond to the Nuclear Age.* Minneapolis, MN: Coffee House Press.

Gillespie, Claire (2020) "What Is Generational Trauma? Here's How Experts Explain It," *Health,* October 20. <www.health.com/condition/ptsd/generational-trauma> (accessed on February 2, 2022).

Hauglann, Maria Wulff (2021) "Autumn Colors at the 400 Years Old Shukkeien Garden, Hiroshima," *Nerd Nomads*, April, 29. <https://nerdnomads.com/shukkeien-garden-hiroshima> (accessed on February 2, 2022).

Hersey, John (2001) *Hiroshima.* London: Penguin Classics.

Hirahara, Naomi (2004) *Summer of the Big Bachi.* New York: Delta Trade Paperback.

Hirahara, Naomi (2005) *Gasa-Gasa Girl.* New York: Delta Trade Paperback.

Hirahara, Naomi (2013) *Strawberry Yellow.* Pasadena, CA: Prospect Park Books.

Hirahara, Naomi (2018) *Hiroshima Boy.* Pasadena, CA: Prospect Park Books.

Hiroshima for Global Peace (2020) "The Reconstruction of Shukkeien Garden and Hiroshima [an interview with Okabe Kikuo]," Hiroshima for Global Peace. <hiroshimaforpeace.com/en/the-reconstruction-of-shukkeien-garden-and-hiroshima/> (accessed on February 2, 2022).

Jacobs, Robert A. (2022) *Nuclear Bodies: The Global Hibakusha.* New Haven: Yale University Press.

Lifton, Robert Jay (1991) *Death in Life: Survivors of Hiroshima.* Chapel Hill: University of North Carolina Press.

Matsunaga, Kyoko (2018) "Radioactive Discourse and Atomic Bomb Tests: Ōta Yōko, Hayashi Kyōko, and Sata Ineko," in Hisaki Wake, Keijiro Suga, and Yuki Masami, (eds.), *Ecocriticism in Japan.* Lanham, MD: Lexington Books, pp. 63-80.

National Park Service (2004) "A History of Japanese Americans in California: Patterns of Settlement and Occupational Characteristics." *Five Views: An Ethnic Historic Site Survey for California* California Department of Parks and Recreation, Office of Historic Preservation, Dec. 1988. NPS.gov, November 17. <https://www.nps.gov/parkhistory/online_books/5views/5views4b.htm> (accessed on February 10, 2022).

Senshin Buddhist Temple (n.d.) "About Jodo Shinshu," *Jodo Shinshu Buddhism: The True Essence of the Pure Land Teaching.* <https://senshintemple.org/teachings/jodoshinshu-buddhism/> (accessed on February 2, 2022).

Teiser, Stephen F. (1988) "'Having Once Died and Returned to Life': Representations of Hell in Medieval China," *Harvard Journal of Asiatic Studies,* 48 (2), pp. 433-464.

Wake, Naoko (2021) *American Survivors: Trans-Pacific Memories of Hiroshima & Nagasaki.* Cambridge: Cambridge University Press.

Wellerstein, Alex (2020) "Counting the Dead at Hiroshima and Nagasaki," *Bulletin of the Atomic Scientists,* August 4. <https://thebulletin.org/2020/08/counting-the-dead-at-hiroshima-and-nagasaki/> (accessed on February 2, 2022).

World War II Magazine (2020) "The Statue That Survived an Atomic Bomb," *World War II Magazine,* Aug 14. <https://www.historynet.com/the-statue-that-survived-an-atomic-bomb/> (accessed on February 2, 2022).

Yehuda, Rachel and Lehrner, Amy (2018) "Intergenerational Transmission of Trauma Effects: Putative Role of Epigenetic Mechanisms," *World Psychiatry,* 17 (3), pp. 243-257.

Chapter 10
(Post)Colonial Atomic Bomb Literatures: Reimagining the Mining Narrative in Han Su-san's *Battleship Island*

Kyoko Matsunaga

1. (Post)Colonial Readings of Atomic Bomb Narratives

On September 29, 2017, an International Workshop entitled "Reading Atomic Bomb Literatures from Perspectives of East Asia" was held at Yeungnam University in Daegu, Korea. Perhaps the first international workshop to explore the possibilities of "East Asian" Atomic Bomb literatures, the workshop examined issues including representations of Korean *hibakusha* in Japanese Atomic Bomb literature, the presence/absence of Korean writings that feature Korean *hibakusha*, a nuclear narrative by an indigenous Taiwanese writer, and the "invisibility" of Okinawan *hibakusha* in literature.

Although the panelists' concerns and approaches varied, there seemed to be a consensus that close examination of the representations (or absence) of "East Asian" *hibakusha* opens a "shared space" for Atomic Bomb narratives that are not limited to "Japanese experiences." Takayuki Kawaguchi, one of the panelists of the workshop, points out how narratives surrounding the atomic bomb experiences in Hiroshima and Nagasaki have often functioned as "collective memories" that have supported the idea of "national identity" in "post-war Japan" (Kawaguchi 2018: 13-14). While the "collective memories" have contributed to strengthen the idea of *hibakusha* "victimhood"—especially that of Japanese—they have obscured connections between *hibakusha* experiences and colonial history. *Hibakusha* experiences, of course, have a relation to Japan's colonization of East Asia. It is no coincidence that about 50,000 people from the Korean Peninsula were exposed to the bomb in Hiroshima, and about 20,000 Koreans experienced the Nagasaki bomb—making almost 10 percent of *hibakusha* people of Korean descent (Ichiba 2000: 27-28). Shoya Unoda, another panelist, states that colonialism, which is inseparable from Korean *hibakusha*'s atomic bomb experiences, helps shape the cognitive framework of Atomic Bomb literatures (Unoda 2018: 20).

The social and literary movement to foreground the connections between the atomic bombs and colonialism started in the late 1960s. For example, Takashi Hiraoka, a former journalist and Hiroshima mayor, had covered stories of Korean *hibakusha* since 1966 and had been involved in the redress movement for Korean *hibakusha* from the beginning. In a seminal article published in 1977, Hiraoka draws attention to the difference between Japanese *hibakusha* testimonies and Korean *hibakusha* testimonies. The former often start from the moment the bomb was detonated while the latter generally start on the day they left, or had been taken from, their homeland:

> The first time I encountered a memoir of Korean *hibakusha* was the summer of 1968. Memoirs of Japanese *hibakusha* often start from "that morning." But Korean *hibakusha* start their stories with "why I came to Japan." This difference is at the core of the issue surrounding Korean *hibakusha*. … The fact that Japanese accounts about the atomic bombs start from "that day"—or the fact that they have been edited in such a way—means nothing but exoneration from the past by breaking off the history before August 6th and by positioning themselves as victims. (Hiraoka 1983: 54, 56)

Hiraoka's comment reveals more than mere "difference" between the narratives of Japanese and Korean *hibakusha*. By noting how (1) Korean *hibakusha* memoirs **include** an explanation of why the authors came to Japan while (2) Japanese *hibakusha* memoirs **exclude** mention of the past before August 6th or 9th of 1945, Hiraoka sees Japanese colonialism— explicitly or implicitly—embedded in both. Hiraoka's insight deconstructs the central axiom that Atomic Bomb Literature starts from the morning of August 6, 1945: Atomic Bomb narratives are shaped by events taking place in East Asia long before "that morning."

This paradigm shift helps us examine the "invisibility" of *hibakusha* in East Asia apart from Japanese *hibakusha*. Referring to the "indifference" to or the "absence" of Korean *hibakusha* in Korean Literature, Kim Munji, another panelist in the workshop, emphasizes that the "subaltern" position of Korean *hibakusha* also relates to the general idea in Korea that the atomic bombs "liberated" East Asia from Japanese colonization. Kim also sees that "the atomic bombs are a pandora box of emotions driven into the corner inside Koreans. In it exists compassion for pain as well as resentment against Japan" (Kim 2018: 33). Although Kim does not specify *whose* "pain," he suggests that the "pain" caused by the atomic bombs dropped by America is inseparable from Japanese crimes and sins of colonization in East Asia, obscuring the individual "pain" of *hibakusha,* including that of Korean *hibakusha*. Reconfiguring Atomic Bomb Literature as (post)colonial literature, which inevitably carries the burden and legacies of colonial history in East Asia, offers opportunities to explore complex layers of individual experiences in East Asia, which are inseparable from both the violence of the Nuclear Age and the violence of colonization.

Although uncommon, Korean writers have attempted to create narratives that highlight the intersection of the atomic bomb's impact and the violence of colonial history. For example, in the above-mentioned workshop, Kim Munji introduced Ko Hyeong-ryeol's epic poem *Little Boy* (1995) and Han Su-san's novel *Battleship Island* (2003/2009).[1] Both works foreground the lives of individual Koreans in Hiroshima or Nagasaki and Korea before "that morning." While Kim lauds *Little Boy*, he criticizes *Battleship Island*. Referring to the film adaptation of *Battleship Island* (2017), Kim attributes the negative reaction to the film to the original novel: "by deploying typical characters of the time to the events on Battleship Island," "the realities of forced labor are masked" (35).[2] Kim condemns the novel's depiction of the Korean miners' "strong desire" to escape the island, the greed of pro-Japanese Koreans and Korean traders eager to benefit from other Koreans, and the "goodwill" of Japanese characters who interact with Koreans "in good faith" (35-36). It is undeniable that some characters in *Battleship Island* are depicted stereotypically to distinguish the different types of people living under Japanese colonization. That said, re-examination of the novel as a (post)colonial atomic bomb narrative offers more than dismissing it for its drawbacks.

Inspired by the images and representations of Korean *hibakusha* by Japanese artists and writers, Han Su-san's *Battleship Island* follows the footsteps of the social and literary movements in Japan since the late 1960s. As Iori Kurokawa points out, the existence of Korean *hibakusha* had become broadly known to the public after the Japan-Republic of Korea Basic Relations Treaty in 1965 was signed, and the depiction of discrimination toward Korean *hibakusha* became common in Atomic Bomb Literature in Japan around the end of the 1960s (Kurokawa 2015: 259). But Han Su-san's novel goes beyond merely representing Korean *hibakusha* "victimhood." Based on testimonies of Korean *hibakusha* as well as voluminous historical records detailing the poverty, discrimination, forced labor, and miners' lives under colonization from the nineteenth century, *Battleship Island* depicts the mine as a dynamic colonial space where various conflicts, alliances, and acts of resistance take place.

The experiences of Korean *hibakusha* depicted in Han's mining narrative evoke comparisons to experiences endured by Indigenous people in Africa, Australia, and North America. In his poetry collection, *Fight Back: For the Sake of People, For the Sake of the Land* (1980), Simon J. Ortiz, an Acoma Pueblo poet from New Mexico, tells stories of uranium miners in the American Southwest. In poems and essays, Ortiz reveals how the US government, corporations, and scientific communities have exploited Indigenous Americans and their territories during the nuclear age. In Ortiz's poetry, uranium mines are sites where different races intersect, cheap labor is exploited, and conflicts/alliances/resistance surface. Just as *Battleship Island* positions Korean *hibakusha* experiences as an extension of Japan's colonization of East Asia, Ortiz portrays the experiences of Indigenous miners as a brief episode in the longer history of the region's colonization at the hands of government, military, and industrial concerns.

This chapter will examine how Han Su-san's *Battleship Island* disrupts the "master narrative" of existing Atomic Bomb Literature by viewing it through the lens of East Asian colonial history. The novel goes beyond the "fixed" images of Korean *hibakusha*, dispicts mines as layered and complex colonial spaces, and offers possible links between (post)colonial East Asian Atomic Bomb Literatures and (post)colonial nuclear narratives in the American Southwest.

2. Crows and Miners: Reconfiguring Representations of Korean *Hibakusha*

In the process of creating *Battleship Island*, Han Su-san was strongly influenced by the testimonies of Korean *hibakusha* and miners via works of Masaharu Oka, a Japanese pastor and the leader of the Association to Protect the Human Rights of Zainichi Koreans in Nagasaki. As Han commented on several occasions, he learned about Korean *hibakusha* for the first time in 1989 when he encountered booklets entitled *Atomic Bombs and Koreans* published by the Association to Protect the Human Rights of Zainichi Koreans in Nagasaki.[3] Since then, Han traveled to Battleship Island (Gunkanjima) with Oka and So Jungwoo, a former miner and *hibakusha* from Gyeongsang Province in Korea.[4] According to Han, the first scene of the novel comes from words So expressed when they visited Battleship Island together in 1990: "Over there is homeland. Across the ocean. Can't remember how many times I thought about it" (Gil 2015). Based on the works of Oka, and testimony of Korean miners/*hibakusha*, Han constructed a fictional story about an actual island where about 500 Koreans worked as coal miners near the end of WWII.

The novel is also informed by the work of Japanese artists, writers, and *hibakusha*. *Crows*, the title of an earlier version of *Battleship Island*, is inspired by one of fifteen Hiroshima Panels created by two Japanese artists, Iri Maruki and Toshi Maruki. *Crows,* a 6 x 24 feet panel painted by the Maruki's, depicts a horde of crows surrounding bodies of *hibakusha* and a white *chima* and *jeogori* ("a skirt" and "shirt" traditional Korean women's clothing). The Maruki's include the following explanation to the panel:

Koreans and Japanese look alike.
In those mercilessly charred faces,
how can one see a difference?

"After the Bomb, the bodies of the Koreans
were left on the streets to the very last.
Some were alive but few. Nothing to be done.
Crows descending from the sky. Hordes of crows.
Coming down to eat the eyes of the Koreans.
Eat the eyes."

Beautiful chima chogori (sic).
Flying through the sky to Korea the homeland.
We respectfully offer this painting.
We pray.[5]

The words in the quotation marks above originally come from the work of Michiko Ishimure, a Japanese writer known for her creative non-fiction about Minamata disease. Maruki's *Crows* was influenced by the description of Korean *hibakusha* and crows in Ishimure's writing.

After completing *The Death of American Prisoners of War* (1971) as Hiroshima Panel #13, the Maruki's felt the need to paint Korean *hibakusha*. They were at a loss, however, since they did not know how to distinguish Koreans from other *hibakusha*. When the Maruki's expressed their concern to Rinjirou Sodei, who had introduced their Hiroshima Panels to the United States in 1970, he recommended they read Ishimure's essay "Chrysanthemum and Nagasaki: Silence of the Remains of Korean *Hibakusha*," which was published in the *Asahi Journal* on August 11, 1968 (Iri Maruki, Toshi, Tsutomu Mizukami 1984: 34). In her essay, Ishimure writes about her visit to Joukouin temple where she heard the remains of Korean *hibakusha* were left, her visit to a hospital to meet a Korean *hibakusha* who was a former miner, and what it means for Koreans to speak Japanese, a colonizer's language.[6] Ishimure also inserts the "voices" of Korean *hibakusha* spoken in Nagasaki dialect: the quotation cited in the Maruki's explanation is one of them.

Although the crows in the painting can be traced back to Ishimure's essay, *chima* and *jeogori* are not mentioned in her essay. In fact, speaking in the "voice" of a Korean *hibakusha*, Ishimure emphasizes the difficulties of finding names of Koreans killed by the bomb: "how can we identify [who's who]? The lists of names were turned into ashes by the bomb. Some died without leaving any bones" (314). Still, the "voice" of Korean *hibakusha* in Ishimure's essay continues to explain that she could tell that the bodies pecked on by crows were Koreans: "we could tell that they were Koreans by where they were placed. They were placed there when they were alive. As if in a prison" (314). This part of Ishimure's essay is omitted from the caption to the painting by the Maruki's. Toshi Maruki explains later that to make it recognizable that the bodies were Korean they decided to include images of *chima* and *jeogori* (Iri Maruki, Toshi, Tsutomu Mizukami 1984: 36). In other words, the painters added *chima* and *jeogori* to *Crows* so viewers of the painting can identify the *hibakusha* in the panel as Koreans.

The powerful imagery of *Crows* is included in Han's novel as well. Jisang, a Korean miner who barely escapes the island, is exposed to the atomic bomb in Nagasaki and witnesses how *hibakusha* who utter Korean words are ignored by the Japanese rescue teams in the ruins. Korean *hibakusha* are not given food or water, they do not receive any treatment, and their bodies are deserted in the aftermath of the destruction. On these Korean bodies, Jisang sees the crows gather:

The bodies that had been left behind until the last were Koreans, too. At a glance, they could be mistaken as Japanese, but from the torn clothes, they were identified as Koreans. The relief corps had sorted out by listening to their moaning words such as "Aigoo" or "Omoni." Then on the deserted Korean bodies, crows flew over

one by one. Under the sweltering August sun, the black crows
swarmed over the decaying Korean bodies. They perched on the
faces, broke the skin and pecked the eyeballs. Koreans were
discriminated against even after they became dead bodies. (Han
2009, vol. 1: 461)

Koreans in this scene are identified by their "torn clothes" and by "moaning
words such as 'Aigoo' or 'Omoni.'" Although "Aigoo" and "Omoni" are
not mentioned by the Maruki's nor in Ishimure's essay, as Iori Kurokawa
points out, in testimonies by Japanese *hibakusha*, Koreans were often
identified by their use of Korean words or the way they spoke Japanese
(255-57). The word "Aigoo" is effectively used in Kenji Nakazawa's
Barefoot Gen (1975-87), one of the most popular atomic bomb comic books
in Japan, as well.[7] In it, doctors postpone treatment to Mr. Pak's father once
they recognize he is Korean by his uttering the word "Aigoo" (Nakazawa
2004: 167). Han's representation of crows and Korean *hibakusha*, then,
faithfully reflects images employed by Japanese artists and writers as well
as *hibakusha* testimony.

It is undeniable that Ishimure's essay, the paintings of the Maruki's, and
Nakazawa's comic book have played an important role in exposing
discrimination against Korean *hibakusha*. Their works have been
instrumental in making Korean *hibakusha* visible to the public. Nevertheless,
as Kurokawa points out, there must have been many other Koreans who
have died without being recognized as Koreans: "some [Koreans] lived as
Japanese with Japanese names under Japanization policies, some spoke
fluent Japanese in order to survive, and others just disappeared without even
uttering a word" (254).

While their tragic representations of Korean *hibakusha* are often in the
spotlight, Han's predecessors—the Maruki's, Ishimure, and Nakazawa—
were conscious of what had happened before "that day" as well. The
Maruki's include the following "note" to the end of their explanation to
Crows: "In the Mitsubishi Shipyards in Nagasaki, there were forced laborers
from Korea numbering more than 5000. There were also many Korean

forced laborers in Hiroshima" (87). In her essay, Ishimure includes Korean "voices" who mention those who died before being exposed to the bomb or explain the reason why Koreans became *hibakusha*: "It's not only the atomic bomb why people died. There were many before that" (337); "Why do you think we were brought here? For Japan and Korea as one. For winning the war. For the country. Not my country. For which country were we brought here?" (341). In Nakazawa's *Barefoot Gen*, Mr. Pak similarly confronts a doctor by saying, "Doctor, we were forced to come to Japan. Yet we've fought right alongside you in this war. We've worked as hard as you for this country!" (167). Although these references are often incidental to the powerful images of Koreans killed by the atomic bombs, Han highlights the history before the bombings in his novel and links the Korean characters' bomb experiences to the longer history of colonization.

Han uses the images of crows not only to depict discrimination against Korean *hibakusha*, but also to explore diverse colonial experiences of Korean miners in Nagasaki before the bomb. In Han's novel, crows are usually not welcomed by Korean characters: they "spit" when they see crows cawing over their heads (Han vol. 1: 29, 145). At one point, the relationship between Koreans and crows is compared to the way Japanese treat Korean miners. Gil Nam, a Korean who came to Japan following his father and works for an "arranger" to transfer Koreans, explains, "Once you are out in the villages, the children will throw rocks at you saying, '*Chosenjin, Chosenjin* (Koreans, Koreans).' It's the same as how we spit when we see crows in Korea" (Han vol. 2, 231). The novel, however, suggests that Koreans are not necessarily considered to be above crows in colonial Japan. Dong-Jin, one of the miners, complains that even the crows disparage Koreans, when bird droppings almost hit him (333). Tsuyoshi Kusuda points out that the novel draws a comparison between Korean miners whose faces are black "with coal dust and sweat" and crows (Han vol.1: 17; Kusuda 2013: 204).[8] There are several scenes where miners joke about how crows think of miners as cousins, brothers, or grandfathers (Han vol.1: 19, 379; Han vol.2: 344). Han uses these imagined similarities between crows and Korean miners to reinforce how some Koreans are opportunists or scavengers, like crows, who take advantage of other Korean miners. In *Battleship Island*, then, the imagery of crows effectively highlights the colonial structure under which communities of Korean miners are simultaneously united and divided.

Like the imagery of the crows in Han's novel, flock of birds are repeatedly conjured up in Ko Hyeong-ryeol's *Little Boy* (1995). Crows, for instance, are compared to 200 heavy bombers in a Tokyo air raid, which "dropped countless bombs/ many of which looked like America's excrement" (52). In Ko's poem, which features Korean characters who had been living in Hiroshima before the bomb, the cry of seagulls evokes "a sense of freedom" as well as an "ominous feeling": "in the far too transparent noon sky/ they by chance forgot that they are in the middle of war/ seagulls need to fly away somewhere quickly/ they resembled souls of something /whole bodies were stiffened with tension and goosebumps" (Ko 2006: 22). Ko's seagull imagery is echoed in *Battleship Island*. At the beginning of the novel, when Thae-bok tells Myong Guk that he is thinking of escaping the island, Myong Guk thinks: "whether it was a seagull crying or a crow flying by, they all look like souls of Koreans. Those tattered souls, who lost their country, seem to fly by like that without being able to go back home, because they are tied up with a string and cannot leave here" (Han vol.1: 8). In both Han's novel and Ko's poem, images of birds embody "souls" who long for freedom to go back home, but are unable, being imprisoned in Japan.

3. Colonial Mining Narrative in *Battleship Island*

Han is not simply inspired by the images of crows in works by Ishimure and the Maruki's; he reimagines them, seeing them through the eyes of Korean miners. To illustrate the diverse experiences of the Korean miners, Han also inserts numerous accounts of colonial history in his novel. For example, he explains how the Japanese invasion of Korea started after Qing China recognized the "full and complete independence and autonomy" of the Kingdom of Korea in the 1895 Treaty of Shimonoseki (Han vol.1: 159). In 1908, two years before the Japanese annexation of Korea, the Oriental

Development Company began sending immigrants to Korea from Japan, making Korea a "new promised land" for impoverished Japanese farmers (244). After the Japanese annexation of Korea, Japan had deprived Korean farmers of their land, forcing them leave their homeland (39). Han writes, "they (Japanese) didn't care at all if one Japanese immigrant to Korea meant five Koreans' loss of land and displacement" (244). For Korean farmers deprived of their land, moving to Japan was their only hope to survive. Some of the Korean miners on Battleship Island, including Myong Guk, one of the main characters in the novel, were dispossessed farmers who came to Japan on their own accord to escape poverty back home.

Other miners had been coerced or tricked into coming to Japan to work. Han devotes pages of his book describing how the Japanese government brought Korean laborers to Japan after the National Mobilization Law of 1938—first in the name of "recruitment," then "official mediation" and finally "drafting." Han emphasizes how the Japanese government colluded with Japanese industries to make this happen: "Japan made monopoly capital—represented by Mitsui, Mitsubishi, Sumitomo, and Noguchi (Japan Chisso)—plot the use of cheap labor and natural resources in Korea. They didn't have any sense of guilt" (Han vol. 2: 362). To fill in the lack of workers in Japan during war, mining and civil engineering companies "recruited" or forcibly brought Koreans to Japan. These tactics were supported by the Japanese government as a national policy. Mitsubishi Mining, for instance, set a target number of laborers to recruit from Korea every year and forced them to work in the mines. To achieve recruitment goals, they collaborated with the Japanese government, police, and pro-Japanese Korean groups such as "Kyowakai" (Han vol. 1: 181-82).

Based on historical documents and testimony from former Korean miners, Han creates stories about the various ways Korean miners in the novel ended up on Battleship Island. Seong-sik, one of the characters, is a 16-year-old Korean farmer, who had been tricked into coming to Japan by a manager of "recruitment." Even pro-Japanese Korean families, who had been involved in "recruitment," are not completely exempt from "drafting." Jisang, another one of the main characters of the novel, is brought to

Battleship Island despite his father's cooperation with the imperial forces. His father had helped send other Korean youths to Japan so that he could avoid sending his sons. Nevertheless, he loses Jisang, the younger son, to expropriation. Whether having been forced by economic circumstances, tricked, or conscripted, the individual background stories of the Korean miners show that leaving their homeland to work in Japan is a result of Japan's colonization of East Asia and is enabled by the Japanese government's collusion with a corrupt capitalist system.

Han's novel also illustrates how the Japanese colonial system divided Korean communities, much to the detriment of the Korean miners. This point is highlighted in the book when Han introduces different phases in the history of Korean miners in Japan. Coal mines were one of the top priorities as Japan extended their control over territories in East Asia. Between 1909 and 1916, Koreans looking for jobs started to move to Japan and worked at coal mines across the nation. Later, some Korean miners who had acquired Japanese language skills became managers who hired, recruited, and supervised other Korean miners working for Japanese companies. By recruiting impoverished and dispossessed Koreans to work in Japanese mines, the Korean managers considerably improved their material circumstances (Han vol. 1: 271-73). For instance, Han describes how the Korean miners who brought laborers from Korea lived in apartments alongside Japanese workers rather than among the Koreans they recruited to work on Battleship Island (280). "Recruited" or "conscripted" Korean miners, on the other hand, lived in quarters located in the lowest and dampest part of the island (10). They were also given "hard and dangerous jobs" at the mine including blasting open mine shafts (68).[9] The novel reflects the obvious divide and hierarchy between Koreans who had started to live in Japan earlier and those who had been "recruited" or forced to come to Japan later. Han also points out in the novel that divisions among Koreans were further deepened by organizations such as "Kyowakai." Originally started by Korean labor leaders, "Kyowakai" was endorsed and controlled by the Japanese government in order to supervise and Japanize Koreans under surveillance of Japanese police (Han vol. 2: 221-23). In other words, the Japanese government used Korean labor leaders to help control Korean laborers in Japan. Han describes the system as the "ingenious dichotomization of Koreans in Japan" (223).[10]

The division among the Korean miners is complex, much more than a simple dichotomy. The novel particularly focuses on the dilemma of Jisang, who speaks Japanese fluently due to his pro-Japanese father's influence. After escaping Battleship Island, Jisang is aided by an elderly Japanese man, Egami, who finds a job for Jisang to teach Japanese at Nagasaki Shipyard owned by Mitsubishi. Ironically for Jisang, working at Nagasaki Shipyard means supporting war effort to expand Japanese control in East Asia. In fact, Nagasaki Shipyard constructed *Musashi*, the biggest battleship in the world at the time, and had made 80 percent of torpedoes used during the Pacific War (Han vol. 2: 172). In order to survive, Jisang takes the teaching job at Nagasaki Shipyard, but he is troubled by the idea of teaching Japanese to fellow Koreans:

> Learning Japanese will force Koreans to obey. But, on the other hand, it will improve the lives of fellow Koreans who had been forced to come to Japan and suffer. Because they don't understand the language, they have been beaten. Also, countless people died because they didn't understand Japanese: they froze when they were told to run from danger. (104)

Teaching Japanese could save lives of Koreans as they daily face physical abuse and harsh working conditions at mines, shipyards, and military factories in Japan. However, it also supports Japan's "imperialization policy," which forced Koreans to use Japanese and to adopt Japanese names. Jisang succeeds in escaping Battleship Island, but he cannot escape the influence of colonialism. In order to survive, he is compelled to support the system that subjugates him and other Korean people.

In *Battleship Island*, Han depicts the mine as a multicultural space, characterized by racial hierarchy and a lack of international alliances. In addition to Japanese and Korean miners, Chinese and American POWs also reside at the mine site.[11] Like the Koreans, Chinese and American POWs are isolated from Japanese miners. While there is usually no interaction between the Korean miners and the Chinese and American POWs, there is one occasion in the novel when Jisang exchanges words with a Chinese miner who says to him, "I can go back home for sure because China will definitely defeat Japan" (Han vol. 1: 254). In the Chinese miner's words, Jisang senses national pride and a different attitude toward the war. There is a chasm between the thinking of Koreans and Americans in the novel as well. Dong-jin, who speaks a little English, shows explicit prejudice against Americans, especially against a Black POW: "Looking at Westerners who gather in a corner, Dong-jin thought what monsters they are. Above all, at a glance, Dong-jin couldn't help laughing at the black man standing in the middle of the crowd. Is he human? His black body was covered with coal dust. The only thing he could recognize were bloodshot eyes and white teeth. They looked like they were floating in air" (252). Unaffected by Dong-jin's racist gaze, the POW refuses to work as hard as other miners, claiming that he is a prisoner of war (rather than a miner), whose status is protected by international agreement (252-53).

Although Battleship Island is a place marked by racial, national, and political division among miners, Han focuses on Korean miners who rise in rebellion and alludes to actual revolts, disputes, and strikes involving Korean miners. Acts of Korean resistance mentioned by Han include the following: 27 Koreans in Gyeongsangnam-do armed with bamboo spears and hoes who resist being taken to Japan; a large strike at Takamatsu coal mine owned by Nissan Chemical Industries; riots at Aso Mine and Furukawa Mine after Korean miners were murdered in 1943 (Han vol. 1: 77-78; Han vol. 2: 331-32). According to the Association to Protect the Human Rights of Zainichi Koreans in Nagasaki (2016), there is no record of riots by Korean miners on Battleship Island (131). However, as former Korean miners testify, Korean miners attempted to escape the island on several occasions, despite the danger of drowning or being tortured if caught (29, 37, 44, 72). Although there is no actual record of an uprising on Battleship Island, Han imagines revolts by Korean miners in the novel, associating them with the actual attempts of escape.

There are at least two memorable scenes in the novel where Korean miners revolt against Japanese miners and Korean labor leaders. The first occurs when Thae-bok is tortured by Japanese labor officers after his attempted escape: Thae-bok stabs one of the officers in the throat and is eventually sent to a prison in Nagasaki (Han vol. 1: 31). The second revolt is conducted by a large group of Korean miners in response to a murder of a Korean miner by a Japanese labor officer and the death of Kumfa, a Korean woman, who had been horribly tortured by Japanese. During this large-scale strike, several Korean miners attempt escape and succeed. Significantly, the two major revolts in the novel occur along with attempts to escape the island. The literary scholar Kim Jeonghun explains its significance as follows:

> There are four times when Korean forced laborers attempt to escape. For them … the fiercest resistance against Mitsubishi Mining workers and laborers, who forcefully promote coal mining, must have been to escape from the island, risking their lives. … Before a full-blown uprising occurs, there are attempts to escape, and we can consider them as part of the process of the uprising. The last escape is carried out at the same time when the uprising occurs. It is impossible to prescind escapes from the uprising. (Kim 2019: 243-44)

As Kim suggests, escaping the island is one of the only ways for the Korean miners to resist, and some resort to it despite the risks. By imagining an uprising among Korean miners and associating it with actual attempts of escape, Han opens up space to envision Korean miners' resistance on Battleship Island, even if only in literarily.

Han's efforts to blend fiction and history can be seen in other parts of the novel as well. The scene where Korean miners repeatedly use the word "Ollagaja! (Agarou!)" (Han vol. 1: 222-25) is one of them. In the western part of Japan, there is a ritual to call out, "Agarou! (Let's go up!)" when a miner dies in a mine so that the soul of the dead will not continue to wander around the place. Accordingly, when one of the Korean miners dies in an accident, fellow Korean miners call out, "Let's go up!" But they refuse to say "Agarou!" in Japanese. Instead, they call out, "Ollagaja!" in Korean. Their action might not change the harsh working and living conditions on Battleship Island, but Han imagines a "spiritual" resistance of Korean miners who deliberately switch languages so that their fellow miner's soul can be guided out of the mine. As Kusuda points out, "the novel can be read as words that guide the dead souls of Korean miners and *hibakusha* out from oblivion" (204).

4. Imagining Transpacific Mining Narratives in a Nuclear Age

Resistance in Han Su-san's mining narrative echoes that of *Fight Back* (1980) by the Acoma Pueblo poet, Simon J. Ortiz. *Fight Back* is a poetry collection based on Ortiz' experiences of working at the Ambrosia Lake uranium mine, which opened during the 1950s near Acoma Pueblo in New Mexico. In *Fight Back*, Ortiz writes about how Acoma and Laguna Pueblo miners were sent to work at the bottom of the mine, where they face more danger than other miners, while they had been placed at the bottom of social ladder outside of the mine.[12] While discussing how Indigenous people have been involved in nuclear production, Ortiz criticizes the ways in which the U.S. government collaborates with industry to make this happen. Even though the jobs at the mines meant creating "bombs and reactors" (Ortiz "Stuff: Chickens and Bombs," 30), "when the exploited Okies, West Virginians, and oilfield workers from the Gulf were trying to get organized," Indigenous people worked as "surplus labor" because "for poor people with low education and no skills and high unemployment, that is the important thing: a job" (Ortiz "No More Sacrifices," 68). While uranium mines were inseparable from national endeavors during the Cold War, Ortiz points out that they are part of the history of the colonization of Native America, which had been taking place in the American Southwest since the sixteenth century. Like Han's novel, which attempts to deconstruct the "master narrative" of the atomic bombs, Ortiz's *Fight Back* recasts the history of the US nuclear narrative by viewing it through the lens of Pueblo history. For the Acoma Pueblo people, nuclear narratives did not start when the world's first nuclear test was conducted at Trinity Site on July 16, 1945. Nor did it start when the atomic bombs were developed at Los Alamos during the 1940s. It started when the people of Acoma Pueblo had been dispossessed of their land, natural resources, religion, and culture after Spain's conquest of the American Southwest more than four centuries ago.

Ortiz does not shy away from illustrating how Indigenous people have been discriminated against or excluded from worker disputes or strikes much of the time; however, he imagines alliances among the workers, evoking the Pueblo Revolt that occurred more than 300 years ago. As a matter of fact, *Fight Back* was written for the Tricentennial commemoration of the 1680 Pueblo Revolt, which was "organized and led by Pueblos" and "joined by mestizos, mulattoes, by captive Indians from many Tribes, by the Mexican Indians brought by the Spanish to New Mexico as servants, by Navajo and Apaches who were hunted down by Spanish slave merchants" (Dunbar-Ortiz "Preface"). In response to the subjugation of Indigenous people in the American Southwest, Ortiz imagines mining narratives where poor whites, Blacks, Mexicans, and Indigenous people forge relationships and work together "to change in a good way" ("To Change in a Good Way," 17).

Acoma Pueblo experiences in Ortiz's poetry and Korean miners' experiences in Han's novel have different cultural and historical backgrounds. That said, these mining narratives from different sides of the Pacific offer possibilities to disrupt "collective memories" of the atomic bombs and nuclear history, going beyond a monolithic "national identity" in "post-war Japan" and America.

Acknowledgements

This chapter is the result of research supported by the Japan Society for the Promotion of Science Grants-in-Aid for Scientific Research (KAKENHI Grant Number 20H01245).

Notes

[1] *Little Boy* was published in 1995 in Korea, and its Japanese translation was published in Japan in 2006. According to Kim Jeonghun, Han Su-san started to publish an earlier version of *Battleship Island* entitled *The Sun Rises, The Sun Sets* as a series in a Korean newspaper from 1993. When it ended up, in Han Su-san's words, as "a miserable failure," he rewrote the story, keeping only the first scene of the novel. Ten years later, it was published in Korea as *Kkamagui* (*Crows*) (Kim 2019: 237, 239). *Battleship Island* [Gunkanjima], which is a translated and compressed version of *Crows*, was published in 2009. In the "Commentary" to *Battleship Island*, Minato Kawamura explains that the omitted parts mostly include Japanese culture and history which Han assumed the audience in Japan would be familiar with (Kawamura 2009: 480-81). The Korean version of *Battleship Island* (*Gunham-do*) was published in Korea in 2016. Battleship Island is known as *Hashima* or *Gunkanjima* in Japanese. Claiming that it looks like the battleship *Tosa*, some started to call it "Gunkanjima" (Battleship Island). Gunkanjima is about 0.1 square kilometers in size and located 18.5 km away from Nagasaki port (The Association to Protect the Human Rights 1986: 33; The Association to Protect the Human Rights 2016: 21).

[2] Released two years after Hashima was designated as one of 23 "Sites of Japan's Meiji Industrial Revolution: Iron and Steel, Shipbuilding and Coal Mining" for the UNESCO World Heritage List, the film *Battleship Island* was created during the controversy over its inclusion because of the forced labor that took place on the island. For more information about the controversy, see Kimura (2013, 2014). For a detailed analysis of the film *Battleship Island*, see Choi and Sakamoto (2021).

[3] There are five volumes of *Atomic Bomb and Koreans* (1982-1986). Han had been living in Japan when he encountered the booklets at a used bookstore in Tokyo (Han 2017).

[4] So's testimony is included in the second volume of *Atomic Bomb and Koreans* (69-77). Han also interviewed So (Han 2015).

[5] Translations by Nancy Hunter with Yasuo Ishikawa, Kimie Itakura, TRANSNET (Maruki Gallery for the Hiroshima Panels 1972: 87).

[6] According to Kurokawa, the remains include those of former Korean miners who died before the atomic bomb. For more details, see Kurokawa (2015).

[7] For an analysis of the representations of "Korean A-bomb Victims" in *Barefoot Gen*,

see Kawaguchi (2010).

[8] Kusuda provides a thorough analysis of the representations of crows in *Battleship Island*. See Kusuda (2013).

[9] Han's references here are based on Oka's work and testimonies by former Korean miners (The Association to Protect the Human Rights 1983).

[10] For information about "Kyowakai," see Higuchi (1986) and Matsumoto (2019).

[11] According to the Association to Protect the Human Rights of Zainichi Koreans in Nagasaki (2016), after 1944 there were 204 Chinese POWs on Battleship Island, and most of them were farmers (121). As a couple of former Korean miners testify, it was not allowed for Korean miners to interact with Chinese miners, and "Chinese were treated worse than Koreans" (37, 449).

[12] For a more detailed analysis of *Fight Back*, see Matsunaga (2019).

References

The Association to Protect the Human Rights of Zainichi Koreans in Nagasaki (1983) *Genbaku to Chousenjin* [Atomic Bomb and Koreans], vol. 2. Nagasaki: The Association to Protect the Human Rights of Zainichi Koreans in Nagasaki.

The Association to Protect the Human Rights of Zainichi Koreans in Nagasaki (1986) *Genbaku to Chousenjin* [Atomic Bomb and Koreans], vol. 4. Nagasaki: The Association to Protect the Human Rights of Zainichi Koreans in Nagasaki.

The Association to Protect the Human Rights of Zainichi Koreans in Nagasaki (2016) *Gunkanjima ni mimi o sumaseba* [Listening to Voices from Battleship Island]. Enlarged and Revised Version. Tokyo: Shakai Hyoronsha.

Choi, Yuujin and Sakamoto, Rumi (2021) "Battleship Island and the Transnational Dynamics of Cultural Memory between South Korea and Japan," *Inter-Asia Cultural Studies*, 22(3), pp. 298-315, DOI: 10.1080/14649373.2021.1962092

Dunbar-Ortiz, Roxanne (1980) "Preface." *Fight Back: For the Sake of the People, For the Sake of the Land*. INAD Literary Journal.

Gil, Yun-hyeong (2015) "Kankou no shima to kashita 'chousenjin no jigokujima' ["Hell Island for Koreans" Turned into Tourist Island]," *Hankyoreh* (June 11), <http://japan.hani.co.kr/arti/politics/20976.html>

Han, Soosan [Su-san] (2009) *Gunkanjima* [Battleship Island], vol. 1 and vol. 2. Translation supervised by Minato Kawamura. Translated by Akiko Yasuoka and Aki Kawamura. Tokyo: Sakuhinsha.

Han, Su-san (2017) Interview. *Korean JoongAng Daily* (August 16), <https://japanese.joins.com/JArticle/232377>

Higuchi, Yuuichi (1984) *Kyowakai: senjika chousenjin tousei soshiki no kenkyuu* [Kyowakai: Study on Korean Control Organization during the War]. Tokyo: Shakai Hyoronsha.

Hiraoka, Takashi (1983) *Muen no kaikyou* [Strait without Support]. Tokyo: Kageshobo.

Ichiba, Junko (2000) *Hiroshima o mochikaetta hitobito* [People Who Brought Back Hiroshima]. Tokyo: Gaifusha.

Ishimure, Michiko (1968) "Kiku to Nagasaki: hibaku chousenjin no ikotsu ha mokusita mama" [Chrysanthemums and Nagasaki: The Remains of Korean Atomic Victims Are Still Silent], *Ishimure Michiko Zenshu* (2004), vol. 1. Tokyo: Fujiwara Shoten.

Kawaguchi, Takayuki (2008) *Genbaku to iu mondai ryouiki.* [Problematique called Genbaku Bungaku]. Osaka: Sougensha.

Kawaguchi, Takayuki (2010) "Barefoot Gen and 'A-Bomb Literature': Re-Recollecting the Nuclear Experience," translated by Nele Noppe. *Global Manga Studies*, 1, pp. 215-225.

Kawaguchi, Takayuki (2018) "Genbaku bungaku kenkyuu no genjou to kadai: higashi ajia to iu shiten kara [Current Situation and Problems of Studies of Atomic Bomb Literature: From East Asian Perspective]," International Workshop: Reexamining Atomic Bomb Literature from East Asian Perspectives, Osaka University Knowledge Archive, pp. 13-18. <http://hdl.handle.net/11094/68042>

Kawamura, Minato (2009) "Commentary," *Gunkanjima* [Battleship Island], vol. 2. Translation supervised by Minato Kawamura. Translated by Akiko Yasuoka and Aki Kawamura. Tokyo: Sakuhinsha, pp. 469-481.

Kim, Jeonghun (2019) *Sensou to bungaku: kankoku kara kangaeru* [War and Literature: From Perspectives of Korea]. Osaka: Kanyou Shuppan.

Kim, Munji (2018) "Kioku no seijigaku to kokkyou o kesu kurushimi no rentai [Politics of Memories and Alliances of Suffering that Erase National Boundaries]," International Workshop: Reexamining Atomic Bomb Literature from East Asian Perspectives, Osaka University Knowledge Archive, pp. 31-38. <http://hdl.handle.net/11094/68042>

Nakazawa, Keiji (2004) *Barefoot Gen*, vol. 2. Translated by Project Gen, San Francisco: Last Gasp.

Kimura, Shisei (2014) *Sangyou isan no kioku to hyoushou: "Gunkanjima" o meguru politikkusu* [Memories and Representations of Industrial Heritage: Politics Surrounding "Gunkanjima"]. Kyoto: Kyoto University Press.

Kimura, Shisei (2018) "Ikou o toushite kangaeru 'tankou' to 'genbaku' [Thinking about Coal Mines and the Atomic Bomb through Remains]," *Genbaku Bungaku Kenkyu*, 17, pp. 67-75.

Kurokawa, Iori (2015) "Hibaku taiken ki ni kakareta chousenjin hibakusha no sugata: 1970 nendai made [Representations of Korean Hibakusha in Atomic Bomb Testimonies: Up to the 1970s]," *Genbaku Bungaku Kenkyuu*, 14, pp. 251-263.

Kusuda, Tsuyoshi (2013) "Chousenjin hibakusha o 'kataru': Han Su-san *Gunkanjima* no baai ["Talking" about Korean Hibakusha: The Case of Han Su-san's *Battleship*

Island]," *Genbaku Bungaku Kenkyu*, 12, pp. 195-204.

Matsumoto, Kunihiko (2019) "'Kyowakai' to kouminka undou no shisouteki haikei: senjika no zainichi chousenjin seisaku [Ideological Background of "Kyowakai" and the Imperialization Movement: Zainichi Korean Policies during the War]," *Yamagata Daigaku Kiyou*, 50 (1), pp. 23-49.

Matsunaga, Kyoko (2019) *Hokubei senjuumin bungaku to kaku bungaku: apokalipusu kara sabaibansu e* [American Indigenous Writers and Nuclear Literature: From Apocalypse to Survivance]. Tokyo: Eihosha.

Ortiz, Simon J (1980) *Fight Back: For the Sake of the People, For the Sake of the Land.* INAD Literary Journal.

Unoda, Shoya (2018) "Genbaku bungaku to chousenjin hibakusha/ zaikan hibakusha: Mishou Hiromi no shigyou o chuushin ni [Atomic Bomb Literature and Korean Hibakusha/ Zainichi Hibakusha: Focusing on Mishou Hiromi's Poetry]," International Workshop: Reexamining Atomic Bomb Literature from East Asian Perspectives, Osaka University Knowledge Archive, pp. 19-28. <http://hdl.handle.net/11094/68042>

Chapter 11
Space and Time of Atomic Bomb Memorials and Monuments in Urban Hiroshima

Gen Tagawa

1. Landscape with Memorials and Monuments in Hiroshima

In Hiroshima city, Peace Memorial Park—where the Cenotaph for the Atomic Bomb Victims (officially named "Hiroshima Peace City Memorial"), Peace Memorial Museum, and the Atomic Bomb Dome are located—is a commemorative space representing the historical tragedy that occurred in Hiroshima on August 6, 1945. For this reason, sociological and historical research on the collective memory of the damage and loss caused by the atomic bombing of Hiroshima and the subsequent reconstruction of the city has focused primarily on the A-bomb Dome and Peace Memorial Park.

Peace Memorial Park is not the only place to commemorate the victims of the atomic bombing and to pray for peace. There are numerous memorials to the victims of the atomic bombing across the entire city of Hiroshima, creating a public space that commemorates this tragic historical event. However, the memorials to the victims of the atomic bombing that exist throughout the city have not been adequately examined. For this reason, in order to clarify how a public space that represents the destruction and carnage caused by the atomic bombing on August 6, 1945 has been constructed, this chapter focuses not only on the Peace Memorial Park, but also on the memorials to the victims of the atomic bombing erected in a public space.

In this chapter, memorials and monuments refer to man-made or natural objects in public spaces that represent the damage caused by the atomic bombings. They include buildings constructed after the bombing to represent the damage caused by the atomic bomb, buildings and trees recognized by the Hiroshima City authorities as having been exposed to the atomic bomb, and explanatory signs in the city center explaining the damage caused by the atomic bomb.

This chapter focuses on how these memorials and monuments representing the A-bomb damage have been created throughout the city, including Peace Memorial Park, focusing on the process of construction over time and their spatial arrangement. The first section will review previous monument studies and examine two main theoretical frameworks. The second section will focus on Peace Memorial Park to clarify the characteristics of its memorial space. The final section will discuss the construction process and spatial arrangement of memorials spread across the urban area of Hiroshima.

2. Memorial and Monument Studies

In recent years, a number of studies have been published in cultural anthropology, history, religious studies, and sociology that focus on memorials and monuments. In particular, studies of war-related monuments have been conducted in Okinawa, Hiroshima, Nagasaki, and areas that were battlefields during the World War II (cf. National Museum of Japanese History ed. 2003; Kitamura 2009; Murakami and Nishimura 2013, etc.). This chapter is part of this stream of research on war monuments.

Mainly in historical research, monuments are treated as mediators that represent past events in a different way from historical documents. Mitsuhiro Wada considers monuments as permanent memory devices inscribed in the landscape, not only representing public memories, but also reproducing and transforming them. Because monuments are often constructed in places related to past events, they are considered to have a strong ideological and message-mediating function, and thus monument studies use the concepts of collective, social, or cultural memory (Wada 2005). Those concepts of the memory mean "shared memories" or "shared narratives" of past events in a "community" and the memory is created and transformed through a process of recalling and forgetting.

Marita Sturken (1997: 45-84), in her analysis of Vietnam War monuments, quotes Danto (1985), who distinguishes between monuments and memorials:

> We erect monuments so that we shall always remember, and build memorials so that we shall never forget…Monuments commemorate the memorable and embody the myths of beginnings. Memorials ritualize remembrance and mark the reality of ends…The memorial is a special precinct, extruded from life, a segregated enclave where we honor the dead. With monuments we honor ourselves (Danto 1985: 152).

Sturken (1997: 47-8) goes on to say that while most monuments show victory and are anonymous with few "explanatory notes," memorials "represent lives and lives sacrificed for a particular value system" and are accompanied by "lists of the dead and special texts."

These words are also cited by Tsuyoshi Kitamura in his analysis of post-World War II memorials in Okinawa. He states that this does not necessarily apply to Okinawan monuments (Kitamura 2009: 113-5). According to Kitamura (2009:114-5), the monuments on Mabuni Hill in Okinawa are characteristic of both memorials, which "honor the dead," and monuments, which "honor ourselves" for the economic triumph of Japan's postwar economic growth.

On the other hand, Kitamura (2009:114) states that the "Cenotaph for the Atomic Bomb Victims" in Hiroshima Peace Memorial Park can be regarded as a typical memorial. However, it is officially called "Memorial Monument for Hiroshima, City of Peace" inscribed with a few impressive words: "Let all the souls here rest in peace; For we shall not repeat the evil." There are also other memorials to the victims of the atomic bombing in Hiroshima, even for the purpose of memorialization, which are not accompanied with some special texts.

Furthermore, in some cases, they are later accompanied by eloquent explanatory notes, as Hiroshima City installed an explanatory board in Japanese and English at the Hiroshima Peace City Monument in 1983 in order to "accurately convey" the content of the inscription (The Hiroshima

City 2019a).[1] This means that their signification changes according to political, economic, and social contexts. Not all artifacts can be divided into what Sturken (1997) calls memorials or monuments, but they may include both characteristics as Kitamura (2009) points out, and their signification must differ depending on who faces to the monument.

Therefore, it is necessary not only to see monuments as expressions of the intent of their builders from the viewpoint of "strong ideological and message-mediating functions (Wada 2005)," but also to grasp what is being practiced by the act of constructing the monument in process.

To this end, it is important to focus on the relationship between monuments representing past events and the landscape that includes their places. Kenneth E. Foote sees the landscape itself as "a sort of communicational resource, a system of signs and symbols, capable of extending the temporal and spatial range of communication" (Foote 2013: 33). He then focused on the relationship between culture, social, or collective memory and landscape with regard to historical events in American society, and pointed out that the landscape of places where violent or tragic events occurred can be changed along a continuum, which he divided into four categories: sanctification, designation, rectification, and obliteration (Foote 2013: 7).

"Sanctification" refers to the construction of memorials and monuments and the performance of rituals at places in order to perpetuate the memory of events, while "obliteration," on the other hand, refers to the desire to forget events and to erase any trace of them (Foote 2013: 7). The intermediate patterns between these two opposites are "designation" and "rectification." The former means that the place in question is memorialized but not sanctified, and the latter refers to the process of "restoring the tragedy to its normal state" and using the place again (Foote 2013: 7). However, it should be noted that while these four patterns described by Foote (2013) indicate the process of "memory" or "forgetting" of historical events, this process is not unidirectional, and people's attitudes toward events vary depending on the social context. It should be noted that these processes are not unidirectional, and that people's attitudes toward the events vary depending on the social context.

Within this framework, I would like to present and discuss the memorials that represent the A-bomb damage in the city of Hiroshima and its surrounding areas. First, we will focus on Hiroshima Peace Memorial Park, the city's central memorial space.

3. Peace Memorial Park

3.1. Memorial and Monumental Space

Peace Memorial Park is the ritual center of postwar Hiroshima. The ritual center means that it is the place where Peace Memorial Ceremony is held by the Hiroshima City every year on August 6. The official name of this ceremony has two names coexisting, "Memorial Ceremony for the Atomic Bomb Victims of the Hiroshima City and Peace Memorial Ceremony," and each has intrinsically a different purpose. The former is to console the souls of those lost to the atomic bombing, and the latter to pray for the realization of lasting world peace. This means that the act of commemorating the victims of the atomic bombing is transformed into sending a message of lasting world peace in Peace Ceremony. It is possible because of the self-evident fact that Hiroshima has been reconstructed and at peace.

This is evident from the fact that Hiroshima Peace Memorial Park was built in accordance with the Hiroshima Peace Memorial City Construction Law, which was enacted for the purpose of "the construction of the city of Hiroshima as a peace memorial city to symbolize the human ideal of sincere pursuit of genuine and lasting peace" on August 6, 1946 (Hiroshima City [City Planning Division of Urban Development Bureau] 2022). Hiroshima Peace Memorial Museum website describes the Peace Memorial City Construction Law as an essential part of the postwar reconstruction of Hiroshima as follows:

> Soon after the war, many plans were proposed for Hiroshima's recovery. In 1946, the city adopted a reconstruction plan, but implementation was hampered by financial and other difficulties. To overcome these obstacles, Hiroshima's municipal government

sought assistance from the national government and secured passage in 1949 of the Hiroshima Peace Memorial City Construction Law. This law promoted the construction of peace memorial facilities, including Peace Memorial Park, as well as roads, bridges, and other urban infrastructure. As land redevelopment progressed and barrack-style housing disappeared, Hiroshima's appearance improved dramatically (Hiroshima Peace Memorial Museum 2022).

The enactment of this special law enabled Hiroshima City to benefit from the free disposal of state-owned land and to achieve postwar reconstruction.

The proposal of Japanese Architect Kenzo Tange was adopted for the design of the Peace Memorial Park. It, however, was essentially designed based on the same concept as the "Greater East Asia Memorial Construction and Management Plan", which praised the Greater East Asia Co-prosperity Sphere (Inoue 1987; Yoneyama 1999). To use Sturken's words, the design of the monument to commemorate the victory of Japanese imperialism was appropriated as a monument to the "beginning of postwar" Hiroshima and its reconstruction under the Peace Memorial City Construction Law, rather than a memorial representing "the end of war and its sacrifice."

However, when Peace Memorial Park began to be built, the area was still devastated with no trees, and there were some barracks in which residents lived, and the A-bomb Dome was also regarded as a "horrific remain" in the early postwar period (Hamada 2014: 23-4; Fukuma 2015a: 131-134; 2015b: 15-22). Thus, Peace Memorial Park could not actually become a monument at that time.

The transformation of Peace Memorial Park into a monument was promoted by the reconstruction of the urban area that included the elimination of the barracks that had been built inside and outside the park. The A-bomb Dome, initially left in ruins and not treated as a monument, became a monument through a preservation movement that began in the mid-1960s (Hamada 2014; Fukuma 2015a; Fukuma 2015b).

As the Peace Memorial Park was being developed as a monument, three memorial elements came into being. The first is the exhibits and texts of the atomic bombing at Peace Memorial Museum. While the building itself within the park is a monument, the exhibits and texts inside it which eloquently describe the damage and loss are characterized as memorials. The second is the list of the dead that is placed in the stone chamber of the Cenotaph for the Atomic Bomb Victims[2]. The third is the memorials and cenotaphs constructed in and around Peace Memorial Park. While the first and second memorial elements are hidden from the park landscape, the third type of monument—the cenotaphs and memorials—have proliferated individually with various intentions, and are not uniform in size, material, or design, and are considered foreign in terms of park design. The most heterogeneous of these memorials is the A-bomb Memorial Mound. The heterogeneity of this monument stands out when compared to the Cenotaph for the Atomic Bomb Victims, which is the centerpiece of Peace Memorial Park.

3.2. Comparison of the Three Memorials

The stone chamber of the Cenotaph for the Atomic Bomb Victims, located in the center of Peace Memorial Park, holds a list of those who died in the bombing. On the other hand, the Atomic Bomb Memorial Mound— located in the northwest section of the park—places the remains of mostly unidentified and unclaimed dead (see Photo 1).

Immediately after the disaster, the precincts of Jisenji Temple—located near the present A-bomb Memorial Mound—were used as a temporary crematorium (Horikawa 2015; Hiroshima City 2019b). The Society for Memorial Services for the War Dead, which was established to collect the remains of the dead scattered throughout the city and hold memorial services, constructed a memorial tower, which was a predecessor of the "A-bomb Memorial Mound," in May 1946 (Hiroshima City 2019b)[3,4]. It was made of papier-mâché due to the lack of wood at the time. In July of the same year, a barracks ossuary and chapel were built with the donations of citizens. And on August 6, 1946, a joint memorial service was held in front of the memorial tower, and memorial services have been held annually since then (Hiroshima City 2019b). The present A-bomb Memorial Mound was built in July 1955, and the remains collected in the city were placed in its chamber, including those found during the construction of Peace Memorial Park, roads and other facilities for the reconstruction of the city (Hiroshima City 2019b). By the end of 1955, several tens of thousands of unidentified remains as well as the remains of 2,434 known victims were deposited there, and memorial services for these remains are held annually on August 6 by various religious groups (Hiroshima City 2019b).

Initially, the remains of the A-bomb victims were planned to be placed in the basement of a cenotaph to be built in Peace Memorial Park (Fukuma 2015b: 37-39; Horikawa 2015: 33-40). However, the Ministry of Construction did not approve the construction of an ossuary in Peace Memorial Park which was officially planned as an urban park. Instead, authorities opted to store a list of A-bomb victims there (Fukuma 2015b; Horikawa 2015). In 1950, a petition was submitted to the mayor of Hiroshima requesting the reconstruction of the aging memorial tower (a predecessor of the A-bomb Memorial Mound), but since the it was located in the planned Peace Memorial Park, the city requested that it be moved off site, and reconstruction at the same location was not easily approved (Horikawa 2015). Therefore,

Photo 1: A-Bomb Memorial Mound on 6 August

the A-bomb Memorial Mound which kept remains was marginalized in the park.

Although both the Cenotaph for the Atomic Bomb Victims and the Atomic Bomb Memorial Mound are a memorial sites for mourning the victims, they are in many ways contrastive. A lists of the dead is stored in the Cenotaph for the A-bomb Victims, while the A-bomb Memorial Mound houses mostly unidentified remains. In addition, while the list in the cenotaph is updated each year with the deaths of A-bomb survivors, there is not such list in the latter. Finally, the list is kept by the city authorities, but the individual names are not publicly displayed. Some of the names of the remains are made public in search of claimants, but most are unidentified remains, and as such are never officially registered their names, and are placed in the ossuary which legally should not be in a city park. These remains continue to be commemorated by religious figures, not by administrative authorities.

Hiroshima National Peace Memorial Hall for the Atomic Bomb Victims was established in 2002 (Hiroshima National Peace Memorial Hall 2022). Visitors see the names and images of the victims in it, and such an exhibition is a different way to commemorate the victims of the atomic bombing than the previous memorials to those directly connected with the victims. There, visitors can come face to face with named portraits of A-bomb victims, and learn about their experiences through audio, video, and text. It is a memorial filled with voices, images, and the written word, not just a list of names of victims.[5] The Peace Memorial Hall for the Atomic Bomb Victims is a memorial site that functions as a complement to the Cenotaph for the Atomic Bomb Victims.

On the other hand, the A-bomb Memorial Mound is a memorial site in which remains of the unidentified dead are kept, and there is no narrative about the dead because they are unidentified. It is precisely in this respect that the A-bomb Memorial Mound differs from the memorial with a "list of dead". It is a site where the memorial the deaths of anonymous victims must forever observed.

4. Memorials and Monuments in Postwar Hiroshima

As mentioned earlier, various memorials and monuments have been constructed in Peace Memorial Park and its vicinity. There are 50 memorials and monuments listed on the website of Hiroshima City (2019c). Other Hiroshima city websites show 61 memorials and monuments with a map of the park and its vicinity (2022a). What does it mean that over 50 memorials and monuments have been created in and around Peace Memorial Park alone? Memorials and monuments are not limited to Peace Memorial Park and its vicinity, but can be found throughout the city. This section will focus on memorials and monuments throughout the city.

4.1. Changes in the Number of Memorials and Monuments Constructed

First, I would like to analyze the date and number of monuments constructed in the urban area of Hiroshima and the surrounding area. Based on the literature survey and field research conducted to date, a total of 217 monuments have been identified. A five-year comparison of the number of monuments constructed since 1945 is shown below (See, Table 1 and Figure 1).[6]

Sixteen memorials and monuments were constructed in total between 1945 to 1949: 21 from 1950 to 1954; 26 from 1955 to 1959; 19 from 1960 to 1964; 27 from 1965 to 1969; 19 from 1970 to 1974; 21 from 1975 to 1979; 11 from 1980 to 1984; 10 from 1985 to 1989; 11 from 1990 to 1994; 14 from 1995 to 1999; eight from 2000 to 2004; 11 from 2005 to 2009; and three from 2010 to 2014.

The data shows a decline in the number of memorials and monuments constructed since 1980. This is assumed to be due to the fact that a sufficient number of them had been constructed by then, as well as the death and aging of the generation with war experience responsible for constructing many of the memorials and monuments.

Table1: Number of Memorials and Monuments Constructed

year	number
1945-49	16
1950-54	21
1955-59	26
1960-64	19
1965-69	27
1970-74	19
1975-79	21
1980-84	11
1985-89	10
1990-94	11
1995-99	14
2000-04	8
2005-09	11
2010-14	3
total	217

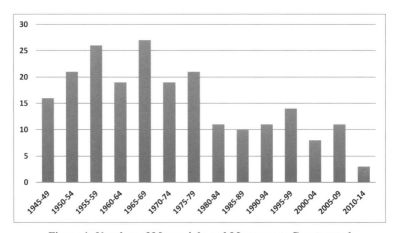

Figure 1: Number of Memorials and Monuments Constructed

4.2. Classification and Comparison of Memorials and Monuments

In this section, the above-mentioned memorials and monuments are divided into five categories: 1) memorials to school teachers, staff, and students; 2) memorials to colleagues in the workplace; 3) memorials to local community residents; and 4) comprehensive memorials reflecting a

Table 2: Number of Memorials and Monuments Constructed by Category

year	school	workplace	community	peace
1945-54	12	9	8	6
1955-64	8	7	8	15
1965-74	6	14	12	7
1975-84	4	6	7	8
1985-94	2	3	4	5
1995-2004	2	2	6	8
2005-14	1	1	2	8
	35	42	47	57

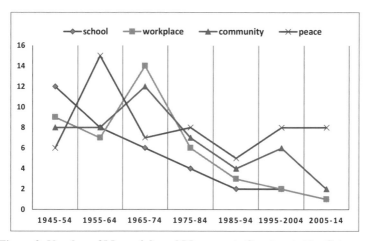

Figure 2: Number of Memorials and Monuments Constructed by Category

desire for peace. Those that did not fit into any of the four categories above were classified as 5) others.

The number of monuments constructed in each since 1945 of the first four categories is shown in the following table (see Table 2 and Figure 2).

The number of memorials constructed for school teachers, staffs, and students ("school memorials") is 35 in total: 12 from 1945 to 1954; eight from 1955 to 1964; six from 1965 to 1974; four from 1975 to 1984; two from 1985 to 1994; two from 1995 to 2004; and one from 2004 to 2015.

The number of memorials constructed for colleagues in the workplace ("workplace memorials") is 42 in total: nine from 1945 to 1954; seven from

1955 to 1964; 14 from 1965 to 1974; six from 1975 to 1984; three from 1985 to 1994; two from 1995 to 2004; and one from 2004 to 2015.

The number of memorials constructed for local community residents ("community memorials") is 47 in total: eight from 1945 to 1954; eight from 1955 to 1964; 12 from 1965 to 1974; seven from 1975 to 1984; four from 1985 to 1994; six from 1995 to 2004; and two from 2005 to 2014.

The number of monuments of comprehensive memorials and desire for peace ("peace monuments") is 57 in total: five from 1945 to 54; 15 from 1955 to 1964; seven from 1965 to 1974; eight from 1975 to 1984; five from 1985 to 1994; eight from 1995 to 2004; and eight from 2005 to 2014.

A comparison of the number of memorials and monuments constructed by category shows that school monuments were most frequently constructed in the decade following the end of the war, and then the number drops off. The number of workplace monuments constructed was the highest between 1965 and 1974 during the late period of rapid economic growth in postwar Japan. The same is true for community monuments, with the highest number (12) constructed in the decade from 1965. The number of monuments constructed in the next two decades decreased, but increased again between 1995 and 2004. The largest number of peace monuments was constructed between 1955 and 1964, but unlike other categories, peace monuments have been constructed continuously with more eight constructed in the period from 2005 to 2014.

It is understandable that school, workplace, and community memorials were constructed to commemorate and memorialize the people associated with their respective organizations. It can be imagined that the reason schools were the first to construct memorials was because monuments were requested by people who lost their children, and it can also be assumed that they needed to provide emotional stability in a school. On the other hand, in the case of workplaces and local communities, the momentum for constructing memorials probably grew after a certain degree of public and economic stability. In this sense, the construction of memorials by such organizations is a monumental act that shows the subsequent recovery as well as the memorial to the victims.

Less easy to interpret are peace monuments constructed without the purpose of memorializing specific people. Many monuments have been constructed in the Peace Memorial Park and its vicinity, beginning with the Cenotaph for the Atomic Bomb Victims in 1952 (officially named the Hiroshima Peace City Monument) and then. This is inevitable in Peace Memorial Park, a space that symbolizes "the human ideal of sincere pursuit of genuine and lasting peace" (Hiroshima City [City Planning Division of Urban Development Bureau] 2022). Furthermore, the reason why so many peace monuments have been constructed from 1945 to the present is that the objective for building the monuments is not achieved by their construction. Construction of monuments to commemorate specific victims decreases in number over time as their purpose is fulfilled, leaving peace monuments, which do not target specific people, as the only monuments that can be constructed. This is reasons for constructing monuments dedicted global "everlasting peace" will never be lost.

Nakamura (2008)—who studied the Nagasaki A-bomb memorials—points out that the number of monuments constructed with the "grave function" of memorializing victims—with whom the builders had direct ties to (who were of the generation that experienced the war)—has decreased over the years, while those with the "function to record a place" and "function to convey peace" have increased in recent years. Using Nakamura's words "function to convey peace," it can be pointed out that in Hiroshima, the importance of monuments with the "peace message" has relatively increased as monuments with a rather "grave function" have been fulfilled.

With the Peace Memorial City Construction Law of 1949, Hiroshima has achieved its goal of reconstruction, which is a synonymous to peace. Therefore, Hiroshima City must continue to convey its desire for peace in perpetuity. As part of this, the city government started a project to construct new monuments that aim to "convey the reality of the atomic bombing," as distinct from memorials for the comfort and remembrance of specific people.

5. New Monuments

The previous section highlighted the transition in the construction of monuments from 1945 to the present, and revealed that the purpose of building monuments has changed from commemorating specific people to expressing a rather abstract desire for peace.

After a peak in the five-year period from 1965 to 1969, the number of memorials constructed declined, especially during the decade from 1985 to 1994 when only a few new memorials were constructed. While construction of monuments has thus slowed to a crawl, Hiroshima City began a project to create new monuments. This section will show that the new monuments constructed by Hiroshima City strengthen the connection between the past event of the atomic bombing and specific places—providing a specific perspective to view the landscape—and thereby creating a spatial image of Hiroshima City that extends in concentric circles from the hypocenter.

5.1. Explanation Board of the A-bomb Damage

In 1980, Hiroshima City began installing "Explanation Board of the A-Bomb Damage" with photographs and explanatory text at various locations in the city (see Photo 2). These boards were installed by the Hiroshima city government "in order to convey the reality of the atomic bombing to as many people as possible and to pass it on from generation to generation" (Hiroshima City 2020). The first of these was installed at "the hypocenter (Shima Hospital)," and in the same year, a total of nine other boards were installed (e.g., "Hondori Shopping Street," "Hiroshima Station," "Fukuromachi Elementary School," "Hiroshima Red Cross Hospital," etc). Ten boards were installed in 1981, ten in 1982, three in 1990, two in 1991, two in 1992, and two in 1999, for a total of 45 by 1999. By 1999, a total of 45 information boards had been installed in the city (Hiroshima City 2020).

For example, the following explanatory text was attached to each board along with a photograph of the damage:

Photo 2: Explanation Board of the A-bomb Damage

Hypocenter
Carried to Hiroshima From Tinian Island by the Enola Gay, a U.S. Army B-29 bomber, the first atomic bomb used in the history of humankind exploded approximately 580 meters above this spot. The city below was hit by heat rays of approximately 3,000 to 4,000 °C along with a blast wind and radiation. Most people in the area lost their lives instantly. The time was 8:15 a.m., August 6, 1945. (View of devastation looking north from hypocenter, November 1945. Photograph by U.S. Army)

Fukuro-machi National People's School (elementary school)(460 meters from the hypocenter)
The school's wooden buildings were completely destroyed and burned by the atomic bombing at 8:15 am on August 6, 1945, leaving only the outer shelf of the three-storied west building, a reinforced concrete structure. Just after the morning assembly, nearly 160 people, including children who had not evacuated and school staff, were exposed to the bombing and almost all died.

After the bombing, the west building was turned into a relief station. During that time, many people wrote messages on the walls of the stairwell passing on the latest news of survivors' whereabouts.

(West building used as a relief station with straw mats in place of windowpanes. October 1945. Photo by Shunkichi Kikuchi)

Onaga Temple (approx. 3,360 meters from the hypocenter)
Though Onaga Temple stood about 3,360 meters northeast of the hypocenter, the severe blast of atomic bomb destroyed the roofing of the temple. Many people who escaped the burning city took refuge in the Onaga area. There injured were given first aid treatment.

(The destroyed Onaga Temple October 20, 1945. Photograph by Shunkichi Kikuchi)

The distance from the hypocenter is marked along with the location. The farthest board from the hypocenter is Onaga Temple.

By reading the photographs and the explanatory text, the landscape of "a street corner you casually pass by" (Hiroshima City 2020) is transformed into something different. However, the landscape shown there is not the difference between before and after the destruction caused by the atomic bomb, but the present landscape after the destruction and reconstruction. The intent of the "A-Bomb Damage Information Board" may be to "record the place," as Nakamura (2008) suggested earlier, but it can rather be seen as an intermediary to monumentalize the landscape of the reconstructed Hiroshima city center.

5.2. A-bombed Buildings and Trees

As mentioned earlier, from 1985 to 1994, the number of monuments constructed to show the damage caused by the atomic bomb reached a plateau, but in 1993, Hiroshima City established the "Guidelines for the Project for the Preservation and Succession of A-bombed Buildings," which registers buildings remaining from the time of the bombing within five kilometers of the hypocenter (Hiroshima City 2019d).

The atomic bomb devastated about 90 percent of the buildings, and the remaining buildings were rebuilt over time (Hiroshima City 2019d). In 1993, 30 A-bombed buildings were registered, and by 1994, the number had risen to 98. As of October 31, 2019, 86 buildings have been registered, 20 of which are publicly owned and 66 of which are privately owned (Hiroshima City 2019d).

Hiroshima City also registers trees (within a radius of approximately two kilometers from the hypocenter) that were damaged by the atomic bomb but did not die by the bombing as A-bombed trees (Hiroshima City 2019d). Hiroshima City bases the two kilometer criterion on reports that about 50 percent of the trees within two kilometers of the hypocenter had their trunks broken, but no trees were damaged beyond two kilometers (Hiroshima City 2019d). Currently, approximately 160 trees are recognized as A-bombed trees in 56 locations within a radius of about two kilometers from the hypocenter (Hiroshima City 2019d).[7]

Like buildings that were exposed to the atomic bomb, A-bombed trees are also marked with an explanatory plaque (see Photo 3). As with the aforementioned "A-bomb Damage Information Board," the distance from the hypocenter is indicated on the board. This distance is a condition for official recognition by Hiroshima City as an A-bombed building or tree, and is the standard for indicating the extent of the damage. For this reason, when an A-bombed building or tree is shown on a map, a concentric circle is always drawn one kilometer (or 500 meters) from the hypocenter, and each monument is plotted within the circle.

5.3. Spatial Organization of the Experience of the Atomic Bomb Damage

Regarding A-bombed buildings, physicists Hiromi Hasai and Kazuo Iwatani have described them as "evidence of radiation exposure," noting that traces of radiation exposure can still be detected physically on buildings today. Similarly, radiation exposure "causes invisible destruction at the

Photo 3: A-bombed Tree

atomic and molecular level inside the body," resulting in health problems (Hasai and Iwatani 1996).

However, people's various experiences of the atomic bombing are not identical to the physical phenomena. The same can be pointed out for A-bombed buildings and trees, where the physical damage to the building or tree itself does not necessarily correspond to the experience of the people in that location. This is because the actual spatial configuration of urban areas and people's ways of life are inherently independent of the concentric shapes of radiation exposure. According to Yoneyama (1999: 92-7), however, not only is the damage caused by the atomic bomb judged by calculating the difference in spatial and temporal proximity from the hypocenter, but even the memories of the witnesses are mediated by the visual image of the city map depicting concentric circles from the hypocenter.[8]

Yoneyama's point (1999: 92-7) also applies to Hiroshima City's project for the installation of A-bomb damage information boards and the recognition and preservation of A-bombed buildings and trees. The installation of A-bomb interpretive plaques with distances from the hypocenter and the identification of A-bombed buildings and trees are acts of marking each location with a concentric circle of spatial imagery from the hypocenter.

The people who come face to face with these information boards experience the place where they stand as a straight line distance from the hypocenter, based on the concentric circle map centered on the hypocenter and the number of distances from the hypocenter marked on the explanatory boards. This experience is mediated by spatial images of a form different from the experience of the people at that time. In other words, the A-bomb explanatory signs, buildings, and trees not only function to differentiate the "casually passing street corner," but also always link the place to the hypocenter or the equivalent Peace Memorial Park. It also means that the site is always moored to the time of 8:15 a.m. on August 6, 1945.

6. Being and Becoming the Peace "Monumental" City

This chapter has shown that Hiroshima Peace Memorial Park is not only a memorial which commemorates victims of the Atomic Bomb, but the monument which praises ourselves in honor of postwar peace and the reconstruction. It has also discussed the temporal and spatial arrangement of the memorials and monuments constructed to commemorate the atomic bombing in the urban area of Hiroshima and explore their meaning. Additionally, this chapter has shown how the projects undertaken by the Hiroshima City to carry on the "reality of the atomic bombing" have made sense of the urban landscape.

In the wake of the atomic bombing, Hiroshima has witnessed stages of "sanctification," "designation," "rectification," and "obliteration," which Foote (2003) defines, stretching from the end of the war to the present day. It has also been a process of reconstruction in the name of peace. In this process, there is "rectification" to restore the original situation and "obliteration" to erase the traces of the tragedy, "sanctification" to perpetuate the memory of the A-bomb damage, and "designation" to preserve traces of the event without making a particular place sacred.

The construction of the Peace Memorial Park made "sanctification" possible only through the "obliteration" of the actual site. There is no trace, which shows the former town except for a few memorials in the park. Alternatively, it could be argued that the "obliteration" as the entire city's reconstruction was made possible by the establishment of the "sanctuary" of the Peace Memorial Park. As examples of recent "selection," this chapter cites the installation of A-bomb damage information boards and the recognition and preservation of A-bombed buildings and trees. The reason for this is the concern over the loss of the function of memorializing and representing the damage of the atomic bomb due to postwar economic reconstruction. Therefore, the newly needed "sanctification" seems to be indicated in the concept of Hijiyama Park "Peace Hill" announced by the Hiroshima City in July 2015, the year making the 70th anniversary of the atomic bombing (Hiroshima City 2015).[9]

In other words, in Hiroshima, various groups and individuals, including the government of Hiroshima City, have been simultaneously employing "sanctification" and "obliteration" to specific places and objects in order to share a collective memory or story of A-bomb damage. This contradictory practice, like the monuments at Mabuni Hill in Okinawa, which Kitamura(2009) discusses, could be described as creating a monument to honor the reconstruction and development of the city by continuing to perform memorial acts to commemorate victims of the A-bombing. This was the inevitable outcome of Hiroshima's reconstruction under a special law after the A-bomb damage, while performing its self-assigned role as "Peace Memorial City" as its self-portrait.

Acknowledgements

While some parts are updated, I would like to thank the Hiroshima Peace Institute of Hiroshima City University for its permission to translate the original article written in Japanese: Gen Tagawa (2014) "Hirosima sigaiti ni okeru Genbakukinennbutu no Jikan to Kukan [Space and Time of Atomic Bomb Memorials and Monuments in Urban Hiroshima]," *Hiroshima Peace Research Journal,* 3, pp. 37-53. This paper is part of the results of the

Hiroshima City University project "An Empirical Study of the 'Monumental Landscape' of Hiroshima as the Peace Memorial City" (2012-2013: 000001030301).

Notes

[1] In 2008, Hiroshima City added new explanatory boards in eight languages (Hiroshima City 2019a).

[2] Each year, names of deceased persons are added by application. As of August 6, 2022, a total of 333,907 names are listed in 123 volumes. Only one of those books lists "many names unknown" (Hiroshima City 2021).

[3] The Hiroshima City Society for Memorial Services for the War Dead, established in 1946, was reorganized as a private organization, the Hiroshima Society for Memorial Services for the War Dead, in 1950 due to the GHQ policy of separation of religion and state (Hirosima sensai kuyoukai 2017:9).

[4] The Hiroshima Society for Memorial Services for the War Dead (Hirosima sensai kuyoukai) compiled records of how the remains were found and collected in and around the city, stored and memorialized at the A-Bomb Memorial Mound, and some were returned to the bereaved families (Hirosima sensai kuyoukai 2017).

[5] In Okinawa's Peace Memorial Park, families eat, drink, and offer incense in front of the Peace Corner, where the names of the victims are engraved. In the absence of such face to face contact with the dead, there is a separation from them.

[6] The data is based on field research conducted between 2013 and 2014, lists provided by Hiroshima City Peace Promotion Division, "Genbaku ireihi tou no gaiyou"(Hiroshima City 2019), "Hirosima burari sanpo" (Masuda 2015), and *Hirosima no ishibumi* (Takuwa 1996). Monuments that existed before 1945 and the war memorial called "*chukonhi*" are excluded from the data. The names of the victims of the atomic bomb were added to some *chukonhi* monuments.

[7] Hiroshima City also recognizes A-bombed bridges.

[8] Akiko Naono (2015) examines historically how the memories of A-bomb survivors came to be mediated by concentric images.

[9] There is an army cemetery in Hijiyama Park. It would remind visitors of prewar Hiroshima, which was once a military city. Therefore, it will have different characteristics from Peace Memorial Park. Hiroshima City continues to promote the projects which convey "the realities of the Atomic Bombing to future generations" (Hiroshima City 2022b).

References

Danto, Arthur (1985) "The Vietnam Veterans Memorial," *The Nation*, August 31, pp.

152-155. <http://hettingern.people.cofc.edu/Aesthetics_Fall_2010/Danto_Vietnam_ Veteran's_Memorial.pdf> (Accessed on October 27, 2022).

Foote, E. Kenneth (2003) *Shadowed Ground: America's Landscapes of Violence and Tragedy (Revised Edition)*. Austin: University of Texas Press.

Fukuma, Yoshiaki (2015a) "Ikou no Hatsumei to Koyuusei no Soushitsu [Invention of Remains and Loss of Uniqueness]," *Shisou*, 1096, pp.130-152.

Fukuma, Yoshiaki (2015b) *"Senseki" no sengosi: Semegiau ikou to monumento* [Postwar History of "War Ruins"]. Tokyo: Iwanamishoten.

Hamada, Takeshi (2014) *"Sensouisan no hozen to heiwakuukan no seisan* [Preservation of War Heritage and Production of Peaceful Spaces]," *Rekisihyouron*, 772, pp.20-34.

Hasai, Hiromi, and Iwatani, Kazuo (1996) *"Genbaku to sono buturiteki eikyou* [The Atomic Bomb and Its Physical Effects]," *Hiroshima no Hibaku Tatemono wa Kataru*, Hiroshima: Hiroshima City.

Hiroshima City (2015) "Hijiyama kouen 'heiwa no oka' kousou [Hijiyama Park 'Hill of Peace' Concept]," <https://www.city.hiroshima.lg.jp/uploaded/attachment/35674. pdf> (Accessed on November 3, 2022).

Hiroshima City (2019a) "Genbaku sibotusha ireihi niha 'yasurakani nemutte kudasai ayamachi ha kurikaemasenkara' to kizamareteimasuga douiuimidesuka? (FAQID-5801) [Meaning of the Words Inscribed on the Cenotaph for the Atomic Bomb Victims] ," (Article ID: 0000009398, updated on 21/10/2019), <https://www.city. hiroshima.lg.jp/site/faq/9398.html> (Accessed on November 2, 2022).

Hiroshima City (2019b) "Genbaku kuyoutou ga dekiru made [How the A-bomb Memorial Mound was built]," (Article ID: 0000015507, updated on 21/10/2019), <https://www. city.hiroshima.lg.jp/site/atomicbomb-peace/15507.html> (Accessed on November 1, 2022).

Hiroshima City (2019c) "Genbaku ireihi tou no gaiyou [Cenotaphs for the A-bomb Victims Overview]," (Article ID: 0000009947, updated on 21/10/2019/), <https://www.city. hiroshima.lg.jp/site/atomicbomb-peace/9947.html> (Accessed on November 2, 2022).

Hiroshima City (2019d) "Hibaku tatemono jumoku kyouryou nituite [About Atomic Bombed Building, Trees and Bridges]," (Article ID: 0000009226, updated on 21/10/2019), <https://www.city.hiroshima.lg.jp/site/atomicbomb-peace/9226.html> (Accessed on November 3, 2022).

Hiroshima City (2020) "Genbaku hisai setsumeiban [Explanation Boards for the Atomic Bomb Damage]," (Article ID: 0011556789, updated on 25/02/2020), <https://www. city.hiroshima.lg.jp/site/atomicbomb-peace/130358.html> (Accessed on November 2, 2022).

Hiroshima City (2021) "Genbaku sibotushameibo nituite [About a list of atomic bomb victims]," (Article ID: 0000015513, updated on 09/11/2021), <https://www.city. hiroshima.lg.jp/site/atomicbomb-peace/15513.html> (Accessed on January 22, 2023).

Hiroshima City (2022a) "Hirosima heiwa kinen kouen shuuhen gaido [Guide Map of Hiroshima Peace Memorial Park and its vicinity]," <https://www.pcf.city.hiroshima. jp/virtual/map/> (Accessed on November 2, 2022).

Hiroshima City (2022b) "Conveying the Realities of the Atomic Bombing to Future Generations," (Article ID: 0000253958, updated on 12/01/2022), <https://www. city.hiroshima.lg.jp/site/english/253958.html> (Accessed on November 3, 2022).

Hiroshima City [City Planning Division of Urban Development Bureau] (2022) "The Hiroshima Peace Memorial City Construction Law and Commentary," <https://www. city.hiroshima.lg.jp/uploaded/attachment/151843.pdf> (Accessed on November 1, 2022).

Hiroshima National Peace Memorial Hall for the Atomic Bomb Victims (2022) "About Memorial Hall", <https://www.hiro-tsuitokinenkan.go.jp/en/> (Accessed on November 2, 2022).

Hiroshima Peace Memorial Museum (2022) "Reconstruction and the Peace Memorial City Construction Law," <https://hpmmuseum.jp/modules/exhibition/index.php? action=ItemView&item_id=63&lang=eng> (Accessed on November 1, 2022).

Hirosima sensai kuyoukai (2017) *Irei no kioku: Genbaku kuyou tou (Zouhoban) [Showa 20nen (1955nen) ~ Heisei 27nen (2015nen)]* [A Chronicle of Atomic Bomb Memorial Mound]. Hiroshima: Hirosima sensai kuyoukai.

Horikawa, Keiko (2015) *Genbaku kuyoutou: Wasurerareta ikotu no nanajuunen* [Atomic Bomb Memorial Mound]. Tokyo: Bungeishunju.

Inoue, Shoichi (1987) *Ato, kicchu, japanesuku: daitoa no posuto modan* [Art, Kitsch, and Japanesque]. Tokyo: Seidosha.

Kitamura, Tsuyoshi (2009) *Shishatachi no sengoshi* [Ethnography of Post battle of Okinawa]. Tokyo: Ochanomizu-shobo.

Masuda, Yutaka (2015) "Hiroshima Burari Sanpo [Walking in Hiroshima]," <http:// masuda901.web.fc2.com> (Accessed on October 27, 2015).

Murakami, Koukyou and Nishimura, Akira, eds. (2013) *Irei no keihu: Sisha wo kioku suru kyoudoutai* [Genealogy of Memorials]. Tokyo: Sinwasha.

Nakamura, Mikiko (2008) *Genbaku no Kioku* [Memory of Atomic Bomb]. Unpublished graduation thesis, submitted to Faculty of Environmental Science, Nagasaki University.

Naono, Akiko (2015) *Genbakutaiken to sengonihon : Kioku no keisei to keishou* [Atomic Bomb Experience and Postwar Japan], Tokyo:Iwanamishoten.

National Museum of Japanese History, ed. (2003) *Kingendai no sensou ni kansuru kinenhi* [Research Report on Monuments of Modern Wars]. Chiba: National

Museum of Japanese History.

Sturken, Marita (1997) *Tangled Memories: The Vietnam War, the AIDS Epidemic, And the Politics of Remembering.* Berkeley: University of California Press.

Takuwa, Jun (1996) *Hirosima no isibumi* [Monuments of Hiroshima]. Hiroshima: Hiroshimaken kyouikuyouhin kabushikigaisha.

Wada, Mitsuhiro (2005) "Kinenhi no tsukuru amerika: Saisho no shokuminchi [Monuments in American History]," in Yuji Wakao and Shoji Haga, (eds.), *Kiroku to kioku no hikaku bunkasi.* Nagoya: The University of Nagoya Press, pp.114-164.

Yoneyama, Lisa (1999) *Hiroshima Traces: Time, Space, and the Dialectics of Memory.* Berkeley: University of California Press.

Yoshiaki Furuzawa

Forgotten Cannon Emplacement Sites on Miyajima

Miyajima—an island in Hatsukaichi City, Hiroshima Prefecture—attracts many tourists from both within and outside of Japan (more than four million in 2018 before the COVID-19 pandemic). It is less than a one-hour train ride from the Hiroshima City center, and today mostly known for Itsukushima Shrine which is named as one of the two UNESCO World Heritage sites in Hiroshima since 1996—the other one is the A-bomb dome in the Peace Memorial Park. There is no cemetery on the island, since the island is historically considered sacred. While Miyajima is one of the popular tourist destinations in Hiroshima, not many people are aware that the Imperial Japanese Army once constructed fixed cannon emplacements on the island in the beginning of the 20th century. Why were these cannons placed on Miyajima?

In 1893, in order to protect Hiroshima Bay and nearby Kure Naval Port, the Imperial Japanese Army decided to build the Hiroshima Bay Fortress, resulting in the construction of eight fixed cannon emplacements and four forts in the Hiroshima Bay area. The eight cannon sites were all built by 1903, and three of them were placed on Miyajima: Takanosu Low Cannon Site (1897-1900, at an altitude of 15 meters), Takanosu High Cannon Site (1898-1900, at an altitude of 143 meters), and Murohama Cannon Site (1898-1899, at an altitude of 10 meters).

While Japan entered into the Russo-Japanese War (1904-1905), the cannons in Miyajima and the greater Hiroshima Bay area were never fired in an actual battle. Following the Russo-Japanese War in 1909, General Staff Headquarter passed a policy to construct fortresses in straits—rather than the Inland Sea—which was implemented after the World War I. As a result, once Hoyo Fortress in Shimonoseki was constructed, all cannon emplacements and forts in the Hiroshima Bay area—including three in Miyajima—were decommissioned in 1926. Almost 100 years has passed since these cannons were abandoned, and they are literally forgotten by many people. One can easily see that these cannon sites are forgotten from looking at how they have been preserved today. While Takanosu Low Cannon Site is literally collapsing, two other sites are also showing signs of damage (See, Photos). They also do not appear on a majority of Miyajima maps. What do these forgotten cannon sites tell us about Hiroshima?

Miyajima has a rich history—which can be easily observed from numerous shrines and temples in the island—and untouched natural reserves —climbing Mount Misen is another popular tourist attractions on the island. Perhaps, former cannon sites may be only one page in the long, rich history of Miyajima since ancient times, however. Former cannon sites in the island reflect a history of Hiroshima as a military city—which led to August 6th, 1945. For example, in 1873, Hiroshima was named as one of the six garrisons, which was later transformed into the 5th Division of the Japanese Imperial Army. In 1894, once the Sino-Japanese War started, Hiroshima (particularly Ujina Port) was a logistics hub for the military since Hiroshima was the westernmost train station at the time. Put differently, the cannon sites on Miyajima reflect the military past of the city.

Today, Hiroshima has transformed from a military city to a city of peace. In Hiroshima, various efforts are made to remember those directly linked to August 6, 1945 (e.g., nurturing storytellers, preserving atomic bombed buildings, spreading seeds of atomic bombed trees, etc.)—thus "…we shall not repeat the evil" as engraved on the Cenotaph for the Victims of the Atomic Bomb in the Hiroshima Peace Memorial Park. But, as our resources are not infinite, we (un)intentionally choose what is to be remembered and what is to be forgotten, which often results in not being able to focus sufficient attention/resources on those indirectly linked to August 6, 1945. Former cannon sites decommissioned more than 20 years before 1945 may be an example of that unfortunately. The future of these former cannon emplacement sites is yet to be determined.

Forgotten cannon sites on Miyajima is a reminder of the military past of Hiroshima City. It reminds us that Hiroshima was not destined to be a peaceful city from the start of its post-war reconstruction process. It was effort of people in Hiroshima that has transformed this former military city into the peaceful city we know today.

Photos: Former Cannon Emplacement Sites on Miyajima in 2019

Takanosu Low Cannon Site

Takanosu High Cannon Site

Murohama Cannon Site

(Photos were taken by the author in May 2019)

Appendix: Chronological Table

Yu Takeda

Date	Japan	World
1938/12		Nuclear fission was discovered.
1939/9		Germany invaded Poland and World War II started.
1941/12	Japan attacked Pearl Harbor and declared war on Allied Powers.	
1942/8		The US set up the Manhattan Engineer District to develop a nuclear weapon.
1943/9	Army-commissioned Ni-Go project started to study the separation of uranium-235.	
1944/9		The US and the UK signed the Hyde Park Aide-Mémoire that kept the atomic bomb secret and suggested possible use of the bomb against Japan.
/10	F-project started to study nuclear weapons in the Navy	
1945/4		The US Target Committee held its first meeting to select targets for atomic bombing, including Hiroshima.
/7		The US conducted the first nuclear test in history.
/8	Japan surrendered and World War II ended.	The US dropped atomic bombs on Hiroshima and Nagasaki.

Date	Japan	World
1945/9	GHQ prohibited nuclear research.	
1946/1		The UN called for the complete elimination of nuclear weapons and set up the Atomic Energy Commission.
/6		The US proposed the Baruch Plan for international control of atomic energy.
1949/8	The Hiroshima Peace Memorial City Construction Law was enacted to provide national assistance for the reconstruction of Hiroshima.	The Soviet Union conducted its first nuclear test.
1952/10		The UK conducted its first nuclear test in Australia.
/11		The US detonated the first hydrogen bomb in the Marshall Islands.
1953/12		US President Dwight D. Eisenhower called for international cooperation for peaceful use of nuclear power in the Atoms for Peace speech.
1954/3	Fishing boats, including Japan's Lucky Dragon No.5, were contaminated during a hydrogen bomb test in Bikini Atoll.	The US detonated a high yield hydrogen bomb at Bikini Atoll in the Marshall Islands.
/4	The Science Council of Japan proposed three principles of Japanese nuclear research of openness, independence, and democracy.	

Date	Japan	World
/6		The Soviet Union's Obninsk Nuclear Power Plant became the first nuclear reactor to produce electricity industrially.
1955/8	The First World Conference against Atomic and Hydrogen Bombs held in Hiroshima. Hiroshima Peace Memorial Museum and Hiroshima Peace Memorial Park were constructed.	The International Conference on the Peaceful Uses of Atomic Energy was held in Geneva.
1957/8		The International Atomic Energy Agency (IAEA) was created.
/9		Nuclear waste exploded in Ozyorsk, Russia, which was called the "Kyshtym Disaster."
1960/2		France conducted its first nuclear test in the Sahara Desert.
1962/10		The Cuban Missile Crisis occurred between the US and the Soviet Union.
1963/8		Partial Test Ban Treaty was opened for signature.
/10	Japan Power Demonstration Reactor became the first Japanese nuclear reactor that produced electricity industrially.	
1964/10		China conducted its first nuclear test.

Date	Japan	World
1966/7	Hiroshima City Council unanimously voted in favor of preserving the Atomic Bomb Dome.	
1967/2		The Treaty of Tlatelolco was signed to prohibit nuclear weapons in Latin America, establishing the first Nuclear-Weapon-Free Zone.
1967/12	Prime Minister Eisaku Sato announced Three Non-Nuclear Principles of not possessing nuclear weapons, not producing them, and not permitting their entry into the country.	
1968/7		The Nuclear Non-Proliferation Treaty (NPT) was opened for signature.
/9	A study group commissioned by the Cabinet Research Office submitted a report on Japan's nuclear weapons capability.	
1970/2	Japan signed the NPT.	
/3		The NPT entered into force.
1972/5		The US and the Soviet Union signed the Anti-Ballistic Missile (ABM) Treaty and the interim Strategic Arms Limitations Talks agreement (SALT I).
1974/5		India conducted its first nuclear test.

Date	Japan	World
/9	The first Japanese nuclear powered ship Mutsu suffered a radiation leak.	
1975/6	Japan participated in a meeting of nuclear suppliers in London, later known as the NSG.	
1977/4	Japan and the US started negotiation on the reprocessing facility in Tokai Mura.	US President Jimmy Carter announced a policy to discourage reprocessing and using plutonium.
/10		The International Nuclear Fuel Cycle Evaluation started to review the nuclear fuel cycle.
1979/3		The Three Mile Island Unit 2 reactor partially melted down.
1982/6		One million people rallied for a nuclear freeze movement in New York.
1986/4		Chernobyl nuclear power plant No. 4 reactor was destroyed in an accident.
1987/12		The US and the Soviet Union signed the Intermediate-Range Nuclear Forces (INF) Treaty.
1988/7	Japan revised a nuclear cooperation agreement with the US to secure its plutonium utilization.	
1990/8		The Gulf War started as Iraq invaded Kuwait.
1991/7		The US and the Soviet Union signed the Strategic Arms Reduction Treaty (START I).
/12		The Soviet Union dissolved.

Date	Japan	World
1992/6		The US authorized the Nunn-Lugar program to secure and dismantle weapons of mass destruction in the former states of the Soviet Union.
1993/1		The US and Russia signed the Strategic Arms Reduction Treaty II (START II).
1994/8	Japan and Russia agreed to cooperate on dismantling decommissioned Russian nuclear submarines.	
/10		The US and North Korea signed the Agreed Framework to freeze the latter's nuclear program in exchange for aid.
/12		Ukraine, which inherited Soviet nuclear weapons, acceded to the NPT as a Non-Nuclear Weapon State.
1995/5		The NPT was extended indefinitely.
/12	Prototype fast breeder reactor Monju suffered sodium leakage.	
1996/9		The Comprehensive Test Ban Treaty was opened for signature.
/12	The Atomic Bomb Dome was designated as a World Heritage Site.	
1998/5		India and Pakistan conducted underground nuclear tests.
2001/9		Hijacked airplanes used for suicide attacks in the United States.

Date	Japan	World
2002/6		The ABM Treaty was terminated as the US withdrew from the treaty.
2003/1		North Korea announced its withdrawal from the NPT.
/8	Japan participated in the first round of the six-party talks to solve the North Korean nuclear weapons problem.	
2006/10		North Korea conducted its first nuclear test.
2009/4		US President Barack Obama delivered an address on nuclear disarmament in Prague.
2010/4		The US and Russia signed the New Strategic Arms Reduction Treaty (New START).
2011/3	Fukushima Daiichi nuclear-power station suffered severe accidents after an earthquake and tsunami.	
/6		Germany announced to shut down all the country's nuclear power plants by 2022.
2015/7		West European countries and its partners agreed with Iran on the Joint Comprehensive Plan of Action to limit the Iranian nuclear program.
2016/12	Prototype fast breeder reactor Monju was decided to be decommissioned.	
2017/9		The Treaty on the Prohibition of Nuclear Weapons (TPNW) was opened for signature.

Date	Japan	World
2019/8		The US withdrew from the INF Treaty, which led to its termination.
2021/1		The TPNW entered into force.

Index